IN SEARCH OF TH

Also by Elizabeth Sutherland

FICTION

Lent Term
The Seer of Kintail
Hannah Hereafter
The Eye of God
The Weeping Tree

NON-FICTION

The Black Isle: a Portrait of the Past
The Prophecies of the Brahan Seer (Editor)
The Rosemarkie Symbol Stones
Ravens and Black Rain: the Story of Highland Second Sight
The Gold Key and the Green Life (Editor)

IN SEARCH OF THE PICTS

A CELTIC DARK AGE NATION

Illustrated by Tom E. Gray

ELIZABETH SUTHERLAND

CONSTABLE · LONDON

First published in Great Britain 1994
by Constable and Company Limited
3 The Lanchesters, 162 Fulham Palace Road
London W6 9ER
Copyright © Elizabeth Sutherland 1994
Illustrations © Tom Gray 1994
Reprinted 1995
The right of Elizabeth Sutherland to be
identified as the author of this work
has been asserted by her in accordance
with the Copyright, Designs and Patents Act 1988
ISBN 0 09 473650 2

A CIP catalogue record for this book
is available from the British Library

Typeset in 11pt Garamond by Servis Filmsetting Ltd
Printed in Great Britain by
St Edmundsbury Press Ltd
Bury St Edmunds, Suffolk

To all Pictophiles everywhere in the hope that this book
will find more

CONTENTS

Acknowledgements xiii

PART THREE: THE FIRST SYMBOL STONES

PART FOUR: CHRISTIANITY AND THE STONES

PART FIVE: IMPORTANT PICTISH PEOPLE

PART SIX: PICTISH LANGUAGE AND THE ARTS

PART SEVEN: DAILY LIFE IN A PICTISH SETTLEMENT

PART EIGHT: THE END OF PICTLAND

CONCLUSION: A GOLDEN AGE

ILLUSTRATIONS

ACKNOWLEDGEMENTS

TEXT

I would like to thank the following: Professor Leslie Alcock, Dr Isabel Henderson, Dr Anna Ritchie, Professor Charles Thomas, the Lloyd Laings, Dr Alfred Smyth, Norman Atkinson, the curator of Angus Museums, Dr Derek Bryce and the many others mentioned within the text without whose scholarship, knowledge and research I could not have begun to write about the Picts.

I am also grateful to the Trustees of Groam House Museum who allowed me – as past curator – twelve inspiring years of living close to the Rosemarkie stones. Thanks too to all those experts who visited the museum, lectured for us and shared their ideas and knowledge.

Much gratitude goes to Tom Gray whose archive of photographs in Groam House Museum brought the whole world of the Picts alive for me.

Thanks to the members of the Pictish Art Society (henceforth PAS), 27 George Street, Edinburgh, who have done so much excellent work in promoting the Picts to a wider audience and especially to Niall M. Robertson, editor of the PAS Journal, who has been particularly helpful and to Davin Hood and Dr I.L. Gordon for their comments on the Bullion Stone.

Thanks to Constable and Co. Ltd for permission to quote from *The Desert Fathers* by Helen Waddell; to Penguin Classics and the estate of H. Mattingly and S.A. Handford for allowing me to quote from Tacitus' *The Agricola and The Germania*.

Above all, I would like to thank Graham Watson, archaeologist, medieval church historian, author and Museums' Officer, Ross & Cromarty District Council, for his encouragement and for kindly reading and commenting on my manuscript.

Elizabeth Sutherland

DRAWINGS, MAPS AND PHOTOGRAPHS

Grateful thanks to Niall M. Robertson, editor of the PAS Journal, for his drawings of the symbols and Ogams.

The three maps showing the distribution of class I, II and III stones are reproduced from *An Historical Atlas of Scotland*, edited by Peter MacNeill and Ranald Nicholson, with permission from the Trustees of the Conference of Scottish Medievalists. Thanks to Dr Whittington of St Andrews University for the map of Pit place-names, reproduced by kind permission of the Society of Antiquaries, Scotland; also to A.B. Cruikshank for permission to use The Royal Scottish Geographical Society's Map of Ptolemy. Our warmest thanks to Eric Nicoll for his map of historical Pictland.

The drawing of Garbeg cemetery and the two aerial photographs of Forteviot and Invergighty are reproduced by kind permission of the National Monuments Record Scotland and the Royal Commission on the Ancient and Historical Monuments of Scotland (RCAHMS).

The six photographs showing Norrie's Law plaques, the replica carnyx, the Grantown and Abernethy stones, the St Ninian's Isle Treasure, and the Monymusk Reliquary were kindly supplied by the National Museums of Scotland (henceforth NMS). Copyright in the stones photographed in NMS are reproduced by permission of the Trustees. Thanks also go to Historic Scotland for allowing me to take photographs within the Meigle, St Vigeans and St Andrews museums.

In the lengthy project to photograph all of the Pictish stones, I received nothing but help and kindness from many people. Graham Ritchie, Lesley Ferguson, Ian Fisher and Ian Fraser of the National Monuments Record, Scotland, Dr David Clarke and Dr Michael Spearman of NMS, Peter Yeoman, Fife Region Archaeologist, Edwina Proudfoot of St Andrews Heritage Services, Mike King of Perth Museum, Ian Shepherd, Grampian Regional Archaeologist, Jocelyn Chamberlain-Mole, Curator of Peterhead Museum, Christine Sangster, Curator of Elgin Museum, Robin Hanley of Inverness Museum and Art Galleries, Groam House Museum Trustees, Lord Strathnaver of Dunrobin Castle Museum, Douglas Scott, Tain. Grateful thanks also to Peter West and staff at H.A. West, Photographic Wholesalers, Edinburgh, who were most helpful at all times.

To the many owners of estates and other private individuals too numerous to mention who allowed us to photograph stones on their property, our grateful thanks.

Elizabeth Sutherland and Tom E. Gray

INTRODUCTION

A GOLDEN AGE?

How tempting it is in these times of awakened awareness of the fragility of the earth to clothe our Pictish ancestors in some misty mantle of nobility.

Sometimes likened to that other mythologized race – the original inhabitants of North America – the Picts too were brave warriors who painted or tattooed their skins, proud nationalists who raised great totem poles of stone, above all respectful tenants of the natural world. Their fate was to be historically obliterated by their Scottish cousins just as the native Americans were either slaughtered or relocated in meagre reservations by incoming Europeans. Even the Pictish name 'Painted Men' was probably a contemptuous invention of the Roman soldiers and as derogatory as the term 'Redskin'.

So the myth persists that somehow those days were better, those people wiser and the world a happier place than it is today. The Mapuches of Chile, the Maoris of New Zealand, the Aborigines still hark back to a golden age. So did the Greeks. So do many Scots today. Our golden age was Pictish.

Anthropologists believe that there is no such thing as primitive man, only primitive conditions.

The Picts therefore were as able to adapt to their surroundings as we are to ours. They had their own way of making sense of the universe. Physically, emotionally, spiritually the Picts were as we are. Surviving skeletons prove they were roughly the same height, their brains the same size. They could be choleric or phlegmatic, artistic or practical, have rheumatism or cancer.

But in their minds, perceptions and beliefs they were different. How different it is impossible for us to know. Therein lies the mystery that has intrigued generations of their descendants. They left behind so much but not enough. The two to three hundred or so sculptured stones and many more fragments that still adorn the kirkyards, museums and the Scottish countryside are like great billboards proclaiming Pictish facts that we – their descendants – can admire but cannot read. Their language is older than the written word – a symbolic code that

Picts and neighbours

contains the beliefs and visions of an ancient world that we can only glimpse in dreams or flashes of insight from the deep well of Jung's collective unconscious mind.

Who, then, were the Picts?

Simply, a collection of Celtic warrior tribes who lived in Scotland north of the Forth-Clyde valley between AD 300 and 843, when they were conquered by the Hiberno/Scottish Celts led by Kenneth mac Alpin, King of Dal Riata (Argyll). Thereafter they became known as Scots.

The main fact to remember about this racial mixture of pre-Celtic (or early Celtic) Neolithic incomers, Bronze Age Celtic metallurgists and Iron Age Brythonic Celts is this: they were essentially Celtic.

Nearly everything else we know about them is controversial.

Although the Roman writer Eumenius first mentioned them in AD 297 as

[xvi]

'Picti' when he referred to them as 'Caledonians and other Picts', we don't know what they called themselves. To the earlier Roman Britons they were known as Priteni. The Irish called them Cruithni – 'People of the Designs'. They have been referred to as Caledonians after one of their largest tribal groups, as Men of Fortriu or Fortrenn after a central tribe, but whether they had a collective name for themselves we simply don't know.

Again we know that they spoke a form of Brittonic Celtic which was not the same as the Goidelic Celtic spoken by the Irish. We know this because the Irish St Colomba needed an interpreter when he visited the court of the Pictish King Brude mac Maelcon in Inverness. But we don't know that language, only the occasional toponymic place-name like Pit, which means a share of land.

Up until recently it was thought that the Picts were illiterate. But there are several stones which have messages written in the old Irish Ogam script and a couple of inscriptions written in an unknown language. Some Picts therefore may have been able to read and write. Again, this is a matter of speculation.

What has survived thanks to annals kept in Irish monasteries such as Ulster and Tighernach is a list in several versions of the names and dates of the Pictish high kings which is thought to be fairly accurate at least from the reign of Brude in AD 550.

But the King List raises as many questions as it answers. None of the early kings inherit from their fathers which suggests that the inheritance might have gone through the female line.

The Venerable Bede, a saintly Northumbrian clergyman who died in AD 735, gives extra credence to the theory of matrilinear descent when he writes in his *Ecclesiastical History of the English People*:

'Having no women with them these Picts asked wives of the Irish who consented on condition that when any dispute arose, they should choose a king from the female royal line rather than the male. This custom continues among the Picts to this day.'

Currently the matrilinear theory is passionately backed by the anthropologist Dr Anthony Jackson who has researched the subject thoroughly, and thoughtfully rejected by such historians as Dr Alfred Smyth. It is still a matter of debate.

The Picts are generally known for the wealth of carved stones that scatter the countryside, kirkyards and museums of Pictland as far north as Shetland. In the definitive book, *The Early Christian Monuments of Scotland* (henceforth ECMS), first published in 1903 and re-issued in 1993, J. Romilly Allen and Joseph Anderson divide the stones into three classes.

Class I consist of undressed slabs incised with a series of geometric, abstract or animal symbols. The origin and meaning of the symbols, the date of the erection

Invergighty barrow cemetery near Arbroath, Angus, revealed by crop marks

of the stones and their purpose are still matters of argument and speculation.

Class II stones are dressed slabs of local stone with the decorated cross carved in relief prominent on the front and a selection of symbols and scenes on the back. These cross slabs date from about AD 700 after the official establishment of Christianity in Pictland. They are crowded with a stunning selection of warriors, monks, hunters, animals, monsters, battle scenes and Old and New Testament iconography.

Class III stones are similar to class II but have no Pictish symbols carved on them.

The crosses, sides and edges in both classes are filled with the most exquisite Celtic interlace consisting of every sort of pattern including knot-work, zoomorphic, key, with snake bosses and spirals, wheels and mazes. All of them are thought to have had their own particular symbolism to do with Christ and creation, death and resurrection and the beauty of the natural world.

Study of these stones tells us three facts about the Picts. Firstly the importance of warriors and hunters in an aristocratic society, secondly the depth of their understanding of and respect for Christianity, and last but not least the brilliance of their sculptural skills which have put the stones at the centre of Dark Age art.

But there is an enigmatic quality about the scenes and figures on the class II and III stones which defy complete understanding. The symbolism is multi-layered and reveals only as much as it conceals. We grope towards knowledge in a dim light.

Although the King List and the stones, some superb metalwork and other archaeological evidence are all that remain to tell us of a nation, there are some tantalizing tit-bits of comment written by such Classical writers as Tacitus, Cassius Dio, Herodian, Eumenius, Ammianus Marcellinus and later St Adamnan, Bede and the Irish monastic annalists. But many of these were collated so much later than the events that they are liable to contain legend, propaganda or plain gossip.

There is speculation too about the end of the Pictish era. How did they come to lose a kingdom that was – through natural inheritance – rightly theirs. How was it that the Kingdom of Pictland became the Kingdom of Scotland under the new dynasty of Kenneth the son of Alpin, an obscure Scottish overlord who had fought his way to power?

There is also speculation on the mainland about where and how the Picts lived. The archaeologist for Highland Region once said to me, 'We know the Picts existed here but where are they?' Now that their wooden dwellings are at last appearing as crop marks in aerial photography, more of their settlements are beginning to appear.

These are some of the questions that throughout the centuries have shrouded

Rosemarkie cross slab, Groam House Museum, Ross & Cromarty

the Picts in the mists of mystery and mythology.

But Pictish study is by no means dead. New stones and fragments turn up every year. Aerial photography is still in its infancy. At any time in any place new information in the form of hidden treasures not necessarily in stone or metalwork may be found.

Above all, interest is alive and growing in and outside the academic world. Organizations such as the Pictish Arts Society flourish. Artists like Marianna Lines have opened the door to a new interest in Pictish art. Photographers like Tom Gray have, through their personal skills, made that art accessible. Museums such as Meigle in Perthshire, St Vigeans in Angus and Groam House in Ross-shire are dedicated to promoting all aspects of the Picts. After years of neglect the Pictish world is beginning to be valued as it deserves to be.

One question I always used to ask the children who visited Groam House Museum was 'Where are the Picts today?' Some would point to the stones, others to story-books, but every so often one would give me the answer I wanted. 'Here, alive and well, in us.'

This book is an attempt not only – in the words of Professor Alcock – to de-mythologize the Picts but also to bring them back to life – a spirited, energetic, red-blooded Celtic race whose genes are in our bodies, whose after-children we are proud to be.

Looking at the great class II red sandstone cross slab in Rosemarkie, the questions crowd in on us. Who was the sculptor? Was his patron some important warlord with wealth to spare, perhaps the local king, or did the monastery engage him for a fee? Who selected the quarry? Who identified and extracted the right slab which would not crack when transported and dressed. Was the artist also the mason? Did he use a template or patterns already painted on vellum or did he invent his own designs? What tools did he use? How long did he take? Did he have assistants? Did the excellence of this commission earn him another? Was his order book full? If so what other stones did he carve? Above all, what do his carvings represent?

Most of these questions are unanswerable. All we know is that this stone, like the others, is an enduring monument not just to an unknown sculptor and his patron, not just to the sophisticated symbolism of a Celtic Dark Age nation, but also solid testimony to the art, beliefs and spirit of our Pictish ancestors. They deserve our curiosity, respect and abiding admiration.

A golden age perhaps.

PART ONE

PICTISH ROOTS

THE FIRST INCOMERS

Mountains and forest, moorland and lochs with rivers threading the black bogs like silver veins in a dark body under a fitful sky: this was what Scotland must have looked like to its first incomers in the seventh millennium.

But the lochs and burns were full of fish, the heather moors and woodlands the home of deer, boar and wild cattle, while the rivers were like roads to the people who were first to explore this land.

Imagine a little fleet of tough skin-covered coracles made water-resistant with fat, and laden dug-out canoes carrying a family of Mesolithic explorers from the south. Driven on to the Island of Jura by a wet wild gale they must have collapsed with exhaustion and slept on the sand in the shelter of their battered boats. Picture them waking to a glorious dawn, a blue and breathless ocean peopled with friendly seals, while the surrounding machair breathed on them the fragrance of wild flowers. So benign and beautiful was the island then – a rarer occurrence than it would be today – that they must have believed that the sun god himself had driven them there. So they stayed.

Recent excavations on Jura by John Mercer have revealed three joined stone rings just over a metre in diameter, thought to be perhaps the outline of a camp-site, perhaps the earliest stone-based dwellings so far recorded. Hazel nuts, bones and shells found in the charcoal have been carbon-dated to the sixth millennium BC. Traces of red ochre suggest that these first men of Scotland might have decorated their bodies for hunting or celebration.

But the stone-based skin-tents of Jura are by no means the only evidence of these first settlers. Middens full of shells and bones of salmon, sea bream, haddock, eel, ray, skate and even shark with hand-axes, bone fish-hooks, and a variety of flint tools have been found in coastal and river-bank sites all over Scotland. Mesolithic nomadic man survived because for his generation he was as wise as we are for ours.

He would know the ways of the forest, the tides, the creatures, the seasons and the stars, not scientifically as we do but as fellow creatures with spirits to be reverenced, avoided and placated. Nature was both bountiful and terrifying. He worshipped it and worked with it while we manipulate it, divide it up and tear it apart.

Lives were short. Mesolithic man was old at thirty if he survived that long. But there was a pattern to his life with seasonal excursions into the forests for hunting, berry-picking and gathering roots and nuts. A rich natural harvest was there for the taking from forest and shore. The idea of ownership probably never occurred to him, yet at the same time he had his particular territory just as the birds and beasts had theirs.

A settlement at Morton in Fife extensively excavated is brought alive by Professor John Morton Coles who was working there in 1969/70.

This promontory, he thought, was occupied by small groups ranging from three to twelve persons who stayed there for short periods in the year to catch birds, mammals, fish, crabs, molluscs and plants. Covered by sand which eventually blanketed the area, traces of hearths, sleeping-hollows and stake-holes for windbreaks, tools and middens were preserved for future speculation.

For such a seemingly simple life to be sustainable, timber too must have been harvested to fashion spears, bows and arrows, snares, traps and stakes, clubs and floats, canoes and rafts, not forgetting trays, boxes and bowls for molluscs, plants and insects.

Stone implements which gave these Pictish ancestors their name probably formed only a part of their necessary raw materials. Stone scrapers, axes, and arrow-heads were of course important, but most of their tools were probably organic and of these next to nothing remains.

The lives of these nomads were necessarily haphazard depending upon the weather, but they were probably contained within a territory of no more than twenty-five kilometres in any direction. Within the two great estuaries of the Tay and the Forth the terrain consisted of uplands threaded by lesser river valleys. The burns, lochs and forests contained more than enough food and shelter for summer or winter occupation. If the February snowfall was heavy inland a return to the coast was always possible. If the coastal storms were too strong in spring, a quick retreat to the forests presented few difficulties. Professor Coles suggests that Morton was probably visited at any time in the year.

A day or two's journey would take them to the limits of their nomadic round. Travelling light, they could move inland or to the coast in a few hours according to their knowledge of where and when the fruit ripened, the herds gathered, the shoals were heaviest, or the cliff nests full of eggs. With such a variety of resources they may have existed here for anything up to twenty generations.

A world of plenty, a world for the young and strong, but no golden age for the

[2]

frail, the elderly and the very young. A world that could not afford the luxury of sentiment.

NEOLITHIC NEWCOMERS

Farming – the first great revolution – began in the areas around Asia Minor as early as 7000 to 6000 BC.

Instead of following the old wandering way of life, families settled to cultivate the land around them. As the population grew, so the more adventurous moved onwards and outwards, overland or overseas, to clear the land, cultivate the soil and establish their own homes. A continual repetition perhaps of Moses in search of the Promised Land.

By about 4000 BC new families arrived in Scotland to settle where the land seemed suitable. There was room for all, and no doubt the nomadic inhabitants either moved on or were content to learn the new skills and intermarry with the incomers.

They first settled, it is thought, in the islands and coastlands around Argyll and gradually moved west to the Outer Hebrides, north to the Orkneys and eastwards up the Great Glen to the fertile firths and coastal shores of the Moray Firth.

Nothing happened in a hurry. No doubt, however, life seemed as short and busy to the settlers as it does to us today. Harder too.

They must have hunted and gathered until the land was cleared in much the same way as Highland emigrants to the Americas conquered that untamed wilderness. Trees had to be felled and the undergrowth slashed and burned, stones and boulders cleared and the soil prepared for the sowing of a primitive wheat called emmer and a kind of barley.

The domestic animals they brought with them had to be cared for and protected from predators and no doubt gradually interbred with the indigenous wild cattle, sheep, goats and boar of the Scottish glens.

Professor Colin Renfrew suggests that by about 3000 BC the Orkneys were populated with dozens of small groups of about twenty people at most on fairly friendly terms with their neighbours. Because of a regular food supply there was time and energy left over to make extra pots, axes, bone and antler tools, not only for their own use but to trade with others in exchange for game, skins, fish, ornaments and flints, depending upon local skills and materials available.

We even know in detail what one of their villages was like. In 1866 a great storm on the west coast of the Orkney mainland blew away the dunes to expose a close-packed group of seven stone houses at Skara Brae which was later extensively excavated by Professor Gordon Childe in 1927.

The covering of sand had protected the walls up to between two and three metres, and although the roofs had long since gone, the contents were intact.

Because of the lack of timber in the islands, the furniture was made of stone. Beds, stools, shelves, dressers, cupboards and water tanks were conveniently arranged around a central hearth decoratively edged with kerbstones.

Between the houses the walls were filled in with household rubbish for insulation. One house only had a window; otherwise the door was the only opening and each hut was connected to the other by narrow twisting lanes.

Dogs were domesticated, cattle kept for milk and bull calves for food. Wool-gathering and weaving, the treatment of skins and furs for clothing were part of the daily chores.

The villagers wore trousers topped by leather tunics with cloaks or mantles of wool or fur. Small containers with traces of red ochre suggest these Pictish ancestors might also have decorated their bodies.

They were craftsmen too. Shell, bone and amber beads have been found in their tombs. Jet buttons, toggles and bone pins together with weapons, tools and pots were skilfully decorated, as were the interior walls of one of the Skara Brae houses.

Skara Brae is not of course the only type of Neolithic dwelling. The stone bases of circular timber huts abound. In Sutherland as many as two thousand have been identified.

A pattern of farming life predominantly based on cattle was laid down in those distant days and was to survive with little change until the glen clearances and enclosures that followed the disaster of Culloden in the eighteenth century. Thus Pictish society too was solidly based on its farming community.

LIFE AFTER LIFE

Although enough archaeological sites remain to indicate the New Stone Age way of life, far more places point specifically to an overwhelming belief in the immortality of man. Hundreds of great burial tombs still adorn the Scottish countryside.

Although these constructions come in a wide variety of shapes and forms, from round to horned, oblong to squarish, the inner design is roughly the same. A small or not so small chamber partitioned and roofed over with upright or corbelled stone slabs is entered by a long low passage lined with more slabs, the

Corrimony chambered cairn, Glenurquhart, Inverness

whole heaped over with stones or earth into a huge circular or bank-shaped mound.

Man has always been religious. The early nomads probably saw everything in nature as full of spirits to be appeased and placated. Farming man was perhaps the first to believe that everything in life including himself was immortal. No doubt he carried in his mind a hodge-podge of terrors, taboos and ceremonies, but most centred on the basic conviction that man was immortal.

Entering the realms of pure speculation, Ward Rutherford suggests that these were the days of the priest/shamans whose primary job was to find the best hunting grounds but who also acted as pacifiers of the spirits of the beasts aroused by killing the flesh.

The spirit of the shaman was able in trance-state and after long periods of endurance to enter the dangerous Otherworld of the spirits. For safety he would wear the hide of the creature he hoped to placate. There were many earthly doors to this world, such as caves, burial cairns and springs, through which he could enter.

[5]

These Otherworld visits made it possible for the shaman to become close to a certain spirit whom he trusted to show favour to his tribe. In return the group adopted the creature as its totem and took its name. It was then taboo to hunt that creature except at festivals sacred to its person.

It is just possible to see these totems as the origins of the Pictish animal symbols.

As a result of his contact with the spirit world the shaman was to become diviner, healer and law-giver to the tribe. In other words he evolved into the Celtic druid.

These primitive priests may have included in their lore the power to communicate with the dead in order to promote the well-being of the living. Respect for ancestors mingled with concern for status in the Otherworld might have led Neolithic man to erect great tombs, specifically the chambered cairns, which still adorn the countryside.

Each small settlement would have had its own tomb or tombs. These were not that different from the houses of the living with rooms, passages and shelves to hold food, weapons and ornaments for the dead to use in the Otherworld. The better the grave-goods the higher the dead man's status in his new life.

Bodies were not immediately buried but left in dank wooden mortuaries or high platforms exposed to the air until the flesh had gone and the bones were ready for burial with fire and ritual.

One of the most exciting of recent finds was at Isbister in South Ronaldsay by the landowner, Mr R. Simison. Together with the bones of 340 people, animal remains, pots, beads, stone tools and flints were found in heaps on the floor. The bones had been sorted into types with most of the skulls stored in two of the side cells and some strewn on the sidewalks. Already, it would seem, the human head was of special significance as it was to be to the Picts and Scots of a later generation.

Study of the bones revealed that the commonest complaint (forty-seven per cent) was degeneration of the spine. Those that survived to adulthood seldom lived longer than thirty years. A man was old at fifty.

Among the fish, animal and bird bones scattered on the floor, joints of cattle, sheep, pig and red deer had been placed in heaps for feasting in the Otherworld. Most intriguing of all were the carcasses of at least ten sea eagles.

A tomb at Cuween on the Orkney mainland contained twenty-four dog skulls while another at Westray had a preponderance of fish bones and antlers.

It is tempting, if fanciful, to think that these creatures were the original tribal totems to surface centuries later as Pictish clan symbols.

Maeshowe is undoubtedly the best known of all the Orkney tombs. Its magnificent structure and sophisticated design are a lasting testimony to the building skills of our Neolithic forefathers. That the passage entrance is – like the others – carefully aligned to catch the midwinter sun shows that these tombs may have had a deeper significance long ago forgotten.

Perhaps the long red rays of the setting sun as it streamed through the passage were the link between this life and the next. Perhaps the sun had a dual existence which led the way to the world of the dead and illuminated it by night just as by day it warmed and lighted the world of the living. Perhaps that linking sun could also lead the ghostly dead back again to the world of the living when the nights were long and the days were short.

Again the temptation is strong to see in that linking sunlight the origin of the Pictish symbol of the double disc, the two faces of the sun that illuminate two worlds and in the tombs link this world to the next.

It has been suggested that the chambered cairn was like the village church of a later generation. Everything of significance to the settlement happened there from the rites of death and burial to celebrations of birth and immortality.

Incredible though it may seem, Stuart Piggott estimated that it would take as many stones to build one cairn as it would to build five parish churches today. Maeshowe is thought to have taken 39,000 man-hours to complete. With a population that was old at thirty, these amazing buildings were probably raised by teenagers. So much time and effort was spent in their construction that they must have been of enormous importance to the community.

So it would seem that Neolithic man was as influenced by his dead fathers as he was by his living neighbours, possibly more so. Those with the gift of story-telling would keep their memory alive through the oral tradition. Those with the gift of seeing would no doubt communicate their wishes.

Although the Picts did not use these cairns for burial, they must have been influenced by Neolithic perceptions of life and death. If their remains are still prominent in the landscape today, imagine how much more dominant they must have looked to the Picts. No doubt some of the old lore and beliefs concerning them would have filtered down through the priests and the oral tradition to Pictish hearths to colour and influence their rites and beliefs.

NEOLITHIC MYSTERIES

There are some nine hundred stone circles in the British Isles, a third of which were probably constructed in Neolithic times. Most of the earliest and best were set within henges.

These latter emerged in the third millennium. They were earthworks, circular

One of the Clava Cairns near Culloden, Inverness

or elliptical in shape with an external bank, an internal ditch and one or more entrance causeways. Though no one knows why they were built, they are generally associated with ritual or sacrificial ceremonies. Aerial photography has discovered the presence of post-holes within the henges which point to the presence of timber rings and buildings together with circles of stone.

Rough estimates suggest that at Stenness in Orkney 20,000 man-hours were needed for excavating the ditch and building up the bank with a further 60,000 man-hours for quarrying and erecting the henge-circle.

Close by, the larger and better-known Ring of Brodgar still contains twenty-seven standing stones. It has been estimated that sixty stones would have been needed to complete the circle. These great sandstone slabs range in height from 2–4.5m (6'6"–15').

Colin Renfrew suggests that these cannot have been built by small settlements but must have been constructed by large and organized groups controlled by a hierarchy of some sort with headmen and priests and centres of administration.

Among those that excel in beauty and significance are the circles at Callanish on the Isle of Lewis where there are no less than four groups of rings arranged on a great wide, watery peat moor under an uninterrupted dome of ever-changing sky. Made of Lewisian gneiss, these tall fingers of stone point to the heavens and it is in the heavens that the answer to their existence is probably to be found.

Just as Mesolithic man had probably seen the shifts and changes in the weather as controlled by the vagaries of spirits, so the Neolithic farmer may have found out what he needed to know – the seasonal changes – by creating solar and lunar observatories. Perhaps the priest-seer saw his stone circle as a temple into which the sun and moon gods – aided by ritual and sacrifice – poured their secrets.

Undoubtedly these long-ago inhabitants of Britain had their own Hawkings and Patrick Moores. What is practised and explored as science today was once unravelled by ritual and performed as powerful magic.

BRONZE AGE CHANGES

As the centuries passed, so fashions in stone circles, burial arrangements, pottery, ornaments and weapons gradually evolved according to the skills of local inventors, growth in trade, and the slow, relentless arrival of newcomers to settle among the farming communities and share their skills.

Between 2500 and 1700 BC changes in ritual burial practice and the design of the cairns varied from area to area. Ring cairns such as those magnificent examples at Clava outside Inverness were surrounded by attached stone kerbs and wider circles of upright stones. At Cullerlie in Aberdeenshire eight small cairns are surrounded by a circle of eight stones.

Cremation rather than the inhumation of unfleshed bones became the practice. Perhaps it was quicker and easier to bury ashes rather than bones. Individual burials of single bodies in stone kists with grave-goods were gradually to follow.

Recumbent stone circles dominate in the Grampian area. Here the stone circle surrounds a stone lying on its back, often enormously heavy. Single monoliths may still be seen in any field, by any road or stark on a windswept hillside. Over the years these have drawn to themselves strange superstitions, fertility rites, tales of nightmare and magic that are still remembered today.

Cup and ring marks at Ormaig, Carnasserie, Argyll

These single stones may once have been part of a long-gone circle, observation stones to do with seasonal forecasting, gravestones honouring some hero's death, or even slabs for measuring distance.

In Caithness at the Hill o' Many Stanes at Mid Clyth about two hundred smallish slabs are arranged in a fan-shaped pattern with the narrow end on a ridge that runs east–west. The ridge is marked by more stones and includes a cairn. Professor Thom suggested that the ridge was for lunar alignments. This stone

Cup marks and symbols on the Dingwall stone, Ross & Cromarty

fan is the largest of four similar sites which Thom suggested might have been Early Bronze Age calculators for extrapolating evidence for the phases of the moon – part of a lunar observatory, in fact.

Nothing similar exists elsewhere in Britain. Only the great stone rows at Carnac in Brittany in any way resemble the stone fans of Caithness.

Many of the standing or recumbent stones were decorated with circular hollows about ten centimetres across. Sometimes these hollows appear surrounded by one or more concentric circles. These are known as cup and ring marks.

Although the finest are to be found in Argyll and Galloway they appear in many places in Scotland. For example, several cup marks appear on a short erect slab (later redecorated by the Picts) in St Clement's Churchyard in Dingwall, while a recumbent stone by a hedge in Newbiggin, Perthshire has both cup and rings as do some kerbstones surrounding the spectacular Clava Cairns near Culloden on the outskirts of Inverness.

Dating to the Early Bronze Age, these enigmatic patterns have inspired countless interpretations.

Some suggest that they were used literally as cups to hold food and drink used in the worship of some god – as they resemble pools with radiating ripples, perhaps a water god. This theory collapses when applied to upright stones, such as those at Dingwall.

They may symbolize eternal life. In every culture the spiral is seen as the symbol of eternity because it follows the pattern of growth. As Dr Bryce suggests, the seed that is planted deep in the body of mother earth spirals upwards to fulfil its potential then falls back to be nurtured into growth again.

Later generations were to develop the symbolism of the spiral, seeing it as a representation of spirit descending into matter and matter rising into spirit.

But these are speculations. Understanding the message of these ancient stones so intrigues the present generation that we see what we want to see, fool ourselves into believing that somehow their wisdom was greater than ours, their understanding of the world more profound. Perhaps it was. We can never know.

POTS AND POTTERS

The earliest pottery cups and bowls arrived with the first farmers in the fourth millennium. Undecorated but sometimes with lugs attached, they were fashioned from clay – most settlements would have identified their nearest clay pit – and probably fired in the domestic hearth. Neither the kiln nor the wheel had yet been invented.

Pots were also used to hold food for the dead and were found among the grave-goods in every type of burial up to the coming of Christianity. Today these are known as food vessels.

Gradually pottery became more sophisticated with impressed or incised decoration, some of it simple with prick-marks or lines, other examples more complicated with twisted and whipped cord impressions, high waists and sloping rims. The art of potting became more sophisticated over the centuries so that it is now possible to link different styles with different areas. Potsherds abound, have been written up, drawn and dated. Some archaeologists become pot-maniacs.

Somewhere towards the beginning of the Bronze Age there appeared the first examples of a new style of pot. These bell beakers as they are called were highly decorated and appeared at about the same time as the introduction of more sophisticated metalwork and a gradual change from communal burial mounds to individual short burial cists. Grave-goods such as those found in Clintery-in-the-Garioch included with the new-style pots a variety of different goods, for example a schist axe, a topaz, a bone awl and a bone pulley or belt ring.

These pots together with new ideas in the crafting of gold, bronze and copper ornaments and artifacts are thought to have been introduced by Celtic immigrants from Belgium, Holland and the Rhine who were to settle in four main areas of Britain, including Wessex, East Anglia, north-east England and south-east and north-east Scotland.

These newcomers probably travelled up the main rivers to encounter the important Neolithic centres where their new skills would either have been welcomed and used to give extra status to their patrons or seen as a threat and the strangers driven off.

The pots can be identified by style and decoration as covering some seven stages. With the seventh group came the end of the Beaker period. By that time no doubt everyone had them so they were no longer in fashion, or possibly their socio-religious functions had died out. The earliest examples may well have been introduced by strangers, but the later ones were doubtless locally crafted.

It is possible that the pots themselves were not as important as their contents. Remember those lovely old Chinese ginger jars? They were bought and treasured not only for their contents but also for their originality and charm. No one thought for a moment that they were locally made or that the makers had any intention of living in Britain. The analogy with beakers and their makers is valid.

Whether the so-called Beaker people were locals who copied the handsome pots imported for their content and kept and valued for their style or whether the pot-makers themselves brought them to Britain and settled locally has not been fully resolved.

A beaker found in Fife is thought to have contained a drink made from lime honey flavoured with meadowsweet. But this may have been used as a food vessel containing sustenance for the journey to the Otherworld. It does not necessarily mean that the drink was imported.

TOOLS AND TREASURE

Copper and gold worked into tools and ornaments were being made in the Balkans as early as 4500 BC. Two thousand years later the inhabitants of Britain were still making flint copies of the copper axes that they had seen brought in by incomers or acquired through barter. These artifacts were still too rare or precious to be buried with the dead, but were rather inherited or captured as objects of power and ritual, for display rather than for use.

The earliest copper-smiths in Britain may have lived in Ireland. The remains of wood felled by their distinctive metal axes date from about 2265 BC. Copper axes have been found in Scotland dating from before 2000 BC and may be associated with the distinctive beaker pots of that period.

Great was the excitement in the small Black Isle village of Rosemarkie when in 1993 a flat copper axehead dating to 2000 BC was found in the bed of an underground stream. Other hoards have been discovered in the north-east area, as have stone moulds for casting the axes.

Halberds (dagger-shaped blades fixed permanently to handles), awls and axes were also being made but not, it is thought, for general use at that time. They are rare objects.

Prehistoric copper mines have been hard to trace in Britain but some have been located in Ireland and one at the Great Orme in Wales. This is an extraordinarily complex system of horizontal shafts and vertical tunnels dug out to a depth of 70m (230'). Michael Parker Pearson believes it may have been one of the largest in Europe. Because the tunnels were so small, Pearson has put forward the interesting theory that they may have been used by children. According to radio-carbon dating the mine was in use between 1800 and 600 BC.

Bronze manufacture arrived in Britain soon after copper, which was not the case generally in Europe. Britain was so late in her use of copper that the one followed the other in quick succession. Bronze is made by mixing copper and tin in a ratio of eight to one. If too much tin is used, the alloy looks silver. The advantage of bronze was its superior hardness. Pure copper tools were not much more efficient than stone.

Bronze-working was not restricted to axes and awls. A hoard found in Migdale in Sutherland produced six armlets with oval section, two moulded armlets, a flat axe, an ear-ring, tubular wooden beads covered with thin bronze, conical bronze objects – toggles, perhaps – and six jet buttons.

Jet necklaces seem to have been a fashion feature of the Bronze Age for they have been found as far apart as Argyll and Angus, and buried with beakers in Fife and Wigtownshire.

Gold was also used to make jewellery. That lovely word *lunulae* describes those flat crescent-shaped neck ornaments decorated with hammered patterns which are thought to have originated in Ireland. The only ear-rings to be found in Scotland came from a cist in Morayshire. Alas, only one has survived. Collars, neck-rings, bracelets, dress-fasteners and chestplates have all survived. A small hoard was ploughed up recently at the Heights of Brae above Dingwall, eleven pieces in all.

[14]

As the Bronze Age developed, so too did the range and sophistication of other metalwork: dirks and rapiers, small bronze razors, chisels and punches, battle-axes, swords, spearheads and occasional ceremonial bronze shields. The latter were not much use in battle but were awesome to look at. Sheet-bronze cauldrons dating from the eighth century BC and flesh-forks suggest gourmandizing Celtic feasts.

Looking through the list of Bronze Age artifacts it becomes obvious that the world was already beginning to change and shrink. No longer was it possible for an enterprising farmer to slash and burn the acres on his doorstep in order to expand his territory. Someone else owned it. If he wanted it he had to fight for it. The increasing range of weapons produced by the metalworkers shows just how hot the arms race had become.

Fighting was now a way of life. Groups of warriors armed to the teeth challenged each other to single combat or battle over territory, cattle and gold.

By 500 BC not only were the bronze-smiths producing new and better battleware, but the Iron Age had arrived and with it changes that were to revolutionize home life, weaponry, warfare and buildings.

IRON AGE FORTS AND HOMES

The Iron Age buildings of Scotland, such as forts, brochs, duns, crannogs, wheel-houses, timber houses and farmsteads, point to a wide variety of dwellings to suit all needs and conditions of climate and terrain. They also demonstrate the prodigious skills of those long-ago master builders.

Unique to Scotland and particularly found in the northern and western isles are the brochs, tall windowless towers most of which were built and occupied – according to carbon dating – during the first century BC and the first two centuries AD.

They were usually but not always located on prominent coastal sites and there are some five hundred of them recorded.

The first question usually asked is who built them? Was it the inspired idea of some incomer who saw them as an improvement on or extension of the small original west-coast duns or the Orkney thick-walled round houses which were similar in size and purpose, but not so tall? Maybe it was the desperate invention of some local family group harassed beyond bearing by a land-hungry local bully.

Certainly once the idea had been conceived it caught on quickly.

Although Mousa in Shetland is the most spectacular of all the surviving brochs at 14m (46') tall and Dun Telve in Glenelg still stands at 10m (33'), Richard

Hingley (Proc. Soc. Antiq. Scot. 1992) points out that not all brochs were towers; some were no taller than strongly built round houses.

The walls were hollow, bonded inside with slabs of stone at various intervals between which there were separate galleries reached by internal stairways. These wall cavities would doubtless have been used for storage purposes.

Ledges – at Dun Telve there are two storeys – jut out from the interior wall which must have supported timber structures and a roof, partial or complete, made of turf or thatch with a hole through which the hearth-smoke could escape. These timber structures would probably have been divided into working compartments and sleeping-quarters for the family.

The purpose of the brochs is not exactly known, but it seems reasonable to suppose they were family keeps comparable to the Peel towers or small fortified castles of a much later generation. Built to protect the family from raiding parties and also no doubt to impress the neighbours, these splendid little fortresses were perhaps the ideal deterrent against the quarrelsome society of the day. Certainly they must have worked, for little or no evidence has been found in them of battle damage.

The brochs have sometimes been called Pictish Towers or Viking strongholds, but this is inaccurate. They went out of use about AD 200 and thus were out of date by the time the Picts entered history. New buildings were to arise around some of the sites using the ruins as useful sources of stone. These can be fairly described as Pictish. The brochs and their associated archaeological finds tell us that proto-Pictish society must have consisted of dozens of small family units headed by comparatively wealthy farmers who were probably related to or under the allegiance of a larger tribal unit – not unlike the clan system of later generations.

WHEELHOUSES

These drystone houses date from the later Iron Age and were particularly popular in the Outer Hebrides where wood was in short supply.

Roundish or trefoil-shaped with stone partitions that radiated from a central hearth like the spokes of a wheel, these are seen as a development of the brochs and belong to the period immediately after the broch era, that is from the third century well into Pictish times.

Anna Ritchie describes a large house at Buckquoy near Birsay in Orkney which she excavated as one in a series of buildings superimposed upon each other dating from the seventh to the end of the ninth centuries AD. Dr Ritchie tells us that the final pre-Norse house (Buckquoy 4) was large and 'uniquely sophisticated'.

[16]

A wheelhouse south of Durness, Sutherland

There were three rooms and two entrances with vestibules, one of which was reached by a paved pathway. In the middle of the house lay the main hall with a central slab-built hearth. On either side of the hearth was low kerbing which must have supported wooden platforms along the walls. A round room that opened off the main hall was built partly below floor level and, as it was the only chamber to be carefully paved, was probably used for storage.

Dr Ritchie tells us that 'A hipped roof is envisaged for the main part of the house, with the couples resting on the inner face of the walls . . . Here then for the first time is a house which may be not only attributed to the northern Picts, but also to the vital eighth century . . . in the Northern Isles.'

HILLFORTS AND DUNS

Although fortified sites were probably being built from late Neolithic times

Extensive vitrification on hill fort at Knockfarril, Strathpeffer

Finavon vitrified fort, Angus

onwards, their use at that time is thought to have been ritual rather than defensive. The bulk of them were built after 600 BC when the population had increased and therefore become more aggressive.

Hillforts are found in the Borders. They measure between one and eight hectares and were thought to be the strongholds of tribal kings. Trapain Law in East Lothian is thought to have been the chief stronghold of the Votadini people.

Vitrified hillforts also abound in the east and north-east of Scotland. These were made of stone walls supported by horizontal wooden beams placed at regular intervals within the walls. Many of these buildings had at some time been burned down, perhaps by accident or deliberately, causing such a heat that the stones fused and clinkered, hence their name – vitrified forts.

The trouble with these fortresses lay in the use of wood which could burn or rot long before the fort had outlived its usefulness. Some were therefore rebuilt with extensive earth and rubble ramparts. As they crowned prominent hill-tops, they required enormous skill to construct. Sometimes whole summits were surrounded by high ramparts within which villages and their livestock could all be contained.

As the years passed construction was strengthened and modified to match the needs of the times. Successive overlords adapted and altered their designs to their personal needs as the Picts themselves were to do in due course.

Duns were small family-sized forts most commonly found in southern and western Scotland, particularly Argyll. They were circular or oval in shape with thick drystone walls enclosing a space of some 375 square metres (4,036 square feet).

Originating perhaps as early as the seventh century BC, duns were one of the most successful of all Iron Age buildings. The Ritchies estimate that their use spanned at least a thousand years.

CRANNOGS

These were timber houses built on artificial or semi-artificial islands in lochs for settlement or defensive purposes. Some were linked to the land by causeways but others were reached by canoes or coracles.

The best sites were small natural islands, but where these were lacking crannogs were built near good grazing shoreland with an eye to protection against encroaching neighbours or predatory animals.

The sites were built up on layers of wood and stones with vertical piles for added support. Roughly round in shape, the area, judging from subsequent excavation, was enclosed by a wooden palisade inside which were several

Dun near Clachan, Kintyre

buildings, some set within their own fences for livestock, and others used as living quarters for the family. The causeway would have been supplemented by a small harbour, for the diet of a crannog dweller would most certainly have been supplemented by fish.

So successful were the crannogs as dwellings that they were inhabited from the late Bronze Age right up to the seventeenth century.

ROUND HOUSES AND FARMSTEADS

The commonest home in south and east Scotland was the round timber house. The average size was about nine metres across and there were various varieties of style.

The commonest type had low walls of wattle and daub or logs and high conical roofs made of thatch or skins. These were supported by a circle of upright posts and sometimes additional central posts. The larger houses had rooms ranged around the central cooking hearth.

More than one house constituted a farmstead which might contain as many as five to nine people. Twenty houses, often protected by ramparts and ditches against bears and wolves and human enemies, made up a village or homestead.

SOUTERRAINS

These underground or partially underground crescent-shaped stone-lined dwellings were the last type of Iron Age building to appear. They are to be traced in their hundreds in eastern Scotland from Caithness and Sutherland south to include the Lothians. They also appear in the northern isles, Ireland and Cornwall and in Europe.

What exactly they were built for is not yet known for certain. Attached to or close beside both timber and stone houses, souterrains are seen as store-rooms for harvest products, byres, or as family shelters in times of attack. They might even have been – like the private chapel of a Christian age – for religious purposes. Stones with cup and ring marks have been built into the occasional wall. Whatever their original purpose, the Picts are thought to have used them as storehouses.

Although all these types of building dated from the Iron Age, the Picts continued to use them or to rebuild in much the same style.

THE CELTIC INHERITANCE

About 1200 BC life in Bronze Age Europe was disrupted, it is thought, by a change in the Russian nomadic way of life. As the hordes pushed westwards, the Mediterranean seethed with warrior pirates. Even Egypt was overwhelmed while Greece entered its own Dark Age. The great Hittite empire in Anatolia was cast down, and its powerful secret monopoly of iron-smelting broken. No doubt some of these strangers found their way to Britain.

Between 1200 and 700 BC the eastern Europeans – displaced by upheavals in Russia – began to spread westwards, eventually to France and Germany, Switzerland and Italy.

Known as the bronze-using Urnfielders from their custom of burying their dead in urns in flat cemeteries, they built hillforts, spoke an early form of the Celtic language, farmed efficiently because of developments in the science of crop rotation, and employed a properly equipped army. They also developed a taste for wine.

These were thought to be the first Celts, though they did not as yet possess the secrets of iron. That came not just from the Hittites but also from the Cimmerians who lived north of the Caucasus, and whose ancestors may have included the Russian nomads who had upset Mediterranean tribal balance in the first place.

From 700 BC the Cimmerians with their knowledge of iron, their fast Steppe ponies and characteristic burial rites, over-ran Europe. They adopted, adapted and developed the farming-fighting culture they found there, and a new phase in Celtic culture began.

THE HALLSTATT CELTS

According to the Greek writer Euphorus, the Keltoi were one of four great barbarian peoples, the others being the Scythians, the Persians and the Lybians.

Too volatile perhaps to have been fused into one nation, they were made up of tribal groups who delighted in taking over and farming new territory, building their hillforts – masterpieces of construction – encouraging craftsmanship and above all revelling in the excitement of battle and looting.

This way of life was not unlike Irish or Pictish practice in the first millennium AD – not at all unlike Scotland in the heyday of the clan system.

The first phase in Celtic culture is named after the village of Hallstatt in the Salzkammergut in Austria where a cemetery was found close to a series of salt mines. Salt and iron together with farming products – improved by the invention of better iron tools and weapons – were the hallmarks of Hallstatt culture.

Hallstatt chiefs became rich and were to grow richer as their tombs suggest. Laid out under their four-wheeled wagons, the bodies – burned or unburned – were equipped with weapons, pottery and food, gold ornaments, personal possessions and horse trappings for their journey to the next world. The whole paraphernalia was enclosed within a wooden chamber and buried beneath a mound.

The Duchess of Mecklenburg in 1917 was the first to identify twenty-six of these lavish graves, but the finest of all at Hochdorf was not opened until the 1970s. Here the skeleton of the chief was found lying on a couch made of sheet bronze. Strewn with gold jewellery, his body still retained fragments of his rich clothing which was embroidered with Chinese silk. He also wore a golden torc or neck-ring. Among the more unusual grave-goods, fish-hooks, nail-clippers and a wooden comb were found together with gold drinking horns, bronze platters and a set of implements used by a butcher to carve meat. These were stored together in a four-wheeled iron-plated wagon. A huge bronze cauldron of Greek origin stood on a wooden stand. Inside it a gold drinking bowl held the dregs of a honey-based drink. Could the drink have been similar to the mead that was found in the Fife grave beaker?

One of the many important results of this archaeological find was to indicate a civilization superior to the Bronze Age – in other words, an Iron Age civilization.

It was also to give some credence to the Irish tales from the oral tradition which describe the enormous wealth and splendour of their heroic ancestors.

New markets were to draw these farmer-warrior-chieftains westwards and south. The Greeks with whom they traded had emerged from their own Dark Age and were to influence and stimulate in them an enthusiastic fascination for the arts.

Then, in 540 BC the Greeks went to war with the Carthaginians for supremacy in the Mediterranean and lost. Without the stimulation of the Greeks for fifty years, Celtic culture changed direction and La Tène heralded a new phase in its development.

LA TÈNE CULTURE

La Tène, meaning 'the shallows', is a place on Lake Neuchatel in Switzerland. In these waters Celts offered gifts of appeasement or thanksgiving to their gods and the hoard found in 1906/7 included iron swords and weapons, other ironwork, wooden objects including a wheel, and the remains of human skeletons.

La Tène Celts buried their chiefs on two-wheeled chariots rather than the farming wagons used at Hallstatt, together with weapons and the usual food offerings for the Otherworld. This might have been a hint perhaps that warriors and farmers were now in separate classes. The war leader and his fighting men had become superior to the farming landowner. Society was shaped like a pyramid with the king, warriors and priesthood élite at the top, farmers and craftsmen, especially the blacksmith, in the middle, and landless men and slaves at the bottom.

La Tène trade and culture were to expand across the Alps into central Europe, France and Britain. Imports and art treasures began to include Italian rather than Greek goods because the focus of civilization had begun to move towards Rome.

CELTS AND ROMANS

In the fifth century BC Celts from France, Germany and Switzerland attacked Italy and settled in the Po Valley. Some years later, in 387 BC, Rome itself was sacked by the Celtic warrior Brennus who with the words 'Vae Victis!' ('Woe to the Defeated!') demanded his weight in gold.

Although Brennus is thought to have had no desire to conquer Rome – he was out for the loot – it was not until over a hundred years later that Rome trounced the Celts at the Battle of Telemon in 225 BC.

The fourth century was one long hot summer for the warrior Celts. They raided the Carpathians, rampaged in the Balkans, ransacked Macedonia, pillaged Greece. They instituted a new way of warfare by hiring themselves out as mercenaries to the Greek princes and any other king who required a fighting force. If the pay was insufficient they mutinied and terrorized their employers.

Interestingly, in 270 BC, they were given territory near Ankara by the Bythinian (Turkish) king who had mistakenly engaged some twenty thousand mercenaries for his own purposes and found them too hard to control. This territory was to be known as Galatia (from the name Gaul) and it survived into Christian times. A form of Celtic was spoken there as well as Greek.

But summer must end and the Celtic rampage drew to a close about 250 BC. A century later the Romans began their long indefatigable advance on Gaul which was to culminate in the invasion of South Britain by Julius Caesar in 54 BC.

Although Celtic culture lingered on in Europe, it was increasingly watered down by Roman influence. But where Rome did not flourish, the Celts survived.

CELTS IN PROTO-PICTLAND

No one is entirely sure when and how the Celticization of the north of Britain began, but it was probably with trade. A few adventurous Hallstatt and later La Tène families with boat-loads of ironware, pottery and wine bartered their goods and either stayed to be assimilated into local Bronze Age life, or returned for more.

Their iron goods were instantly copied by local metalworkers, for the coming of iron must have revolutionized every aspect of life from the battlefield to the kitchen hearth.

As time passed and trade increased, more incomers settled and the indigenous population gradually absorbed into their own culture new ways of burial, building and warfare.

Although the incomers tried to preserve their own customs into future generations, the influence of the local culture was equally powerful. In turn the incomers adopted many of the beliefs and practices of the various parts of Britain where they settled. A two-way threading together of local usages and new continental habits was eventually to emerge as a Celtic culture with a Celtic language.

Although proto-Pictland was not an exact replica of Celtic Ireland in language and, as far as we know, in ritual and custom, by the coming of Rome in the first century AD, however, all British society including Ireland and proto-Pictland was thoroughly Celtic.

[24]

It is usually thought that in Scotland the Celtic language was introduced around 500 BC. If so, the inhabitants must have spoken two languages for a while – their own indigenous tongue with tribal variations and the language of the incomers.

Gradually over the early centuries BC the tribal dialects disappeared in favour of the more universally understood Celtic tongue. An analogy can be found in today's Scotland where Gaelic is fast dying out in favour of English. Some would go so far as to say that it was all but driven out by educationalists in the nineteenth and early twentieth centuries. The same might possibly have happened towards the end of the first millennium BC, where the élite spoke Celtic and the rest were either forced or chose to speak the language of opportunity.

It is possible that the pre-Celtic oral tradition survived well beyond Celtic times, that it remained the language of ritual and magic. Just as the Mass survived in its Latin form well into the twentieth century, so the old priests and ritualists may have continued to use the dead language on ceremonial occasions. But this is sheer speculation.

Recently a new and exciting argument over the origin and language of the Celts in Scotland has been proposed by Professor Colin Renfrew.

He suggests that the introduction of the Celtic language into Scotland coincided with the arrival of the Neolithic farmers.

This is a plausible if radical explanation of the problem of how the population of Scotland became Celtic. Those first farmers had always been Celts. Thus the dialects spoken locally would not have needed the domination of later immigrants to change them to Celtic. They already were.

A modification of this new thinking suggests that the Indo-European language may have reached the British Isles during the Early Bronze Age. It was linked to those first few élitist incomers already mentioned and their eventual domination of proto-Pictish society.

A CELTIC SOCIETY

Dr Binchy described the Irish Celtic world as 'tribal, rural, hierarchical and familiar'. Stuart Piggott, in his definitive book on the druids, said that this description could equally apply to the pre-Roman Celtic world in general.

If you read Frank Adam's account of the *Clans, Septs and Regiments of the Scottish Highlands* you will find some remarkable analogies between the clan system and Gaulish tribal life.

Tribes were more or less the same as clans (*clann* translates as children) and the clan system survived in Scotland up till Culloden (1746). To a lesser extent it is still alive and well.

Tribal or family groups were led by a hierarchy of kings, warriors and priests whose way of maintaining their aristocratic lifestyle was by battle for booty or territory. A good king was judged by how successful he was in protecting his own territory against the predation of neighbours and by his ability to ransack the herds and treasures of these same neighbours. A successful king or chief provided his tribe with peace to get on with their farming and crafting way of life.

In Scotland, the clan or tribal territory was divided up into parcels of land run by the sons and descendants of the chief, but still owned by him. Thus the clan was literally a family. The farmers and labourers were also for the most part members of the same family, so that when a chief sat down to feast, the whole clan had the right to be present, though the humbler members were placed below the salt and ate and drank less expensively.

Some looked upon the high chief as a senior officer, others as a provider of work and shelter to be paid for in produce, but all had the right to regard him as a father. He had the divine right of a king to command loyalty, the legal rights of 'pit and gallows' in disputes, and the power of a benign despot to order the lives of his clansmen. A group of advisers – usually close relatives – were chosen to guide the king and could depose him if he disgraced himself.

The Irish Celts are thought to have elected their high king from one of a number of chieftains who could be a third-generation descendant from a high king. The rules on eligibility for kingship were strict in that the chosen one should not be blemished in body, mind or spirit and should have proved his courage in battle.

On a par with the warrior élite, the druids were of great importance in the Celtic hierarchy. They not only presided at sacrifices, but were the administrators and makers of the law, the teachers and scholars, the keepers of the oral tradition which included the genealogies of the kings and the myths and legends of the tribe. They were the men of wisdom, the seers and diviners who knew how to interpret visions and omens in relation to battles, journeys, marriages and the general well-being of the clan.

Druids in Ireland were peripatetic and could travel freely across boundaries from one tribal group to another. The druids of Ireland and Pictland and pre-Roman Britain must have shared a similar knowledge right into Christian times.

A third group of importance to Celtic society consisted of the craftsmen. The bards were the wordsmiths, poets, musicians and guardians of the language and the complicated techniques of expression.

Blacksmiths, carpenters and metalworkers had their own gods, their own trade secrets and position in society.

[26]

Below the farmers were the landless men, the servants and, before Christianity, the slaves whose lives must have been harsh indeed.

Evidence points to a certain mobility between the classes. The children of warriors could enter the druid profession and vice versa. No doubt the son of a landless labourer could rise to personal glory by patronage and courage in battle. Folklore stories which in Scotland owe their origin to the oral tradition are full of the sons of poor wood-cutters or penniless widows who earn by a blend of moral courage and good luck the hand of the king's daughter. Equally, dowryless maidens through their beauty and goodness could win the king's son.

Feasting, fighting, raiding cattle and hunting occupied the lives of the warriors. They probably spent much of their time practising with their weapons and getting drunk at the noisy feasts. The druids must have spent most of their time rehearsing the laws and myths of the oral tradition. The craftsmen produced the weapons and adornments for the warriors while the ordinary folk got on with the business of farming and ranching to provide the feasts – an exhausting existence.

One of several Gaulish customs to survive into eighteenth century Scotland was that of fostering. A king or chief fostered his children out from an early age to humbler members of his clan. They lived with the family and the sons were taught the necessary skills of warfare, hunting, genealogy and horsemanship while the daughters learned the womanly arts of needlework, music and household tasks. This system cemented bonds of friendship and loyalty within the clan. Should the king or chief be killed or his fortress raided, his sons at least were safe.

This, then, was the society confronted by the Romans on their first venture beyond the Forth/Clyde valley, not so very different from the one they had subdued in Gaul and conquered in southern Britain under Julius Caesar.

ROMAN INVADERS

In certain Scottish schools of good reputation during the first half of this century, it was taught that the Picts were savages, not worth discussing because they had not been civilized by Rome.

Roman propaganda, it would seem, was still very much alive in the twentieth century. There is of course an element of truth in the statement. Roman civilization was a superb culture on which we still rely. Hopefully the Latin and Greek of the Classical writers will return to our schools again.

Those countries that were virtually untouched by Roman civilization, however, retain a strong element of Celtic culture which has a glamour and grandeur demanding equal attention. Sadly it is true to say that in Scotland at least this culture is often ignored in the classrooms of today.

Why was Rome compelled continually to expand its boundaries to the outermost parts of the known world? Dr David Breeze suggests that the reason was fear of being subjugated itself. Pride and politics perhaps also played their part. Suetonius wrote that after the murder of Caligula the Emperor Claudius required a triumph. Britain was chosen. The southern tribes of Britain bravely resisted the four attacking legions under the generalship of Julius Caesar, but Claudius was able to visit Colchester to celebrate his required victory in due course. Claudius may not have been aware of it, but Caesar's invasion of Britain was at bottom his own path to personal power.

The Roman army was indeed a formidable organization. Each legion consisted of about five thousand soldiers who were either Romans or farmers of Roman territory. When they were not fighting they were administrators. The army pervaded most of the civilian professions.

The other main branch of the army was the auxilia. Auxiliaries were originally recruited from friends or allies of Rome who were formed into various units to support the legions. Latterly these units were made up of men from defeated frontier tribes locally recruited. According to Breeze the auxilia in Britain between AD 98 and 138 consisted of between 33,000 and 35,000 men. They served for about twenty-five years and were honoured with Roman citizenship when they retired.

As the conquest widened so too did the need for extra recruitment. In Gaul, Cretan archers, Balearic slingers, North African and German foot soldiers were all employed by Julius Caesar.

Campaigns took place in the spring and summer months. First the governor would try to locate the local tribes by using spies, scouts and travelling traders. Temporary camps were erected overnight. Then, after a successful attack, hostages would be taken, forts built to keep the peace and roads levelled to link the forts. Conquered tribes were grouped into city-states. A group of these *civitates* eventually formed a province.

This, then, was the unconquered and no doubt dreaded force that began its push northward to invade the territory and deal death to the Caledonians and proto-Picts living in the AD 80s.

Such organization, such power, such determination must have come as a culture shock to the proto-Picts. Nothing that they had previously heard could have matched the reality. One way of avoiding a fatal confrontation was by evasion. This was not the coward's way out, but deliberate Celtic strategy. Sensible too, for they knew the difficult terrain. They also saw the advantage of stealthy night attacks, some of which were spectacularly successful. But the Roman army was not to be distracted from final confrontation. Their road north was firmly planted with camps and forts. Their intention was resolute.

AGRICOLA'S ADVANCE

Gnaeus Iulius Agricola was born on 13 June AD 40. As the son of a praetor he hoped at least to rise to the position of a first consul. He did much better.

That we know so much about him is due to his son-in-law and biographer, Cornelius Tacitus, who wrote an account of his life and campaigns in Scotland shortly after Agricola was recalled to Rome.

Agricola's rise was rapid. In AD 69, after a series of excellent appointments, he was sent to Britain as a legate in the 20th Legion. After a period as governor of Aquitania he was returned to Britain in AD 77 or 78 as governor and a year later he advanced into Scotland with some twenty thousand men and the emperor Vespasian's blessing.

AD 79 saw the death of Vespasian and the proclamation of Titus as emperor. Titus extended Agricola's period of service (normally three years), probably for a further three years, and ordered him to move north.

Dr Breeze notes that the move north was celebrated at the Roman Colosseum by the appearance of a Caledonian bear.

Tacitus opens his description of the fourth season with these words: 'If the courage of the army and the glory of the Roman name had allowed it, a terminus would have been found within the island.'

This is the first hint that the Romans – at that time – did not intend to conquer the whole of Scotland but to establish a frontier in the Clyde-Forth valley. Perhaps Agricola's scouts had penetrated north of the Tay and had seen the mountainous country that lay beyond and Agricola had suggested to Titus a halt at the most convenient site.

For whatever reason this decision was reached, the Forth-Clyde line was consolidated with forts and in the spring of AD 81 Agricola turned his attention to south-west Scotland. Here he garrisoned the coast facing Ireland, and contemplated an Irish invasion which he believed he could accomplish with a single legion and some auxiliaries. He may have explored the western sea-route northwards only to realize that the country was impassable.

This was the year of Titus's death and with the acclamation of Domitian the policy was again changed and Agricola was ordered to challenge the Caledones.

In AD 82 or 83, he entered the territory of these proto-Pict warriors, crossed the Forth, and advanced north to Strathmore. The pretext – Roman generals liked to provide a civilized reason for unprovoked attacks – given by Tacitus was that 'he feared a rising of the northern tribes'.

He spent two summers using his fleet to supplement and back up his army as he penetrated the east-coast route north. That first season he was attacked by barbarians and lost about a third of his army, including the 9th Legion, in a surprise assault by night on a temporary camp.

He also had to deal with a mutiny of recruits, the Usipi, raised as auxiliaries in Frankfurt. These wretched men, beaten into rebellion by harsh centurions, seized three boats and sailed – as they thought – for home. They rounded the coast of north-west Scotland driven on by storms and such a severe hunger that they resorted to cannibalism. The few survivors to reach Germany were seized and enslaved by unfriendly German tribes.

The following season Agricola sent his fleet ahead to plunder, hassle and provoke the Caledones and other tribes into a confrontation. His time in Britain was soon to run out and where was the enemy? He pushed past the Grampians northwards to Moray and Nairn and the Spey valley where camp-sites have been identified, and beyond, as Professor Barri Jones has identified from aerial photography and excavation.

Meanwhile, in a remarkable act of solidarity, the Caledones and other tribes put aside their previous internal feuds and assembled, according to Tacitus, the somewhat unrealistic figure of thirty thousand men on a site of their own choosing under their warrior leader Calgacus. Word of their position reached Agricola who hastened to confront these ancestors of the Picts on the slopes of the Graupian (Grampian) Mountain.

DEFEAT AT MONS GRAUPIUS

Lawrence Keppie tells us that Mons Graupius should have been Mons Grampius, the Grampian Mountain. When the text of Tacitus's *Agricola* was first printed in the 1470s, Grampius was written as Graupius, as it has remained ever since.

Although Tacitus devotes ten chapters of his biography to a description of one of the most famous battles on Scottish soil, no one to this day can say with certainty where Mons Graupius was located. All we know is that according to Tacitus it was close to the sea and far to the north.

Locations have been suggested as far south as Ardoch and the Lomond Hills and as far north as Caithness and Sutherland. The aerial photography of

Professor J.K. St Joseph suggested to him that the battle was fought on the slope below Mither Tap O'Bennachie, already the site of a hillfort some twenty-five miles north-west of Aberdeen.

Among the many other sites proposed have been Raedykes, south of Stonehaven, and Knockhill, Strathcathro and Cat Law.

The aerial photography of Professor Barri Jones suggests a number of northern sites still to be considered, such as the Pass of Grange, Knockhill and Bin of Cullen in Morayshire, where traces of camp-sites have been seen from the air.

Tacitus begins his account of the battle by reporting the death of Agricola's year-old son. Nevertheless, in true Roman style, he 'sought remedies for his grief and one of them was war'. He hastened in light marching order to confront the enemy already assembled.

Sending his fleet ahead to harass the enemy, he marched his men without the usual baggage train to meet the assembled tribes. 'Already more than 30,000 could be seen flocking to the colours, all the young men in their prime and famous warriors whose old age was fresh and green, every man wearing the decorations he had earned.'

The great exhortations to battle delivered by the two generals, Agricola and Calgacus, before the fight, were obviously given their fine phrases by Tacitus. Probably Agricola exhorted his troops in customary Roman style, and passed on the gist of what he had said to his son-in-law. Calgacus may also have harangued his followers. If so Agricola would probably not have understood him, and thus it was left to Tacitus to invent fine anti-Roman sentiments about how the Romans created desolation and called it peace.

'We', cried Calgacus in the words of Tacitus, 'the choicest flower of British manhood were hidden away in her most secret places ... we, the most distant dwellers upon earth, the last of the free have been shielded by our very remoteness ... But there are no more nations beyond us; nothing is there but waves and rocks and the Romans, more deadly still than these – for there is in them an arrogance which no submission or good behaviour can escape.'

The Caledonian war leader is described as 'a man of courage and high lineage'. His name translates as 'swordsman' but this may have been his title rather than his personal name.

Facing his 30,000 warriors and warlords were 8,000 auxiliaries with 3,000 cavalry in the battle line and 2,000 cavalry in reserve. The four legions – considerably reduced in numbers because extra troops were needed to control rebellions in other parts of the empire – were held in reserve. The auxiliaries consisted of Batavians, Tungrians and soldiers recruited in Britain. Agricola's army has been estimated by Dr Breeze to have numbered no more than 28,000 men at best, and may have been considerably less.

It is unlikely too that Calgacus's forces were anything like the 30,000 mentioned.

Meanwhile the Caledonian chariots – long obsolete in the Roman world – raced up and down between the armies making a lot of noise but not achieving much.

Agricola, afraid of being outflanked, spread his auxilia in a long thin line. Weapons flew while the Batavian and Tungrian forces were the first to advance.

The Romans were armed with short swords and protected by large shields with bosses, while the Caledonians had small shields and longer swords not fitted for close encounter. The Romans advanced too quickly uphill towards the enemy hillfort and soon they were face to face with the main Caledonian forces who had the advantage of the higher ground.

Meanwhile the cavalry reserve, having first disposed of the chariots, were ordered by Agricola to support the infantrymen, who were now having trouble with the Caledonian advance.

Confronted by the Roman army on both sides, the Caledonians broke ranks and retreated to nearby woodlands. Here they rallied, but by now the dismounted cavalry had encircled the woods. Thrusting forwards, they forced the Caledonians to flee and closely followed their retreat. By nightfall it was all over. Tacitus records that only 360 auxiliaries fell – none of them Romans – as against 10,000 Caledonians and their allies.

The proto-Picts lost as a result of the superior weapons and armour, the better discipline and tactics and the experienced leadership of the Roman general.

When Agricola sent scouts to locate the remains of the Caledonian army, he learned that all had fled while some had set fire to their homes rather than let the enemy take possession of them. He then led his army into the unlocated Boresti territory where he took hostages, ordered his fleet to sail round Britain, where they discovered the Orkneys, while he marched south and was almost immediately recalled to Rome.

There his achievements were recognized as a triumph. A statue was raised and he was offered the proconsulship of Asia, which he declined. He died in AD 93 aged fifty-six.

Although the Caledones suffered a major defeat at Mons Graupius, it could perhaps be said that the battle was the foundation on which the Pictish nation was built.

Forced to unite among themselves, the ancient tribes gradually began to form themselves into a united nation. At the same time, they no doubt learned much of Roman art, culture and warfare which they were to absorb into their own society.

[32]

Ptolemy's map showing Pictland.

THE CELTIC TRIBES OF PTOLEMY

Claudius Ptolemaeus was an Alexandrian geographer writing in about AD 150. He wrote two books, the *Almagest* and the *Geography*. The latter, written in Greek, contains references to Britain, its tribes, its main features, latitudes and longitudes.

There are however three difficulties where the map of north Britain is concerned.

Firstly, Scotland beyond the Forth has been rotated ninety degrees so that its main axis runs west–east instead of south–north. Thus the Mull of Kintyre

[33]

becomes the most northerly point rather than Caithness and Sutherland.

Secondly, Ptolemy's use of latitude and longitude is inaccurate owing to the fact that he took Thule (Shetland), whose position had been fixed by Agricola, as his furthest fixed point north. He probably had no astronomical data for Britain as he never visited the British Isles.

Thirdly, he must have read names from other available documents and located places in the general area of the tribe. He calls his locations *poleis*, Greek for towns. He does not tell us whether these were forts, Roman cities or native settlements.

He places in Scotland eighteen tribes, seventeen rivers, sixteen settlements, ten islands, seven capes, three bays and four other names. Professor Watson has identified as far as possible the meaning of the Latinized tribal names of the proto-Picts, which make interesting reading.

South of the Forth

1 The **Votadini** lived in the Lothians and south-east Scotland. Irish Gaelic changed the name to Fothudan and the Welsh version became Goddodin.
2 The **Selgovae** were in the centre between the Cheviots and the Tweed. The name may mean 'hunters'.
3 The **Novantae** or 'vigorous people' occupied part of Dumfries-shire and Galloway.
4 The **Damnonii** lived in Ayr, Renfrewshire, Dumbarton and Lanark, extending into Stirlingshire. There were also Damnonii in Devon, in Brittany and in Ireland, where they were known as 'the men who used to deepen the earth'. Watson suggests they came north as miners from the Devon peninsula. The name literally means 'men under the care of the goddess of the deep', which hints at a mining background.

North and East of the Forth

5 The **Venicones** would seem to have inhabited land extending from north of the Forth to south of Aberdeenshire. The name is too uncertain for interpretation. 'Vernicones' would mean 'swamp or alder hounds'.
6 The **Taezali** may have occupied Grampian region north to Peterhead. Ptolemy mentions one settlement in their territory, Deetown after the river goddess Deva.
7 The **Vacomagi** are thought to have occupied the southern shore of the Moray Firth. The name could mean 'men of the open plains'.
8 Further north-east, the **Decantae** or 'noblemen' probably lived in Easter Ross and the Black Isle.

9 The **Lugi** in Ross-shire may have derived their name from the Gaulish word for 'ravens'. These people are thought to have been dark in hair and skin colouring like the Silures in Wales. Lochcarron folk are still called 'the black ravens of Lochcarron' in the Gaelic.

10 The **Smertae** lived around the River Oykel, a remote and mountainous region of Sutherland. Watson tells us that the name may mean 'smeared folk'. In Gaulish inscriptions, a goddess called Rosmerta was associated with Tuetates, a terrifying war god who demanded sacrifices by thrusting a man head-first into a vat of blood to be drowned. Rosmerta translates as 'the greatly smeared goddess', smeared that is with blood. Thus the 'smeared folk' may refer to her worship or to the fact that the Smertae daubed themselves with the blood of their enemies.

11 The **Cornavii** in Caithness translate as the 'folk of the horn'.

South-west of Caithness

12, 13, 14 The **Caereni** ('sheep folk'), the **Carnonacae** ('folk of the trumpets (or the cairns)') and the **Creones** ('people of the rugged boundaries') spread down the north-west coast. South of the Creones as far as the Mull of Kintyre were the **Epidii**. Virgil's tutor was called Epidius, a Gaulish name which means 'horseman'. The Epidii translate therefore as 'horse-breeders (or horse-trainers)'. Kintyre is the clanland of the MacEacherns whose name means 'children of the horse-lord'.

The Central Highlands

16 South of the Great Glen and occupying the whole of the Central Highlands stretched the great tribe of the **Caledonii** from which the name Caledonia – synonomous for today's Scotland – is taken. The origins of the name are obscure, but Watson thinks it may have derived from the old Irish *caled*, meaning hard, or *cal*, from the Latin word for 'clamour'. There is a possibility suggested by Nicolaisen that the origins of the name may go back to a pre-Celtic language.

Unlocated

17 The **Boresti**. Dr Breeze suggests that Ptolemy and his sources acquired much of their information from the records of Agricola's campaigns. As we have seen, Tacitus refers to a tribe called the Boresti which Agricola attacked after the Battle of Mons Graupius. So far this territory has not been located.

BREACHED WALLS AND ABANDONED FRONTIERS

After the departure of Agricola, Roman problems in other parts of the empire were responsible for the withdrawal of troops from north Britain. The invaders retreated to the Forth-Clyde isthmus and from thence south to the Cheviots.

In the AD 120s the emperor Hadrian ordered a great wall to be built of turf and stone just north of the Tyne and Solway line.

It looked as if proto-Pictland was at last free of the troublesome invaders. However, in AD 138 Hadrian was succeeded by the great Antoninus Pius. The army was again ordered north and the British frontier pushed forward to the Clyde/Forth valley where a new wall was raised in AD 142/3.

The Antonine Wall was constructed of turf or occasionally, where turf was scarce, clay blocks on a base of sandstone boulders. It stretched for 60 kilometres (37 miles) between Bo-ness on the Forth and Old Kilpatrick on the Clyde. The base was about fifteen Roman feet wide while the height is not known, although experiments suggest it may have been nearly three metres. Fortlets capable of garrisoning forty to eighty men were added every mile with larger forts each housing a regiment of auxiliaries at wider intervals. A road – the Military Way – ran alongside the wall.

Carved stone distance slabs commemorating the work of the legionaries who built the wall were set up at regular intervals. These slabs depicted scenes of triumph such as Roman soldiers trampling naked barbarians, sacrificing animals probably to the war god Mars, and accepting laurel wreaths.

Meanwhile a network of forts and fortlets connected by roads was set up in Lowland Scotland along the main travel routes, many of them built on old Agricolan sites.

However, by about AD 155 the great wall system, which must have seemed impregnable when first built, was in trouble. Forts were abandoned and burned (perhaps by the proto-Picts, perhaps by the retreating Romans themselves), and although many were rebuilt, by the time of the accession of Marcus Aurelius in AD 161, the Romans had more or less retreated back behind Hadrian's Wall. By AD 180 the enemy were virtually out of Scotland.

The frontier at Hadrian's Wall was thereafter continually under attack by Caledonians who refused to honour treaties, preferring to join forces with the Maeatae, a major tribe who lived near the wall. The Roman governor cunningly bribed the Maeatae to ditch the Caledonians and there followed almost ten years of peace.

Dr Breeze suggests that the Romans played the Caledonians and Maeatae off against each other, a strategy that worked until the late 190s when the two major tribes decided to unite their forces against the common enemy.

By AD 208 historians such as Cassius Dio and Herodian were giving a much clearer account of events. Septimus Severus, the emperor, with his sons Caracalla and Geta, arrived in Britain with a large force, ostensibly to repair and maintain the frontier at Hadrian's Wall. In fact, a year later, with some forty thousand men and an accompanying fleet, he crossed the wall and invaded Caledonia.

Accounts of the campaign concentrate more on the landscape and dreary weather conditions than the invasion. Casualties were heavy, but eventually they reached 'almost the end of the island'. There were no major battles. It seemed that the proto-Picts preferred guerilla tactics. Dio suggests that the barbarians may deliberately have lured them north. However, treaties were made, peace negotiated and Severus, Caracalla and Geta adopted the joint title 'Britannicus' ('conqueror of Britain').

Their glory was short-lived. A year later the Maeatae, shortly to be joined by the Caledonians, rebelled. Caracalla was put in charge of the army which was ordered to kill everyone in sight.

When Severus died at York in AD 211, Caracalla lost interest. He made peace with the natives and abandoned his forts at Carpow near Perth on the Tay and Cramond on the Forth. With his mother and brother he returned to Rome bearing his father's ashes.

For the next ninety years peace appears to have endured in the north. This was probably a time to take stock of the horrors of Roman trespass, to settle internal rivalries among the warrior kingdoms, to consolidate and form what was soon to become a proud and powerful nation – the Picts.

THE PICTISH INHERITANCE

The first part of this book has been an attempt to trace the ancestry of the Picts through archaeology, Classical comment and decades of dedicated academic research.

From their Mesolithic forefathers, the Picts must have inherited a profound knowledge of their flora – the edible, healing, poisonous plants, roots and berries that carpeted the countryside.

They would have known the best ways to hunt, stalk, chase, trap and kill the forest fauna for food and clothing. But they had also learned to hunt not just for the pot but for pleasure, the prerogative of the élite. They would have respected the taboos and rituals that still surrounded all aspects of the kill.

From Neolithic ancestors they would have inherited their farming knowledge

[37]

The Clootie Well, Munlochy. A Pictish legacy?

– how best to breed and rear cattle, the importance of feeding the land, crop rotation, when to sow and reap according to the phases of the moon.

They might well have retained the secrets of the stone circles, how to calculate the changing seasons, how to predict the weather, how to practise the charms and incantations that called up winds and storms.

Although they had no sense of history with dates and facts as we do today, they would most certainly have known about the lineages and deeds of their forebears reaching back perhaps for hundreds of years. Tales of battles and heroes would have been repeated at Pictish hearths and halls through the oral tradition.

Their prodigious building skills were also inherited, while their use of decorated stones might have derived from the Romans.

Pictish heroic society was directly inherited from their Celtic ancestors of Indo-European origin. Already it had begun to evolve into the clan system which survived into eighteenth-century Scotland.

Iron-smithing, at that time still shrouded in magic and mystery, was another important Celtic inheritance, while their skills in metal craftsmanship came straight from their Bronze Age ancestors.

Good horsemanship and breeding were again of Celtic origin, although they probably learned much from the Romans. The same could be said of their fighting and battle skills.

Their love of finery, feasting and drinking, their generosity in the giving and receiving of gifts and hospitality, their volatile nature and love of combat can all be traced to the Gauls.

They were grounded in superstition. The coming of Christianity certainly tempered some of their terrors but it never succeeded in driving them all out. Such fears belonged to the first inhabitants of Scotland, which is still a superstitious nation today. Many of the old Pictish beliefs are still practised throughout the country. People still attach clouts or rags to springs or visit healing wells such as Munlochy in the Black Isle. Plenty of folk still believe in the Pictish monster of Loch Ness. Festivals such as Hallowe'en, that great celebration of the dead, the Burning of the Clavie in Burghead, and a host of other ancient beliefs, customs, wells and pagan sites can probably be traced back to those distant times.

Now that we have given the Picts a past and learned that much of what they inherited we also share, the time has come to enter their world and try to discover them as far as is possible in an age which as far as records go is as dark as night, with the occasional illumination of a fitful moon.

PART TWO

THE PICTISH KINGDOM

'PEOPLE OF THE DESIGNS'

I N 325 BC a Greek explorer call Pytheas sailed round Britain and referred to the British Isles as the Pretanic Islands, from the word 'Priteni' or 'Pretani'.

At first the name Pretanic applied to all the islands but in the south it probably became Romanized into Britanni, with the people calling themselves Brittones. However, it would seem that the name Priteni remained in its old form to describe the people north of the Antonine Wall. Like the ancient Irish variation of the same name, Cruithni, it means 'People of the Designs' – possibly referring to the custom of tattooing rather than painting the skin.

At first the old Irish name for all Britain was 'Cruthen'. Later its use was restricted to the people who had not been conquered by Rome north of the Antonine Wall. Thus Cruthentuath and Pictland as names became interchangeable.

Although the panegyricist Eumenius appears to be the first to mention in AD 297 that the Britons were only accustomed to fighting the Picts and the Hibernians (Irish), both still 'half-naked enemies', he was not the only Classical writer to call them by that name.

A Roman poet states in AD 310 that the emperor Constantius Augustus did not deign to acquire the woods and marshes of the 'Caledones and other Picti'.

The Caledonians were certainly one tribe in Pictland, whereas it would seem that the Picti consisted of a group of other tribes north of the Forth/Clyde frontier, not all culturally alike but by this time loosely allied to each other. It could be argued that today not all regions of Scotland are culturally alike, nor do they always agree, though their mumblings and rumblings are no longer resolved by battle.

Dio Cassius informs us (in the abridgement of his writings by Xiphilinus) that by 208 'the two most important tribes of the Britons [in the North] are the Caledonians and the Maeatae; the names of all the tribes have been practically absorbed in these. The Maeatae dwell close to the wall which divides the island into two parts and the Caledones next to them.'

According to Watson the word Maeatae translates as 'warriors', and the name survives in Dunmyat (Fort of the Maeatae) and Myothill in Stirlingshire.

The historian Ammianus Marcellinus, referring to a Pictish attack on Hadrian's Wall in AD 367, says that the Picts were later divided into two peoples, the Verturiones and the Dycaledones (double Caledonians). The Verturiones were to reappear as the people of the Pictish kingdom of Fortriu, centred on Strathearn and Menteith. Marjorie Anderson reckons that the Verturiones were sea raiders from Fortriu and Fife. It seems then that the Maeatae and the Verturiones were the same people as the Venicones of Ptolemy's map.

St Patrick was the first Briton to use the Pictish name in the fifth century when he referred to them as 'most shameful, wicked and apostate Picts' because they had bought some of his Christian converts from slave dealers.

Gildas the Sage, another Briton, who died about 570, referred to 'marauding Picts' who had raided post-Roman Britain and who came from the north by sea. He describes them as savage men with more hair on their villainous faces than decent clothing on their bodies.

The Venerable Bede in the eighth century believed that the Picts at the time of St Columba's mission were divided into two groups, northern and southern, and that the southern Picts had been converted to Christianity by St Ninian. If Bede is correct the division between them was therefore in operation from about AD 400 and may have continued at least until AD 550. The boundary line is not known but is thought to be the Mounth, an area just south and west of Aberdeen.

The origins of the Pictish name – Painted People – would seem to be fairly obvious. From Julius Caesar, who wrote, referring only to Britons in the south, 'all the Britanni paint themselves with woad which produces a bluish colouring', to Ovid, Martial, Solinus, Herodian, Claudian and Jordanes, there are numerous references to the fact that the Britons coloured their skins. However, some early writers mention that the Picts were tattooed rather than painted.

Isadore of Seville, writing about AD 600, says that the Picts took their name from the fact that their bodies had designs pricked into their skins by needles.

So Picts they were to the Dark Age world and Picts they remain today, but the question is, what did they call themselves? Did they have a collective name or did they continue to call themselves by their tribal names, as, for example, the Caledonians?

It is possible that the term Picti was the Latinized version of their own collective name. Marcellinus was to speak of the Pecti, along with the Saxones, the Scotti (Irish) and the Attacotti, as continually harassing the Britons.

Professor Watson tells us that in old Norse the name is 'Pettr', in old English 'Peohta', and in old Scots 'Pecht'. In Fife and Aberdeenshire today, the Picts are still referred to as the 'Pechs' or 'Pechties'. These forms suggest Pect instead of Pict, with an entirely different meaning.

Whatever the truth behind the name, one fact emerges – that the Latin term Pict is historically correct to describe the people who lived in Scotland north of the Forth/Clyde valley for nearly six hundred years between AD 297 and 840.

FOUNDATION MYTHS

Once upon a time there was a king called Cruithne, son of Cing the Champion, who reigned for a hundred years. He had seven sons who were called Fib, Fidach, Floclaid (or Fotla), Fortrenn, Cat (or Caitt), Ce and Circenn.

These seven brothers divided Alba into seven portions of land each called after himself.

Fib ruled for twenty-four years over Fife and Kinross. Professor Watson suggests the name may be personal and the meaning obscure. In the *Book of Deer* the people of Fife are called the *cu-sidhe* – the fairy hounds.

Fidach ruled for forty years over Moray and Ross. The name translates as 'woodsman'.

Foltlaig or *Fotla* ruled for thirty years over Atholl and Gowrie. Fotla was a goddess of Ireland and a name for that country. Thus Atholl means 'new Ireland'.

Fortriu (*Fortrenn*) ruled for seventy years over Strathearn and Menteith. The name is thought to be the gaelicized form of Verturiones. Its meaning is obscure but may be connected to the River Forth. It might mean 'people of the slow winding river'.

Cat (*Caitt*) ruled for twelve years over Caithness and Sutherland. The name means 'cat people'.

Ce ruled for fifteen years over part of Aberdeenshire including Bennachie. *Ce* may survive in the name of Keith in Banffshire. An ancient Irish legend tells of a certain Frigriu who eloped to Ireland with the daughter of a man from Iona. Frigriu is called the 'artificer of the Pictish plain of Ce'.

Cirech or *Circenn* ruled for sixty years over Angus and the Mearns. The name may mean 'crest-headed'. A battle was fought on the Plain of Circinn against the Scots. W.F. Skene mentions a certain Crus, son of Cirech, who was a chief warrior of the Picts.

A little like the Jewish story of the rise of the Children of Israel, this was perhaps the Pictish way of accounting for their past. The story of Cruithne appears with variations in three of the texts of the Pictish King List, and the seven provinces are listed in a survey called *De Situ Albanie* attached to List One.

[42]

Professor Watson performed a tremendous feat when he translated as far as possible the meanings of these tribal names, some of which were directly descended from the Romanized tribal names on Ptolemy's map, and many of which are rooted in today's place names.

In *Historia Brittonum*, Ninnius, who was writing in the early ninth century, said that the Picts occupied the Orkney Islands and from there devastated and conquered many parts of north Britain where they remained to the present day.

In the Irish version of the same history, dating from the eleventh century, Cruithne's grandson Aenbecan, son of Caitt, became high-king over the seven provinces while five of Cruithne's brothers went from Orkney to France to found the city of Pictavis or Poitiers.

Another ancient legend recorded in *Chronicles of the Picts and Scots* edited by W.F. Skene comes from a poem in the *Book of Ballymote*. This tells us that Cruithne's people first came from Thrace to France, where they founded Poitiers, and then moved on to Ireland during the time of the fifth mythical invasion, where they defeated the king of Leinster's enemies. Drostan the Pictish Druid cured the Irish warriors who had been poisoned by enemy weapons.

But Eremon the high-king of Ireland decreed that King Gub of the Picts was not to settle in his country. Instead he and his men were given as wives the widows of those Irish warriors who had perished in battle during the invasion on condition that succession to high-kingship should be derived from the women not the men. King Gub and his warlords swore by the sun and the moon to keep this promise.

Cathluan, son of Gub, was the first high-king of the Cruithnig to rule Alba. He was followed by sixty-nine kings until Drust IX who, as the last king of the Picts, was allegedly killed at the instigation of Kenneth mac Alpin in about AD 842.

Another legend makes no mention of Cathluan but tells us that King Cruithne crossed to Alba and there accompanied the Britons of Fortriu to war with the Saxons. He successfully defended their land, but as there were no women in Alba he returned to the high-king of Ireland who gave him twelve widows on condition that inheritance passed through the female line.

The third legend found in *Picts and Scots* relates that the Irish king obtained thirty-six warriors from the people of Thrace as mercenaries. After the Thracians had cleared 'sword-land' for themselves in Fortriu and Circinn they were given 150 maidens of the Irish nobility, provided inheritance thereafter went through the female line.

The Venerable Bede repeats a version of this old legend. He writes in his *Ecclesiastical History* in 731 that the Picts came from Scythia to North Ireland where the king advised them to go east to Britain and then north, which advice they took. As they had no women with them, the Irish king agreed to oblige them

[43]

with wives provided they henceforth chose their rulers by the female rather than the male ancestry of their kings. 'And all know', wrote Bede, 'that this custom is still maintained among the Picts.'

But these latter stories with their strong Irish point of view originated in Ireland, where they were carefully preserved and passed from generation to generation through the oral tradition by those druids who were known as seers and who probably invented them.

The name seer implies the use of dreams, revelations and imagination rather than fact. The myths are not Pictish. Professor H.M. Chadwick asks the question 'Could the Picts really have believed that their law of inheritance had its origin in such a transaction as the story relates?' (If indeed this was their law of inheritance.)

No doubt the Picts had their own way of recording the origin and history of their people, but none of it exists as fact in written form. Scraps of evidence may lie hidden in the legends, old festivals and perhaps in the symbols themselves.

Such records as do exist are from Irish sources and were mostly compiled long after the events and are therefore coloured by the perceptions of a later age.

THE KING LIST

In the bigger and better-organized monasteries the monks kept annals which were year-by-year entries of important facts; together they went to make up a chronicle. These year-books or diaries, which were basically annotated Easter Tables, recorded important national events such as accessions and deaths of kings, dates of battles, and whatever was considered momentous in the life of that particular monastery.

Lists of the names and dates of Pictish kings in succession are to be found in the only surviving native source, known as the King List. This survives in seven or eight texts, most of which were edited by W.F. Skene and which were found in Irish records.

These eight lists have been divided into two major texts, of which List One would seem to be the most important. It starts with the mythical Cruithne and his descendants, who are not mentioned in List Two, and includes a certain Brude Bont, who reigned for forty-eight years and was succeeded by thirty kings all called Brude, with distinguishing descriptive styles, who 'ruled over Ireland and Albania [Scotland] for 150 years'.

List One was found along with other sources on early Scottish history in a fourteenth-century manuscript discovered in Paris along with a later Scottish

Chronicle, and both are thought to date from the tenth century.

Where did the Irish chroniclers get the information on the List, much of which is to be found in the annals of Tigernach and Ulster among other sources?

Not, Isabel Henderson suggests, originally from Ireland, as the names of the kings were written in their Pictish forms; nor from Northumbria or other parts of Britain. Why should they bother? Which leaves the possibility of a Pictish monastic source, long ago lost but not necessarily beyond recovery.

Iona would be the obvious choice, but not the only one. Dr Henderson suggests that Applecross, founded by St Maelrubha in AD 672 from its parent monastery at Bangor in Ireland, might have been the source. Another possibility, according to the fifteenth-century historian Bower, is Abernethy in Perthshire. He claimed to have seen a chronicle of the church there that cited Abernethy as the chief royal palace of both Pictish kings and bishops.

It seems possible that the original Pictish material – which must have existed somewhere – may well have been destroyed by the conquering Scots for the purpose of suppressing all things Pictish, or burned perhaps by marauding Vikings. The manuscripts may well have mouldered away in the damp Scottish climate at some much later date, or simply have been lost. There always remains the possibility – however remote – that more information will turn up buried in the walls or crypts of some ruined Pictish monastic site – an exciting thought.

KING BRUDE AND SAINT COLUMBA

The first Pictish king to be established as a documented historical figure, and not mythic as many of the earlier names on the King List are thought to be, is Brude, son of Maelcon.

Professor Chadwick tells us about the variations of that name which occur in the different versions of the King List. Brude or Bruide appear in the Irish annals and Bredei or Bridei would seem to be the Pictish spelling, with the accent on the final syllable. However, the commonest form of the name these days would seem to be Brude. Inverness has a street called King Brude Road.

Maelcon, his father, is associated with Maelgwn, a powerful king of Gwynedd in North Wales whose family may have descended from Cunedda, a Briton from south of the Forth.

Gildas the Sage, a British religious historian thought to have been a member of the sub-Roman civilian élite living south of the Thames, had harsh words to say about the Welsh kings, and particularly King Maelgwn, in his *De Excideo*.

Writing in about 540 he calls him the dragon of the island, wallowing like a

St Columba's Cave, Ellary, Argyll

fool in the ancient ink of his crimes 'like a man drunk on wine pressed from the vine of the Sodomites' – splendid vituperation with perhaps more than a modicum of truth. Maelgwn died in AD 547.

Gildas was equally insulting to the Picts, calling them and the Scots 'foul hordes like dark throngs of worms who wriggle out of narrow cracks in the rock when the sun is high and the weather grows warm'.

About 550 Brude inherited or was elected to the high-kingship of Pictland and he ruled for about thirty-three years. Some five years into his reign he defeated King Gabran of the Scots who died in the same year.

In AD 500 the Scots from Ulster under King Fergus Mor mac Eirc had secured a foothold in Argyll and called it Dal Riata, which was the name of his kingdom in Ireland. From that time on until 840 they were to become an increasingly penetrating thorn in the flesh of the Pictish rulers. They probably deserved their Roman name of *Scotti*, which translates as 'bandits'.

However, the victory over Gabran was to secure peace between the two peoples for fifteen years. Had Brude pressed on to expel the Scots from Pictish shores, the course of history might well have been changed.

But possibly the urge was not there. The Picts and the Scots had known each other intimately for many centuries. The two kingdoms had intermarried and had fought side by side in numerous battles. Gildas reports three Pictish wars against the Romans, the third of which ended in a Pictish defeat. The Picts and the Scots were allies then, possibly for the last time for many centuries to come.

Argyll was sparsely populated. The country was rugged and not easy to cultivate. Perhaps Brude no longer saw the Dal Riatans as a realistic threat to his fertile eastern realms. Or perhaps, as we shall see, he was persuaded to this point of view by St Columba.

At the mature age of forty-two, Columba with twelve companions 'resolving to seek a foreign country for the love of Christ sailed from Scotia [Ireland] to Britain, where he lived for 34 years, an island soldier'. So St Adamnan wrote in his famous hagiography of the saint.

He arrived at Iona perhaps before, perhaps after making contact with Conall, the Scottish King of Dal Riatan Argyll, to seek his permission to settle on the island. But Iona was still Pictish territory, certainly in the eyes of Brude. Permission would be needed from this 'rex potentissimus' as Bede described him, before he could settle.

Had Columba not been of royal descent – his mother Eithne was eleventh in line from Cathair Mor, King of Leinster, and his father's great-grandfather was the celebrated Niall of the Nine Hostages – it is doubtful that he would have had any access at all to the Pictish court. Presumably Brude had heard of him and was curious to meet this colourful aristocrat who was also a Christian monk. Ian

[47]

Finlay suggests that Brude may have regarded him first and foremost as an ambassador similar to the great statesmen clerics of a later age. No doubt too rumours of his miraculous powers had gone before him and Brude was curious to test these skills against those of his own magicians.

It is too easy to see Columba as a modern muscular Christian marching through the Dark Ages scattering superstition and enlightening the heathen. He was a high-born Celt who could have been elected king through his aristocratic descent. He had the soul of a poet, the imagination of a writer and the voice of a musician. He enjoyed travel, he excelled in organisation and he cared deeply about people and the God-given world.

How did Columba see Christ? Ian Finlay suggests that because of his pagan heritage he could think of God only in symbolic terms. The cross was that all-important symbol, as the Pictish class II, III and IV stones will show.

Perhaps he saw Christ as a latter-day Cu Chulainn with his warrior band of angels storming through the heavens to attack evil in the form of monsters and devils wherever it was to be found.

It was no easy task to cross the Highlands in those days. Wolves and hostile Picts added to atrocious weather must have made the journey hard and hazardous. He and his companions probably travelled as far as possible by boat through the Sound of Lorne, up Loch Linnhe, then by foot along the banks of the River Lochy into the Great Glen, through Loch Lochy, Loch Oich and Loch Ness and finally to the court of Brude in Inverness.

On the way, Adamnan tells us that he encountered the mythical monster of Loch Ness. Making the sign of the symbol of Christ he invoked the name of God, and commanded the creature to depart. Many of the early saints conquered monsters of this sort and in this manner. Highland folklore was and is full of lochs that sheltered the dreaded water-horse (kelpie) or the water-bull, symbols of power over water to the pagan. Adamnan's inclusion of the story was no doubt to prove that the power of Christ was greater than any pagan spirit. The water-horse as we shall see may have emerged as one of the pre-Christian symbols on the class I and II stones.

Brude's fortress has usually been associated with the vitrified fort of Craig Phadraig about two miles west of the mouth of the River Ness and some five hundred feet above sea-level. Professor Alcock suggests that the site of Brude and Columba's encounter was Castle Hill on the River Ness in the centre of Inverness, but that his main fortress may have been Castle Urquhart on Loch Ness.

Skene believed that the fort was sited at Torvean, a gravelly ridge a little south of the town where the golf course is today. When the Caledonian Canal was cut in 1808, workmen found in this area a heavy silver chain, the most beautiful and élitist object imaginable, with thirty-three doubled links, eighteen inches long and weighing ninety-two ounces.

Other chains have been excavated over the years in other parts of Scotland, some with terminals bearing Pictish symbols. Welsh kings such as Brude's father wore chains instead of crowns. Although this chain was probably not Brude's as it has been dated to the seventh century, and Brude died in 584, it is possible that Brude brought the fashion north from Wales and that the chain was commissioned by a successor.

When Columba reached the fortress, he and his companions sang vespers outside Brude's gates. Although the druids objected to the noise, Columba chanted the 46th Psalm in his powerful voice.

'God is our hope and strength: a very present help in trouble.

'Therefore will we not fear, though the earth be moved; and though the hills be carried into the midst of the sea ...

'The Lord of hosts is with us; the God of Jacob is our refuge.'

Columba's voice was one of his great talents. The fourteenth century *Leabhar Breac* records that:

> The sound of the voice of Colum Cille
> Great was its sweetness above all clerics:
> To the end of fifteen hundred paces,
> Though great the distance, it was distinctly heard.

When his voice was raised in anger towards one of Iona's monks, it was said that it could be heard in Mull.

Thus at the sound of his voice and against all the Celtic laws of hospitality, Brude ordered the gate to be locked. Maybe he was curious to know how his visitor would react.

More likely Adamnan saw another opportunity to record a miracle and adjusted his account to that effect, so he wrote that the saint strode up to the entrance, made the sign of Christ, knocked and 'laid his hand upon the gate which instantly flew open of its own accord, the bolts having been driven back with great force'. The Christians passed through and the king and his advisers, alarmed, left the palace to meet 'the blessed man with reverence and address him with the most respectful and conciliatory language. And ever after from that day, so long as he lived, the king held this holy and reverend man in very great honour, as was due.'

No doubt Brude would have been as superstitious as any of his contemporaries, but he was also a politician, a warrior and no doubt a realist. It is hard to believe that the high-king of Pictland would have been as alarmed as Adamnan suggests.

[49]

He would have known about Christianity, shown a diplomatic interest and decided to leave religious matters in the hands of his chief priest and adviser, Broichan.

It is obvious that Brude respected and admired Columba, but not I think for his Christianity. Their dealings as man to man were of a more political nature. Although Bede and Adamnan gloss over the matter of Brude's personal conversion, it is generally thought that neither he nor the Pictish aristocracy were ready for Christianity.

What Columba did do was to win Brude's goodwill, to pave the way for future missionary expeditions into Pictland, to secure Iona as a Christian centre, and to negotiate the safety of some of his monks who were hostages in Orkney. This request was made in the presence of the king of Orkney – a vassal of Brude – and granted. Most important, he was able to prevent Brude from hustling King Conall, thus giving the Scots time to recover from defeat and further establish their kingdom of Dal Riata in Argyll and the Isles.

Adamnan records in detail more about Columba's encounters with Broichan than with Brude, for he knew that it was with the magicians of Pictland that the real power lay. To establish Christianity as a credible alternative to the old religion he must first discredit the magicians.

As a man of his generation, Columba did not disbelieve in the old gods and their powers. What he needed to do was to prove that they were less potent than Christ. He used the only way possible, the only way he knew, by pitting miracle against magic in what we might call today a demonstration of psychology and auto-suggestion.

Broichan was not only chief magician but also foster father or tutor in the true Celtic tradition to Brude. The relationship was close, for Celtic kings relied not only on the advice of their chief druids but also on the wisdom and influence of their foster families. In Brude's presence, Columba started the contest by requesting that Broichan set free an Irish slave girl in his possession.

When Broichan refused – an overt sign of hostility because the laws of hospitality required the host to be more than generous to his guest – Columba warned him of his imminent death. Accompanied by his companions and no doubt by curious members of Brude's court, he went down to the River Ness, selected a white pebble and predicted that God would cure many heathens by its use. He added that Broichan was at that moment about to be smitten by the angel of death. Immediately messengers from Brude arrived to confirm Columba's words and to beg him to save the magician's life. Columba sent the stone to Brude and told him to dip it in water and give the drink to Broichan. If the slave was freed then Broichan would recover.

The stone was placed in water where it floated 'contrary to nature'. When the magician drank, he lost his hand-maid but gained his life.

Again Broichan was bested when he tried to raise a magic mist and storm to drown Columba on Loch Ness. The wind rose and the sky darkened. Undaunted, Columba entered his boat, sailed into the wind, which then changed direction and bore him safely to his destination. Columba was himself a skilled sailor, but Broichan was not to know that.

Brude must have witnessed his foster father's discomfiture but it was not enough to make him convert.

It is wise to remember that Adamnan's hagiography is shrouded in symbolism. What he wanted to do was prove the superiority of Columba and Christianity over Broichan and paganism. Where his own and centuries of successive generations were concerned, he certainly succeeded.

The death of Brude in 584 was a blow to the infant Christian Church in the north-west. Adamnan makes excuses for the fact that any friend of Columba's should have died at all. His reason was that the white pebble, 'a certain cure for all diseases' which Columba had given him to cure Broichan, had been lost 'when looked for by those persons whose term of life had arrived'. When needed 'it was not to be found in the place where previously it had been laid', probably the treasury. Thus Brude died, having ruled for some thirty-three years, a surprisingly long reign for those volatile days.

There is a possibility that he was killed in the battle of Asreth in the land of Circinn (Angus) between Picts on both sides. Dr Henderson suggests that he may have had trouble controlling the southern Picts and that the north of Pictland as the royal centre declined in importance after his death.

BRUDE'S SUCCESSORS

Brude, who may have been the last high-king to rule from the Moray Firth area, was succeeded by *Gartnait IV*, son of Domech (thirty-seventh in succession), who reigned for either eleven or twenty years.

Peace with the Dal Riatan Scots so carefully bargained for by Columba could not last for ever. During the final years of Brude's long life and during Garnait's reign, Aedan mac Gabran, King of the Dal Riatan Scots, a great warrior who had at least four or five sons, fought against the Picts and others over a period of thirteen years.

Aedan was consecrated king by a reluctant Columba, who preferred his brother Eoganan. They must have become reconciled for Columba prayed for his victory at a battle against – according to Adamnan – the Miathi. These were the

Abernethy, Perth & Kinross, was an important Pictish site.
The round tower dates from the eleventh century

same people as the Maeatae mentioned by Cassius Dio. They lived near the Antonine Wall and the location is thought to have been Stirlingshire. Although Aedan won this battle it was an unhappy victory as two of his sons were killed, together with 303 warriors, some time around 590. A further skirmish against the Picts north of the Tay, known as the Battle of Circinn, saw the death of yet another son, but the records are hazy. The two battles may have been one.

Aedan, tradition suggests, was born near the Forth. Allegedly he gave his fortress of Eperpuill (Aberfoyle) to found a monastery. According to one tradition he may have married a Pictish princess.

In 603, according to Bede, for no known reason, he tackled the Angles under King Ethelfrid at the Battle of Degsastan, perhaps because he was alarmed by the Northumbrians' growing threat to the Britons of Strathclyde. Another tradition suggests that his wife was the daughter of the king of Strathclyde and their son was Artur, a rare British name and the first historical reference to an Arthur in Strathclyde. Aedan's daughter Gemma was allegedly the mother of Saint Lasrian.

The Battle of Degsastan was a disaster. Two more of Aedan's sons were killed and his army was wiped out. As a result he may have abdicated or been deposed.

According to 'Scelo Cano meic Gartnain', compiled in the eleventh century from material dating from the ninth, there was war between Aedan and a certain Gartnan mac Aeda meic Gabrain. Aedan killed Gartnan and would have killed his son Cano who lived in Skye if he had not escaped to Ireland.

It looks as if Gartnan son of Aeda son of Gabrain was none other than Gartnait IV.

Gartnait's successor was *Nechtan II* (thirty-eighth), son of Irb according to the King Lists but named as Cano's son in Irish records. He may well have been Gartnait's grandson.

Both Gartnait IV and his successor Nechtan II, son of Canonn or Cano, are credited with building the church at Abernethy, although the Aberdeen Breviary states that a certain Domath, a local king, was responsible.

Traditionally, however, the church of St Brigit of Kildare was founded about AD 625 by Nechtan II (Nectonius Magnus), with Darlugdath the abbess of Kildare present with a following of nuns who founded the convent at Abernethy.

Dr Smyth suggests this Nechtan was the same ruler as Neithon, king of Strathclyde, and that southern Pictland was very much under the influence of the Strathclyde Britons in the early seventh century. Considering the close family ties between Aedan and Strathclyde, this seems more than possible.

Thirty-ninth in line, *Ciniath*, son of Lutrin, ruled for nineteen years. His reign roughly paralleled that of King Edwin of Northumberland, who was killed at the Battle of Hatfield by the British king Cadwalla of Gwynedd about AD 633. Bede tells us that during Edwin's reign the sons of his predecessor, Ethelfrid, lived in exile with many of their followers among the 'Irish or Picts' and were there converted to Irish Christianity. As soon as Edwin was killed, Eanfrid, the eldest son of Ethelfrid, inherited the Northumbrian province of Bernicia and with his brother was killed by Cadwalla.

Little is known about Pictish affairs in the first half of the seventh century. Three brothers ruled in succession between approximately AD 630 and 650. These were *Nechtan III* (fortieth), son of Uuid or Foith, *Brude II* (forty-first) and *Talorc IV* (forty-second). During part of that period, the Dal Riatan king Domnall Brecc had a disastrous reign, losing five important battles, some in Ireland but at least one against the Picts. He was eventually killed in battle by the king of Strathclyde, an indication that the friendship between the Britons and the Scots was over.

However, the Picts were in no position to be complacent. Northumberland was on the move.

On Eanfrid's death at the hands of Cadwalla, Oswald – the Saintly King – ruled over a reunited Northumbria, having first killed the hated Cadwalla. Bede admired Oswald as a true Christian. It was Oswald who sent to Ireland for a bishop to convert his people, and chief of those who came was Aidan, a monk from Iona. Bede tells us that Columba's foundation was 'for a long time the principal monastery of nearly all the northern Irish and all the Picts and exercised a widespread authority'. Oswald was killed in battle in 642 and was succeeded by his brother Oswiu, aged about thirty. He was to rule for twenty-eight years.

During Eanfrid's exile in Pictland he had married a Pictish princess. Their son *Talorcen* (forty-third) inherited the Pictish throne in AD 653 and reigned for four years. Talorcen is said to have fought successfully against the Scots in the Battle of Strath Ethairt in AD 654, and for the next thirty years or so there were no skirmishes between the Picts and the Scots.

There was a good reason for this. At the end of Talorcen's reign his uncle Oswiu 'subdued and made tributary' a large part of southern Pictland, which was to be occupied for thirty years.

Gartnait VI (forty-fourth), son of Domnall, inherited that part of Pictland which was not occupied by the English. He is thought to have been a son of Domnall Brecc and his death is recorded six years later in 663.

In the year of his death a great event took place in Northumbria. The famous Synod of Whitby, presided over by King Oswiu, was called to debate two hot controversies within the Church. One was concerned with the cut of the monastic tonsure, the other was over the complicated issue of when to observe Easter. Oswiu had found himself celebrating the great festival under the Bishop of Lindisfarne while his queen, Eanfled, was still fasting for Lent under the

Part of an Anglian cross-shaft at Abercorn, West Lothian

spiritual direction of her Kentish priest.

So the Celtic Church founded by St Columba was up against the Church led by the Pope in Rome. St Colman, a Celt, found himself in stolid opposition to the quick-witted St Wilfrid, representing the Petrine church of Rome. Wilfrid won the vote. He became not only Bishop of York and the Northumbrians but – as Bede tells us – 'likewise of the Picts', at least that part of Pictland under Northumbrian rule.

By AD 678 an Anglian bishopric had been created in Pictland under Bishop Trumwine at Abercorn on the south shore of the River Forth.

[55]

These were dark times indeed for the Picts and nothing is known about their reactions to occupation, but we can guess that it was universally loathed.

King Oswiu had died in 670 during the reign of the Pictish *Drust V* (forty-fifth), brother of Gartnait VI. Oswiu was succeeded by Ecgfrid, who was probably responsible for Drust's expulsion from his kingdom in 672.

Dr Henderson suggests that this might have had something to do with an incident recorded in the eighth-century *Life of St Wilfrid* by Eddius Stephanus. The Picts, eager to be free of the hated enemy, collected an army and attempted a rebellion, probably under Drust. Ecgfrid, quashing the rising, was said to have made a bridge of Pictish corpses across two rivers so that his army could pass over them dry-shod and thus slaughter the remains of the Pictish warriors.

Eddius tells us that it was proud Wilfrid who goaded Ecgfrid towards this appalling massacre because he hated the thought of losing any part of his diocese to the 'bestial tribes of the Picts'.

The deposed Drust was followed in 672 by *Brude III* (forty-sixth), son of Bili, a king rightly remembered by foreign chroniclers for his courage and battle skills. Brude had interesting ancestors. His father is thought to have been a son of Neithon, the king of Strathclyde, and his mother a daughter of the Northumbrian Eanfrid. Thus Brude III was a first cousin of Ecgfrid.

No doubt as a result of Northumbrian occupation and the leadership of a loser (Drust), Pictland needed the courage and discipline of a strong ruler. According to the Irish annals and Skene, Brude is thought to have been responsible for besieging the great fortress of Dunottar just south of Aberdeen in AD 681. A year later he may have taken his fleet north and devastated Orkney. On his way there he possibly attacked Dunbeath in Caithness, and a year later, in 683, conceivably assaulted the great Scottish fortresses of Dunadd in Dal Riata and Dundurn in Pictland.

But his laurel wreath was truly earned on 20 May 685 when he routed the Northumbrians under Ecgfrid at the *Bellum Duin Nectain* – the Battle of Dunnichen or Nechtansmere – near Forfar. Had he not won that day, Pictland might have been destroyed for ever and the Kingdom of Scotland never existed. We would all have been English. More of Dunnichen later.

Ecgfrid was killed and his body taken to Iona. Bishop Trumwine and his monks left Abercorn, some Anglian nuns fled to St Cuthbert for safety, and the Picts recovered their lost territory. They were free once more.

Brude reigned for some twenty-one years and on his death he was taken for burial to Iona. According to an old legend recorded in the *Life of Adamnan*, the latter was a friend of the king. As abbot, he watched over the corpse, praying all night for its recovery. At dawn the body began to revive until one of the old monks warned Adamnan that such a miracle would set too high a standard for his

Dal Riatan fortress of Dunadd in Argyll, captured by Oengus I, showing footprint on left and basin on right. The metal box protects the incised carving of a boar. The rock surface is now protected by a replica

successors. The king was allowed to rest in peace.

According to the Irish annal that recorded his death he was called the 'King of Fortriu', a clue to the belief that his administrative centre was in the south.

Taran or *Tarain* (forty-seventh), son of Enfidach, inherited in 693. Dr Smyth thinks that he may have been called after the Gaulish thunder-god. His father was killed in AD 693 and he himself was deposed in 697. A couple of years later he was forced into exile in Ireland. Dr Smyth writes that he probably took with him a sizable following. A court in exile such as this would have the opportunity to pick up new ideas in art, artifacts and literature which later would strongly influence the craftsmen at home.

Brude IV (forty-eighth) *mac Derile* succeeded Taran in 697. Dr Henderson suggests that he might have been the grandson of Brude mac Bili. He seems to have defeated the Northumbrians in a battle against the Bernicians and killed Berht, thought to have been a sub-king in the Lothians. He is remembered for ratifying Adamnan's famous Law of the Innocents, which was promulgated to protect women, children and the clergy from the horrors of war and to exempt women from actually fighting in battle.

Perhaps the law was inspired by Adamnan's mother, Ronait, who, according to a medieval Irish legend, saw a woman with an iron reaping hook dragging another woman out of enemy ranks with the hook in her breast 'for men and women went equally to battle at that time'. Ronait is said to have sat down and refused to move until Adamnan promised to make a law exempting women from fighting.

Together with Brude, Eochaid of the Scots, the Bishop of Iona and Curadan of Rosemarkie, forty clergymen, and fifty-one kings and overlords ratified the new law.

Brude mac Derile died in 706 and was succeeded by his brother, *Nechtan mac Derile* (forty-ninth), who was to reign for eighteen years. Although five years into his reign the Picts were defeated by the Northumbrians on the plain of Manaw, thought to be near Falkirk, it seems that Nechtan came to the conclusion that the Northumbrian Church with its Roman usages had more of the truth or possibly was of greater use to him politically than the Columban Church which still adhered to the old Celtic ways.

After Brude mac Bili's expulsion of the Northumbrians, the Celtic Church celebrated a huge revival and resurgence of power, perhaps too much for Nechtan's liking. The Scots were gaining territory in the north-west and Iona was in the heart of Scottish territory.

He decided to accept Northumbrian ways and in AD 710 asked Abbot Caolfrid to send him information and architects to build him a stone church 'in the Roman fashion' which he promised to dedicate to St Peter.

In AD 717 or possibly earlier he expelled the Columban monks beyond 'Dorsum Brittaniae', the Spine of Britain.

But his move may also have been due to personal religious conviction. He was a Christian and considered himself to be head of the Pictish Church. His reign was to establish Pictland officially as a Christian country with himself as head of the Church.

Thereafter he is thought to have entered the religious life, for a while at least.

The King List at this juncture becomes very confused owing to a series of squabbles to do with succession. *Drust VI* (fiftieth) and *Alpin I* (fifty-first) are mentioned as ruling together for five years. The Irish annals show how disturbed these times were. According to them Drust ruled alone in AD 724 when Nechtan took up religion, but when two years later Nechtan wanted his throne again, Drust arrested him and was himself deposed in favour of Alpin I, son of the Scottish Eochu.

There were four internal skirmishes fought between 728 and 729. The first is thought to have taken place at Moncrieffe Hill, south of Perth. The final champion to emerge victorious between Drust and yet another contestant, was

Oengus I (Onuist) mac Fergus (fifty-second), the founder of a new Pictish dynasty.

Oengus, one of the most powerful of all the Pictish kings, reigned for thirty blood-encrusted years. Bede called him 'a tyrannical murderer who from the beginning to the end of his reign persisted in the performance of bloody crime'. Though Bede was biased, he was speaking the literal truth.

Oengus first turned his attention to Dal Riata, where his son, Brude, flighted a Scottish warrior, in 731. Two years later Brude was captured by a certain Dungal of Lorn who in turn was wounded by Oengus and fled to Ireland. An incident that shows Oengus to have been ruthless occurred when he drowned a king's son sent to him by his own brother as a hostage, or perhaps as a result of a Dal Riatan family feud.

The Irish annals state that Oengus laid waste the districts of Dal Riata. He captured Dunadd and other fortresses, captured Dungal and his brother, and lost his son Brude, which was a great sorrow to him, for Brude would seem to have been as ruthless a warrior as his father.

After a lull of three years Oengus ordered the drowning of the king of Atholl, and in 741 he defeated his remaining enemies in two battles that may have been fought in Ireland. Thus, after ten years of conflict, Oengus defeated Dal Riata and became the first King of the Picts and the Scots.

Drunk with victory, he unwisely looked for more territory to conquer rather than settling down to consolidate his gains. This was his great mistake. Strathclyde and the Britons tempted him to greater feats of daring and in 744 a first skirmish was fought, although the result was not recorded. By 750 he had allied himself unsuccessfully with the kings of Wessex and Mercia against Strathclyde, but the Britons under his brother Talorcan were victorious, although Talorcan was killed in the fighting. Oengus, ruthless as ever, joined with the Northumbrians in 756 to take Dumbarton fortress and Strathclyde. This time his army and the Northumbrians were exterminated.

Oengus died in 761. What a waste of men and time and power his reign had proved to be.

He was succeeded by his brother *Brude V* (fifty-third), who reigned for two years and who was followed by *Ciniod (Kenneth)* (fifty-fourth), son of Wredech, who died in 775.

During Ciniod's reign Dal Riata began to recover under the kingship of Aed Find who, according to the Irish annals, died in 778 after a reign of thirty years. Aed overthrew the Pictish laws of Oengus and substituted his own Dal Riatan 'Laws of Aed'. He managed to throw off Pictish domination in a battle fought in Fortriu in 768, and by the time of his death Dal Riata was independent once more.

The records now become increasingly confused, so that it is hard to understand just what is going on in the two neighbouring kingdoms. Three

Pictish kings are listed, *Alpin II* (fifty-fifth), son of Wroid, *Drust VII* (fifty-sixth), son of Talorcen, and *Talorcen II* (fifty-seventh), son of Drustan, all of whom reigned in a short period of seven years.

Talorcen III (fifty-eighth) is listed as a son of Oengus. If his father was Oengus I then here is the first instance of a son inheriting from his father. He or his predecessor Talorcen II may have been called Dubthalorc, described as 'a king of the Picts on this side of the Mounth', who died, according to the Annals of Ulster, in 782.

Canual (Conall) mac Tadg (fifty-ninth) is a shadowy figure mentioned in the Ulster Annals in 789 as having been 'defeated and fled, and Constantine was victorious'. In 807 he was killed by Conall mac Aedan in Kintyre.

Then follows the great *Constantine mac Fergus* (sixtieth) also known as *Castantin son of Uurguist*, a Pict or half-Pict who won the Pictish throne by killing Conall mac Tadg, and who was to rule for thirty-five years. The records are obscure but Dr Henderson has worked out that while his son Donald ruled Dal Riata he was king of Pictland from about 789 to 820. For the last nine years of his reign – Donald having predeceased him – he was also king of Dal Riata. In other words Constantine was the second king to rule over the Picts and the Scots, Oengus having been the first.

He is remembered as the founder of the church at Dunkeld.

By this time the Vikings had arrived. During Constantine's reign in 794 the Irish annals record the 'devastation of all the islands of Britain by the gentiles [Norse heathen]', with the first sacking of Iona in 802. But these attacks were coming on all sides of Pictland. The warriors had to spread themselves thinly.

Oengus II mac Fergus (sixty-first), or *Unuist son of Uurguist*, succeeded his brother in AD and ruled for about fourteen years. He is thought to have been responsible for bringing the relics of St Andrew to Kilrimont and establishing the great church centre at St Andrews, though it may have been an earlier foundation.

Legend records that both he and his father had their base in Fortriu and ruled from Forteviot. In the Ulster Annals they are both described as kings of Fortriv.

After the death of Oengus the kingship seems to have been shared by *Drust VIII* (sixty-second), son of Constantine, and *Talorc* (sixty-third), son of Uuthoil. They reigned for three or four years between them.

According to the *Chronicle of Huntingdon* (a history of the united Picts and Scots) it was about this time that Alpin, an obscure Scottish figure who may have been a lesser king in Dal Riata, began to harry the Picts.

Meanwhile *Uven* or *Eoganan* (sixty-fourth), son of Oengus II, also listed as a king of Dal Riata, became king of the Picts for three years only. He is recorded as having been slain in a great disaster at the hands of the Norse invaders in 839. Along with numbers 'beyond counting of men of Fortriu', his brother Bran and a

Dal Riatan king called Aed were also killed.

The only king to be killed by the Norse, Eoganan is also the last king of the Picts to be recorded as such in the Irish annals.

Two further kings with Pictish names succeeded each other in one version of the King List. These are *Uurad or Ferath* (sixty-fifth), son of Bargot, and *Brude VI* (sixty-sixth), son of Ferath, who may have been *his* son. They ruled for about four years between them.

Other texts include three more kings, *Kenneth* (sixty-seventh), son of Ferath, probably a brother of his predecessor, *Brude VII* (sixty-eighth), son of Fethal, and *Drust IX* (sixty-ninth), another son of Ferath, who between them ruled for six years.

Drust is thought to have been killed by the Scots either at Forteviot or by trickery at Scone. More of that later.

During the last phase of Pictish kingship the succession to the Pictish throne seems to have fluctuated between three major families, that of Constantine and Oengus II, that of the sons of Fethal, and that of the sons of Ferath. If matriliny had ever been the practice of the Picts it seems that it had now passed out of use.

What it also shows is how closely intertwined the two dynasties of Scottish Dal Riata and the Pictish nation had become, so closely linked that it would have been impossible to say that this king was purely Pictish and the other Irish. The time was ripe for union.

The list of sixty-nine Pictish kings reflects an heroic era that was to end with the crowning of *Kenneth mac Alpin* as the creator of a new dynasty, the first king of the Scots, now a united nation that included the old kingdom of the Picts. Scotland was born.

MATRILINEAR SUCCESSION

Looking back over the life of Brude and the other kings, the question arises as to how he and most of the others happened to have fathers who were not until the end of the Pictish era high-kings of Pictland themselves. From whom did they accede?

Through their mothers presumably, or so it would seem, and so it has been assumed by a majority of Pictish scholars in the past.

There are three reasons for this assumption.

The Venerable Bede in Chapter One of his *Ecclesiastical History* repeats the Irish version of the Pictish foundation legend which says that as they had no women they asked for Irish brides. The Irish agreed on condition that when the need arose 'they should choose a king from the female royal line rather than the male. This custom continues among the Picts to this day.'

The second reason is to be found, as we have seen, in the King List. Except for some instances towards the end of the Pictish nation, no king appears to have inherited his kingdom through his father.

Thirdly, not only Brude mac Maelcon but a number of other Pictish kings had non-Pictish fathers. Talorgen (d. AD 647) and Brude mac Bili (d. 693) both had fathers who were not Picts. Talorgen's father Eanfrith was an Anglo-Saxon king of Bernicia. Bili, father of Brude, is thought to have been a king of Strathclyde.

However, other students of the matrilinear theory, such as Dr Alfred Smyth, are not so certain. Bede's source came from Ireland. It was not a Pictish legend and indeed it may have sprung from Iona itself at a time when the Dal Riatan Scots were attempting to claim Pictland for themselves. This Irish propaganda may or may not have been fact. Or it may have been true of certain Pictish families, especially those with strong Irish ties, but not of all.

Irish succession depended upon the fitness of the man for the job. Any one of three generations from a high-king could be chosen. In Leinster there were about thirty-five tribes, each with its own overlord, six of whom were powerful enough to provide kings for the province.

The situation in Pictland may have been similar. According to *De Situ Albanie* there were seven districts each with its own king, and under him seven further divisions under lesser lords. This situation could be compared with Leinster. If the high-kingship rotated between the more important of these seven regional kingdoms, or even if there were only two – one north of the Mounth and the other south – then this might account for the unusual method of succession found in the King List.

Smyth suggests another reason why the sons of non-Pictish kings might have ruled in Pictland. Possibly they were imposed upon them by other more successful kingdoms. Brude mac Bili persuaded the Picts to rally to the cause of his grandfather and thus they reverted to Strathclyde domination. Haggling and feuding between the tribal groups, with constant quarrels between the élite families for the office of high-king, could have led to the promotion of the strongest and most ruthless men as rulers.

Whether or not the inheritance went through the female line, with the woman's lineage producing kings in a series of complicated marriages of cross-cousins, as Anthony Jackson believes, one fact emerges from the surviving King List. No woman was ever queen in her own right. No king's mother is mentioned, only his father. Surely in a matrilinear society this would have been important.

There may of course have been other lists lost over the centuries. In Ireland – a patrilinear society – the *Ban-Senchus* contained the pedigrees of royal women and the importance of dynastic marriage where property and prestige were concerned. Arranged marriages are no doubt as old as marriage itself, but these are not matrilineal.

Perhaps only certain kings who had married into stronger dynasties were compelled to hand over their rights of succession to their wives.

A question arises over élite marriages in general. Did regional kings and their underlords, the warrior and druid classes, also practise matriliny? Presumably so.

F.T. Wainwright states 'that the right of succession among the Picts was different from the right of succession among other nations in Britain may be accepted as a fact'. Perhaps. Perhaps not. Certainly if the Picts practised matrilinear succession they were the only Celts in Britain to do so. In Scottish terms the case, in my opinion, is 'non-proven'.

FORTS, PALACES AND PIT-PLACES

Pictland, as we have seen, was roughly divided into seven provinces, each ruled by a king who may have been capable of becoming a high-king. Each provincial king is said to have ruled over seven lesser lords, and there were about half a million subjects scattered throughout the country with the bulk of them living in the north and east.

The number seven may have had a mystical meaning not to be taken literally, but the point is that each province had its own king and under him a number of lesser landowners and their retainers.

These lesser landowners may have been relatives of the provincial king. Apart from administering their territory and collecting dues in kind from the local farmers, they may have paid taxes to their overlords and provided warriors for battles and the small inter-tribal or inter-family skirmishes which were part of daily life.

Of course borders would shift from time to time, overlords would be overthrown and kings killed or deposed. Each regional set-up seems to have been a minor reflection of the national system where the high-kings would have expected the backing of the provincial kings. The clan system of later years was itself a modified reflection of Pictish society.

Much of Pictish territory can be accurately defined through the study of place-names. Dr Watson, W.F.H. Nicolaisen and Kenneth Jackson – the acknowledged experts – have done superb work in this field.

This is an enormous subject and it is possible only to look at a few places where

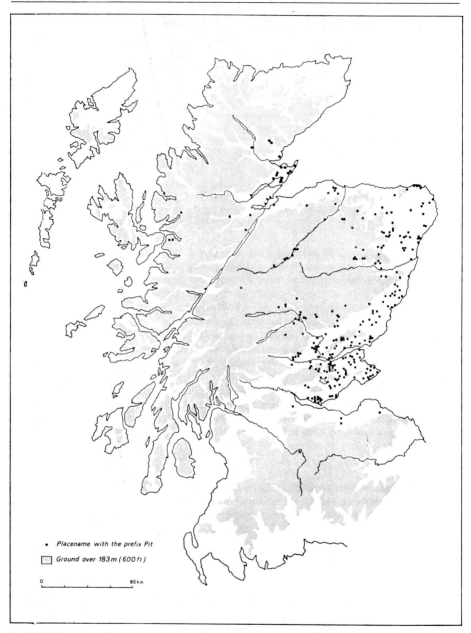

Pit place-names

The Birsay stone, from Orkney, now in the National Museums
of Scotland (NMS) Edinburgh

the Picts may have lived, including their royal fortified and non-fortified palaces.

In Orkney the *Brough of Birsay* may have been the seat of the ruler who was mentioned as a subject-king to Brude mac Maelcon in the late sixth century. A stone carved with what would seem to be the symbols of kingship was found at Birsay. The site stands on a tidal island and was not enclosed.

[65]

Dundurn, Perth & Kinross. An important Dark Age fort. View from the graveyard which contains at least one Class III stone

Fortified hill-tops, many of them Iron Age in origin but rebuilt and inhabited by the Picts, are mostly to be found in the north.

The great trivallate fortress at *Burghead* in Moray, thought to have been built in the fourth or fifth centuries and occupied at least for a further five hundred years, is believed to have been a Pictish naval base, and one of the most important sites in the north.

Coastal sites like *Green Castle, Portknockie*, on the southern shores of the Moray Firth, and *Dunnottar*, south of Aberdeen, were important naval defensive sites.

Dunnottar is mentioned twice in the Annals of Ulster as being besieged in 681 and 694. Sally Foster suggests it may have been significant because of its closeness to the stack at *Dunnicaer* where class I stones have been found, a cult-focus perhaps.

Stone-walled forts in Aberdeenshire such as *Bruce's Camp*, Inverurie with its concentration of Pictish stones, *Mither Tap* and *Tillymuick of Bennachie* may all have been used in the Pictish era. The biggest site is *Tap o' Noth* near Rhynie which Ralston suggests could be a prime candidate for a central palace for the north-eastern Picts. The whole Rhynie area is full of class I stones. *Doon Hill* has been described by Professor Alcock as 'a princely site'.

Dunnichen in Angus, Nechtan's Fort, may have derived its name from Nechtan I, son of Erp, whose dates are uncertain but who may have reigned for twenty-four years in the fifth century. A curious legend recorded by Skene tells us that St Boethius (Buitte) arrived by sea to find that Nechtan had just died. He restored him to life and in gratitude for his life the king gave him the old Roman fort at *Kirkbuddo*, a few miles south-east of Forfar. The site is not that far from Dunnichen.

Dunkeld in Perthshire was the fortress of the Caledonians, along with *Rohallion*, the Rath of the Caledonians, and *Shiehallion*, the Fairy Hill of the Caledonians. Later Dunkeld was established as a Christian centre by King Constantine in the ninth century.

Dundurn, near the lower end of Loch Earn in Perthshire, may have been one of the royal fortresses of Fortriu centred on Strathearn. Its importance lay in the fact that it guarded the approach to the major royal sites in the Pictish heartland beyond.

Professor and Mrs Alcock (*et al*) excavated Dundurn and found in spite of the damp conditions a remarkable collection of both imported and locally produced objects including a complete leather shoe, an unparalleled find in Pictland.

Forteviot in Perthshire, where the Water of May joins the River Earn, was an unenclosed royal site which became the centre of the kings of Pictland in the early ninth century. Constantine and his brother Oengas ruled from here. Recent aerial photography has shown extensive evidence of a ritual nature including graves around the area together with class II and class III carved stones.

Crop marks have fairly recently indicated other possible Pictish sites which Gordon Maxwell wittily calls in a paper on the subject 'a new overview'. One category of these is the presumed rectangular wooden building or timber hall. Maxwell has identified six south of the Forth, a group of at least five in *Lathrisk*, Fife, single ones near *Scone*, in *Strathmore*, in upper *Strathearn*, at Friockheim in Angus, on the Dee at *Crathes*, and on the Don at *West Fintray*, with a couple at *Balmachree* near Inverness. These may well have been royal palaces.

Much of Pictland seems to have been loosely divided into farmsteads, small parcels of land or settlements easily identified by the toponym 'pit' or 'pett', which means a share or portion of land, equivalent to the word *baile* in Scottish Gaelic.

Pit-names proliferate in eastern Scotland with approximately seven in Sutherland, seventeen in Ross-shire, ten in Inverness-shire, one in Nairnshire, twelve in Moray, fifteen in Banffshire, sixty-seven in Aberdeenshire, twenty-five in Kincardineshire, thirty-one in Angus, fifty-seven in Fife and Kinross, one in Clackmannanshire, sixty-nine in Perthshire, and three in Stirlingshire. On the

Aerial view of Forteviot, a royal site

west side of Scotland the term is extremely rare.

Pit can be associated with personal names, such as *Pitkenny* in Fife, which means 'Kenneth's stead'. *Pitmiclardie* means 'Maclaverty's share', and Laverty means 'rule-bearing'. *Pitgersie* in Aberdeenshire, 'the shoemaker's share', and the three *Pitskellys* in Kincardine, Forfar and Perthshire, all mean 'the story-teller's share'.

Many relate to farming, such as *Pitmaglassy* in Lochaber, which means 'a clump of green land', or *Pitlochry* in Perthshire, meaning 'stony ground'. Animal names occur, such as *Pettmuck* and *Pitcaple* in Aberdeenshire, which refer to pigs and horses respectively. Some relate to trees, such as *Pitchirn* in Badenoch – the 'rowan-tree farmstead'. How many Rowan-tree cottages could we count throughout Scotland today? Thousands.

Some of these sites, like *Pittenweem* and *Pitlochry*, have become important towns today; others remain as villages or farms to form an important link with our ancestors. All have Scottish Gaelic names too, many of which are straight translations of the literal meaning, but the Pictish versions have remained.

Apart from 'pit', there are other toponyms that apply to Pictland. One of these is 'aber', the old British term for a confluence of rivers. Important sites such as *Aberlemno*, *Abernethy*, *Aberfoyle* and *Applecross* probably all had royal connections.

Aberfoyle on the Forth was once thought to be Aedan's stronghold of Eperpuill, which he gave to St Berach for a monastery. Aedan was allegedly the son of the Dal Riatan King Gabran and a Pictish princess named Ingheanach or Luan, the daughter of the lesser king Brachan in Angus, who may have had his particular territory in that district known as the *Gowrie*. *Brachan* is remembered in the name of the diocese of Brechin.

Applecross or Aporcrossan is the only 'aber' name to survive on the west coast of Scotland opposite the Isle of Raasay. It is associated with the foundation of the Pictish monastery by St Maelrubha in the seventh century.

'Dol', 'dul' and 'dal' are toponyms that describe meadows, dales or valleys. W.M. Alexander lists thirty-eight in Aberdeenshire. The simplest forms are found in *Dull* in Aberfeldy, *Doll* in Sutherland, *Dallas* in Ross and Moray, and of course *Dollar* in Clackmannanshire.

Many terms relate to forests: 'pren' is tree as in *Prinlaws* in Fife meaning 'a green tree'. '*Lanerc*' is a glade as in Lanarkshire. '*Cardden*' is a copse as in Kincardine. This would apply to a settlement on the edge of a forest. 'Preas', a Gaelic term adopted from old British, means 'thicket' or 'covert', as in *Pressmuk* in Perth and *Pressley* in Moray.

Although so little is known of the Pictish kings, their territory, strongholds and royal seats survive hidden in a host of place-names that connect us to the Pictish people before the conquest of the Scots by Kenneth mac Alpin. In one small chapter it is impossible to do justice to the variety of place-names. In their own way they have much to tell us of the Pictish way of life.

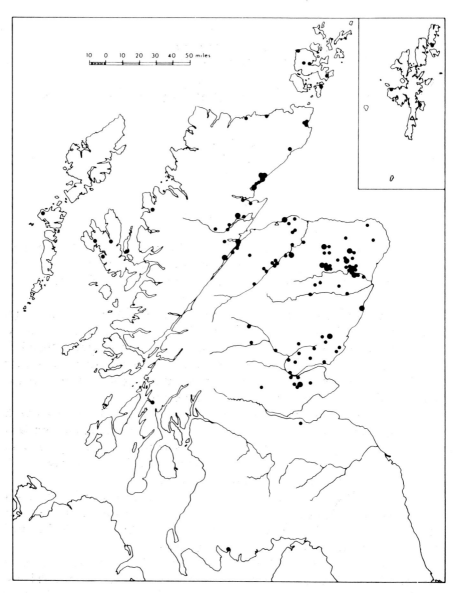

Distribution of stones incised with Pictish symbols

• Single incised stones
● Two or more stones

Class I stones

PART THREE

THE FIRST SYMBOL STONES

A UNIQUE DISPLAY

So far we have tried to find out about the Picts by looking at their history as far as we know it, by examining the only piece of documentary evidence to survive – the King List – and looking at the names and sites of some of the places where they lived.

We have found a group of Celtic warrior tribes united under a high-king. Society was similar in many ways to other Celtic groups in Britain, with an aristocracy that relied on farmers and craftsmen to support their traditional élitist lifestyle. But just as no two persons are the same, so no two nations are entirely alike. The Picts are distinguished from other British tribes by the design, sculpture and erection of unique symbol-bearing stones.

J. Romilly Allen and Joseph Anderson were not the first to describe the wealth of carved symbol stones virtually ignored and left to ruin throughout Scotland for centuries. The Spalding Club of Aberdeen sponsored a study by Dr John Stuart in two volumes which came out in 1856 and 1867. These were widely read, admired in their time, and are well worth looking at today.

Dr Joseph Anderson, 'unquestionably one of the most remarkable Scotsmen of his generation' according to his obituary in the *Scotsman* newspaper, was Keeper of the National Museum of Antiquities of Scotland. He believed passionately that archaeology should begin at home.

J. Romilly Allen was a Welsh civil engineer with a fascination for early Scottish sculpture. Together they produced what was to become and still is the definitive book on the subject, entitled *The Early Christian Monuments of Scotland* (ECMS), published by the Society of Antiquaries of Scotland in 1903. Hardly obtainable outside the major libraries, it was reprinted in 1993 by the Pinkfoot Press in Angus with a foreword by Dr Anna Ritchie and an introduction by Dr Isabel Henderson, both leading authorities on Pictish archaeology and art respectively.

It was Joseph Anderson who first divided the stones into three classes.

Class I consists of undressed stones with incised symbols only.

Class II are dressed slabs with symbols and Celtic ornament carved in relief.

Class III are monuments with Celtic ornament in relief but without the symbols on Class I and II.

This classification is still valid.

Isabel Henderson has, however, tentatively suggested a fourth class to describe what Allen called 'stones with crosses but no ornaments', which because of their extreme simplicity are very hard to date.

It was first thought that the three categories fell into a fairly rigid time sequence. Thus class I stones were being carved in the sixth and seventh centuries, class II appeared with the conversion of the aristocracy to Christianity in the eighth and ninth, and class III in the ninth and tenth centuries after the conquest of the Picts by the Scots. This would seem to assume that class I and II stones were erected for the same reasons. All three classes may well have overlapped and class I and II may well have been erected for different reasons.

In spite of the scholarly volumes of Allen and Anderson, followed by a fair number of books, academic papers, theories and statements, no one has yet been able to find out for certain when and why class I stones were first erected, who or what was responsible for their erection, where the symbols originated, and what they meant.

So when were class I stones first erected?

Many authorities believe that, comparing the symbols with Anglian art, the answer must be that they first appeared in the seventh century and their motifs were borrowed from the Northumbrians.

There is certainly a similarity between some of the evangelistic animals in the exquisite Gospel books, such as the *Book of Durrow*, and the class I symbols. More so when you study the creatures on the gold grave-goods belonging to the pagan Anglo-Saxon king found in the ship-burial mound at Sutton Hoo in Suffolk. These date from the mid seventh century.

Authorities such as Robert Stevenson were convinced that the stylized animal symbols were invented and appeared within the Christian era. He saw nothing incompatible between the symbols and Christianity. In his opinion they corresponded in many details to the Irish- or Hiberno-Saxon art style of the seventh to mid eighth centuries. Pictish animal art therefore was influenced by Anglo-Saxons as depicted in Sutton Hoo and the *Books of Durrow* and *Echternach*, all of which were devised in the seventh century.

Certainly some of the Pictish animals share details with the manuscript beasts, but only the eagle is found entire in both.

Isabel Henderson, with her special gifts of insight, suggests that the Northumbrian artists were influenced by the Picts. Class II ideas were certainly

Kildonan Cross (Class III) by Kildonan manse, Sutherland

The Eagle stone, Strathpeffer

borrowed from the other cults of the day, particularly Irish and Northumbrian, but the animals on class I stones are so fresh and free, so uniquely alive as they stride across the stones, that it seems – to me at least – that they must be the original designs that influenced the neighbouring nations.

If, as is supposed by many students in the field today, the symbols and the stones predate the seventh century, then it would have been impossible for the Picts to have copied from the Northumbrians. The Gospels had not been written and the Sutton Hoo king neither born nor buried.

The hoard of treasure found at Norrie's Law in Fife has also been regarded as a pointer to the dating of the symbol stones. The treasure included a pair of leaf-

Dunrobin 1, Dunrobin Castle Museum

shaped silver plaques and some hand-pins adorned with Pictish symbols. Decorated hand-pins were being made in Roman Britain in the fourth century and the silver plaques may have been Pictish versions of Roman objects, possibly *phalerae*. The Laings and Charles Thomas both consider that the hoard is older than the seventh century, possibly dating from before AD 600. The treasure cannot therefore act as an accurate device for dating the stones.

Anderson and Allen argue that because there were no symbol stones found in Dal Riata, they must therefore have been raised after AD 500.

Dr Henderson believes that the earliest symbol stones may have originated in the Golspie area of the Moray Firth. If this is true – and certainly the quality and confident simplicity of the incised symbols in that area are compatible with the theory – then their date could be before Dal Riata was colonized by the Irish. They simply never reached Argyll.

The Laings suggest it is possible that the symbol stones could be considered as part of an Iron Age tradition discernible before the Picts entered history.

They point out that the symbol stones must have been produced over a long rather than a short period to allow the major symbols to evolve from the earliest norm to the later more elaborate designs.

This theory of the declining symbol first proposed by Stevenson must be obvious to any student of the stones. The difference between the earliest crescents and double discs in the Moray Firth area and those on the elaborate class II cross slabs such as Rosemarkie, south of the same area, would make one suppose that the sculptors and their patrons no longer remembered the deep symbolism behind the original designs. The pattern had become more important than the meaning. A seventh-century date for the earliest would not, I believe, give enough time for the spread of the stones throughout Scotland and for the designs of the major symbols to decline.

The idea that the early symbols were Christian or even compatible with Christianity because they appear in such close contact with the cross on class II stones seems strange. The few animals represented are, as Dr Anne Ross points out, important in pagan Celtic culture, as would appear to be several of the abstract symbols. Others could be traced to Roman artifacts as the Laings suggest and some – as Thomas proposes – possibly to unrecognizable Iron Age or even older cult objects.

That these ancient pagan symbols were to be found on Christian class II stones is neither offensive, as some Christians maintain, or unusual. Christians often borrowed pagan symbols to make a Christian point. The Classical centaur prefigures Christ the healer on several class II stones.

Proximity to the Cross ensured conversion, for the Cross was the mightiest of all symbols, capable of driving the devil out of any heathen totem, and it dominates in size and splendour all the class II stones. Early Christian saints preferred to bless the paganism out of old sites and objects by conversion rather than by destruction. Look at how Columba treated the mythical monster in Loch Ness.

Of course, it does rather depend on the original interpretation of the symbols. If they were to do with pagan rites and magic, they probably would not have survived the Christian era in any form, but if they were to do with clans and people, they would have been regarded by Christians as being as harmless as heraldry.

Although it is impossible to date the first symbol stones with any accuracy, we

[76]

The Daniel stone, Meigle Museum. Detail showing centaur

do know that they were also being carved after class II stones appeared in the eighth century. The fourth-century Irish Ogam alphabet appears in a late version dated by K.H. Jackson to the eighth century on several Aberdeenshire stones.

So who erected the first stones?

The answer seems obvious. Surely the Picts were responsible for the invention, carving and distribution of the symbol stones. Unlike Roman slabs, they were carved of local stone in situ by local sculptors or sculptors travelling from a Pictish school.

However, the anthropologist Dr Anthony Jackson, in a recent lecture to Friends of Grampian Stones (FOGS) at the Marischal Museum, Aberdeen in 1993, suggested that the stones were probably all carved by Anglo-Saxon masons because the Picts had no experience in sculpture of this sort. 'There is no such thing as Pictish art,' he announced to a staggered audience. He could find no

[77]

evidence that the Picts carved any of the stones that adorn Pictland. It will be interesting to read his forthcoming publication on the matter.

Although Jackson's idea is thought-provoking, I believe there is proof that the Picts were well capable of carving class I stones. They may have been illiterate, inaccessible, non-Christian and never civilized by Rome, but they were artistic and innovative and perfectly capable of incising the simple lines required to decorate a stone.

The proof may lie hidden in the name itself, the Painted People (Picts) – the People of the Designs (Priteni). Herodian, writing in 208, said of the Caledones, 'They tattoo their bodies not only with likenesses of animals of all kinds, but with all sorts of drawings.'

Thus it is accepted that the Picts coloured and/or tattooed their bodies. Papal legates reporting a visit to Mercia in 786 told Pope Hadrian that they had to warn against the pagan custom of disfiguring the body by 'hideous scars – defiling and disfiguring the body – injury of staining'. Perhaps this was a reference to Mercian neighbours, the Picts.

It was F.C. Diack who in 1944 suggested that the symbols were devised from the tattoos that denoted the status of the individual.

The art of tattooing is at least as skilled as the art of sculpting. A good tattooist would surely find no difficulty in adapting and transferring his designs to stone, or so I am assured by my artist friends.

The symbols are so honed-down, complete, finished and confident that Charles Thomas believes they must pre-date the stones. On Sanday in the Orkneys alterations to a structure were dated to the sixth century and involved the re-use of two stones, one of which bore what the excavator Dr John Hunter suggested might be a proto-symbol of the double disc and a snake's head. As the stone had been laid face down during its re-use, the symbol could have been of a much earlier date. The progression might therefore have been skin, metal, wood, and finally stone.

The symbols may have been carved or painted on wooden shields, lintels and doorposts long before they appeared on stone. We know they were etched on jewellery. What of those decorations that Tacitus tells us were worn by the Caledonian warriors at Mons Graupius? Might they not have been connected with the symbols?

Two further and credible suggestions as to who might be responsible for the erection of the stones come from Dr Henderson.

The first is Brude mac Maelcon, who ruled from 550 until 583. A reign of over thirty years would have given him the necessary time to establish the custom, and the first stones are believed to have been erected in the vicinity of his court, the Moray Firth area. Not only had he the time but also the power, and if the symbolism is connected – as many believe – with matriliny, he had a motive. The date too would be about right.

The other candidate is King Brude mac Bili, the victor of Dunnichen in 685, who freed the southern Picts from thirty years of Northumbrian domination. The stones might be seen as expressions of nationalism starting in the north and proliferating in the south after the departure of the Northumbrians in 685. The date, however, would seem to be too late.

Perhaps the two kings were both responsible. Brude mac Maelcon may have authorized their erection in the first place while Brude mac Bili might have encouraged their spread in the south for the reasons already given.

Perhaps indeed all the kings were responsible for the continual erection of class I stones for reasons common to each generation. But why?

The simple answer must be to convey a message, some form of communication. To a people who had no written language, the stones might be seen as billboards erected to make public statements that were meant to be understood by all who saw them and to endure beyond the current generation.

We have already seen from studying the Pictish past that stone was a common medium for communication. Stone circles, monoliths, cairns with their inner chambers of stone, cist burial slabs and recumbents with their cup and ring decorations were all of deep ritual significance to Pictish ancestors. Because standing stones were still prominent in the Pictish landscape, they must have continued to be of interest and significance. Many of the ancient monoliths were used again by the Picts who added their own symbols which appear side by side with the old Bronze Age cup marks.

Then along came the Romans with a whole new range of ideas in stone usage. Milestones, gravestones, colourful carved distance slabs that marked the route of the Antonine Wall, altars, effigies of gods, dedication stones with lettering all proliferated on Roman territory. After Rome there were tombstones in Wales, the Isle of Man, southern Scotland and Iona with lettering, occasional pictures and simple incised crosses – Christian grave markers – all of which would have been seen and noted by Pictish seafaring warriors and travellers. The Picts were no more confined to their own borders than any other nation of the times.

Therefore, far from being a new idea, stone would have been an obvious medium for the message they conveyed.

But what is the message?

Theories have changed and developed over the years, and Pictophiles have their own strongly held beliefs, prejudices and convictions as to what the stones might mean.

There remain some two hundred or so symbol stones spread about a country which consisted of about half a million Picts. There must have been many more, as surviving fragments indicate, perhaps that same amount again or even twice as many that have not survived the rigours of fifteen hundred years. They were obviously of tremendous importance in their day, but why?

An early theory was that they might have been to do with ownership, stone notice-boards that marked out the territory of a person and included a description of that territory. A salmon, for instance, might mean that the territory included a river, an eagle that there were mountains. However, study of the distribution of the symbols in ECMS gives no clue whatsoever. The commonest symbols appear in most if not every area of Pictland. The distribution seems entirely haphazard.

A popular and ingenious theory postulated by the anthropologist Dr Anthony Jackson depends upon the validity of the matrilinear system of inheritance. Pictland, he insists, was divided into matrilinear clans practising patrilinear cross-cousin marriage. In other words, although the inheritance came through the female line, males were kings. There is no evidence in the King List that any queen reigned in her own right.

The rules of matriliny mean that power is not handed down by a king to his son (patriliny) or by a woman to her daughter (matriarchy) but goes instead to a man's sister's son.

But how would a chief inheriting through his mother's line retain his status if his father came from a lesser lineage? Jackson suggests that a payment was made. That payment might be represented on the stones by a mirror or mirror-and-comb symbol.

This is matrilinear inheritance in its simplest form. The rules become more and more complicated as the generations pass. Jackson suggests that the symbols which for the most part appear in pairs with the occasional addition of the mirror and comb were raised to describe and explain political alliances of lineages by marriage.

The idea is exciting and has many followers but it leaves a lot unexplained. What about the stones whose number of symbols does not conform to his ideas of pairing? The Golspie stone with its seven or eight symbols, and Craigton with three symbols, are both in Dunrobin Museum. Inverurie 1 has four symbols while the Ulbster Stone in Thurso boasts eight.

Why, Charles Thomas asks, should the stones appear only at a secondary stage in Pictish history, and why does Jackson pay so little attention to the date and derivation?

In *The Symbol Stones of Scotland* (a title I don't much care for because the symbol stones came from Pictland), Jackson has written a passionate and difficult book supporting his theory that 'In 683 AD king Bridei (son of Bili) proclaimed that all lineages should erect stones recording their alliance/marriages'.

This tongue-in-cheek statement is based on an edict that was never proclaimed, but should have been, says Jackson. The proof is to be found on the symbol stones themselves.

A new theory caused an upsurge of interest in 1992. Dr Ross Sampson, a Glasgow archaeologist, sees the distribution of symbols on a given stone as hieroglyphs representing the name of the person they commemorate.

He came to this conclusion by comparing the frequency of individual symbol combinations with the frequency with which individual Celtic names occurred in ancient Ireland and Wales. He found that Dark Age Irish and Welsh personal name frequencies closely matched the frequency with which different symbol combinations occur on Pictish stones. Thus he came to the conclusion that the symbols represented the names of Pictish kings and the aristocracy, but the names themselves remain a mystery.

Most of them are two-part names represented by two hieroglyphic symbols. Some of the less common symbols could be adjectives. For example, a typical élite warrior might have been called 'wise eagle' or 'shining salmon' or 'brave wolf', expressed in a long-lost form of British hieroglyphs.

This is another tempting theory that cannot be proved. The more you look at it, the more interesting it appears, although it has not found strong support among experts in the field. The trouble is that not all Pictish kings had names of two or more syllables. Drust and Brude, for example, would not seem to fit the theory, although Talorcen might.

What the supposition does do is take for granted the original theory that the stones are to do with the dead rather than the living.

Since the days of cairns and cist burials, stones have been connected with memorials to the dead. From the earliest times, as we have seen, Pictish ancestors, whether Celtic or pre-Celtic, expended great energy in celebrating their fathers and forefathers. Roman stones recorded the official position or military rank of the deceased together with information about the tribe and family of the dead. Iona slabs recorded abbots, priors and prioresses and social rank.

On medieval West Highland slabs symbolism proliferated, with swords, weapons, shears, hatchets, hammers, tongs and anvils, galleys, castles, harps, heraldic devices on shields and figures in pleated tunics. Mirrors and combs symbolized women.

Thomas studied tombstones through the ages to find out what they have in common. A name, of course, status in society and position in the family, occupation, possibly the commemorator. (Note how in Scottish memorials the woman keeps her maiden name. Could this be a relic of matriliny?)

So death was celebrated in the beginning, as it is today. We don't know for certain how pre-Christian Picts marked their important graves, yet the answer

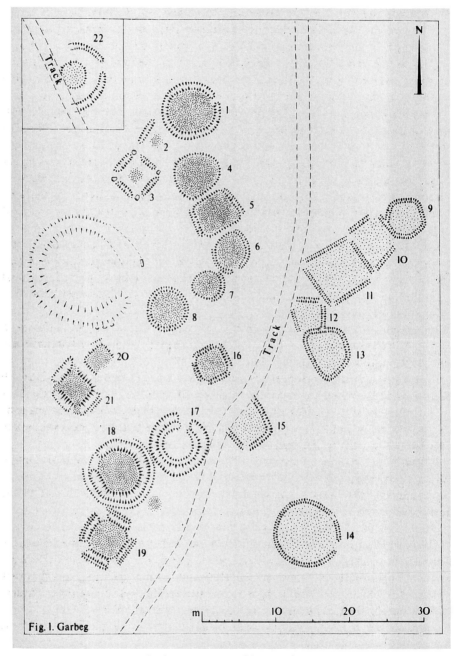

Fig. l. Garbeg

Garbeg cemetery, Glenurquhart

might have been standing in the landscape unrecognized for centuries.

The Picts would have been well aware of the practice of marking Christian graves in other parts of Britain. Charles Thomas and Joanna Close-Brooks suggest that maybe they were consciously imitating the funerary stone practices of their Irish or British neighbours. Perhaps. Or maybe they were merely continuing the age-old natural inclination of man to remember his dead.

Of course, this theory can't be proved and has been resisted on that account. One of the problems has been the lack of graves beneath the commemorative stones.

Some certainly have had graves attached, like the Princess Stone found by Dr Close-Brooks at Dunrobin Dairy Park and now in Dunrobin Museum. Others may have been set up within the vicinity of much older burial sites, such as cist or low-cairn burials, or pagan ritual sites. Very few class I stones have been found close to or in Christian graveyards.

Remember that many stones have been shifted over the centuries from their original sites. The Eagle Stone in Strathpeffer is a classic example. Moved at least three times, its original site is unknown, but Robert Gourlay, Highland Regional Archaeologist, thinks it may have been at the ancient graveyard of Fodderty a mile or so away.

In conclusion, it would seem that in spite of all the interesting suppositions to explain the erection of class I stones, we still don't really know whether they were commemorations of the dead or the living.

If they were tombstones, then what exactly is the information given? Does the top symbol indicate the clan and the symbol beneath it the profession, the mirror and comb the female sex with additional symbols providing further information?

If they were marriage-alliance stones, do the two symbols give the two lineages with the mirror and comb standing for bride-gifts?

Or are the symbols bye-names of the élite dead, reminiscent of native American names.

Or are the stones posters proclaiming land ownership and descriptive of the territory?

We don't know.

The origin of the symbols themselves would seem to date back into the remote Pictish past, perhaps as far as La Tène and the Early Scottish Iron Age. Probably some of the symbols were so full of tribal and religious significance that they first emerged as tattoos, eventually to appear on stone either side of the sixth century.

So what do the class I symbol stones tell us about the Picts?

Firstly, that they were artistic and inventive, well able to carve stones as beautiful as most of them are.

Secondly, that they relied on a powerful and probably ancient system of mass

Edderton Bronze Age monolith reused by Picts, Ross & Cromarty

communication which may have derived from their tattoos and/or other ancient rituals of their own past.

Thirdly, that if they practised matriliny as many suppose, then the stones were a highly intelligent method of explanation.

Lastly, the stones may indicate a powerful respect for the élite dead in the common tradition of mankind, but indicating a unique method of demonstration.

It is possible that the stones might represent a combination of the above suggestions or none of them. An anthropologist working with native Americans on the Oregon River studied the impression by Marianna Lines of the Edderton stone with its salmon and double disc and said, 'My chief could tell you what that means. It tells you the times of the year when the salmon are running.'

So the truth is we don't yet know the answer to why the stones were raised. It is one of the first questions I shall be asking at the Pearly Gates!

THE INCISED SYMBOLS

Thomas Carlyle wrote, 'In a symbol lies concealment or revelation'. Where the Pictish symbols are concerned, there is certainly concealment. Can there ever be revelation?

In 1903 Romilly Allen identified forty-six different symbols and divided them into groups as follows:

1. Certain geometric forms that may either be purely conventional or intended to represent natural objects.
2. Figures of inanimate objects of known use.
3. Figures of birds, beasts, fish, reptiles, imaginary creatures and plants.

Since 1903 other stones have been discovered at the rate of about one or two a year, but only two further symbols have been identified.

Five of the geometric figures and one of the reptiles are often but not always crossed with floriated rods bent once or twice to resemble the letters V or Z or a twisted Z.

The class I symbols appear on undressed slabs of local stone, on Neolithic standing stones, on cave walls in East Wemyss, Fife and Covesea near Elgin, on metalwork and occasionally on rock surfaces such as the boar at Dunadd.

The majority come in pairs with or without the addition of a mirror or mirror and comb, but there are major exceptions to what would seem to be the norm.

Although Allen identified as many as forty-six symbols, and by other reckonings there are some sixty or so designs that might be called symbols, Anthony Jackson suggests that the true definition of a Pictish symbol is a design that combines more than once with another design. If you use this criterion then there are only twenty-eight true symbols and you have to omit five of the animal designs.

The figure of twenty-eight fits in neatly with his assumption that the number seven was of magical importance. By tradition there were seven Pictish kingdoms, and Skene wrote that each of those seven kingdoms had seven lesser divisions.

A seventh son in later Scottish tradition, according to the Reverend Robert Kirk writing in the late seventeenth century, received through some virtue in his mother's womb the gift of second sight. It is possible that such a belief dates back to Pictish times.

Bearing this in mind, interpretations of other symbols may still be found hidden in the legends and fairy-tales of Scotland inherited from a remote past.

In the Highlands the oral tradition continued at least until the nineteenth century, with folklorists like J.G. Campbell, J.F. Campbell, Andrew Lang and a host of others up to the present day seeing the necessity of preserving the old tales and beliefs for future generations. This may be particularly true of the animal symbols.

My own count of class I symbols comes to thirty.

THE PICTISH BEAST

There are some eighty stones with animals incised on them. Some of these appear to be fantastic, others are marvellously real.

Looking at them in the order of their occurrence on the stones, the Pictish beast is far ahead of the others with twenty-four appearances.

What a beautiful creature he is, with his reverentially bowed neck, curved snout, scrolled feet and flowing mane. Sometimes likened to a dolphin, he does not in my opinion resemble any real creature. The usual description of 'swimming elephant' is ridiculous and patronizing.

Dr Henderson has pointed out its likeness to the fantastic creature on the design of the king's purse from Sutton Hoo, while C.L. Curle compares it with the long-snouted beast on Folio 192v in the *Book of Durrow*.

Dr Carola Hicks suggests that the Pictish animals were selected to make appropriate statements for two reasons: firstly because similar animals were being or had been used on other monuments, and secondly because these

'Craw Stane', Rhynie, Gordon

particular animals were significant to the Picts.

Most significant of all was probably the Pictish beast.

Ask any child what they think it might be. Most will answer – apart from the occasional aardvark or crocodile – sea-horse. From there it is only a step to water-horse.

The *eich uisge* (water-horse), also known as the kelpie and *tarve uisge* (water-bull), dominated Scottish folklore. It is usually seen in the form of a young horse. F. Marian McNeill tells us that the kelpie would strike the water three times with his tail so heavily that the sound was like thunder, while his disappearance into a pool was like a lightning flash.

Loch Morar had its monster, and the loch at Pitlundie in the Black Isle still has its *tarve uisge* heard to bellow under ice. A pool in North Esk in Angus was a haunt of the dreaded water-horse. These are only a few of the many place-names throughout the country.

The kelpie is a Caledonian spirit described as the personification of water. It

[87]

can be as gentle as a rock-pool, as unpredictable as a squall, and as dangerous as a torrent.

Just as Nessie is the biggest tourist attraction in the Highlands today, with photographers, scientists and sightseers scouring the loch for a glimpse, so the Picts may have regarded the water-horse as real. The graceful beast depicted on the stones may well have been their interpretation of the mythic water-horse, at least as realistic as the hazy blown-up photographs that adorn the visitor centre of Loch Ness and a good deal more artistic.

Water fascinated the Celt. He recognized that this was a living beneficent force, essential not only for life, fertility and healing but also for travel and for food. But water could also be destructive. Polluted wells brought sickness, storms wrecked ships, floods drowned cattle and crops.

The Pictish beast, then, might well be symbolic of power over the restless spirits that roughened or calmed the sea, that sweetened or harmed the wells, that spared or shared the rain. As a group symbol it may well have represented a provincial kingdom or the office of kingship.

THE SALMON

The salmon symbol appears fourteen times. Like the other creatures (apart from the snake when crossed by a Z-rod) it faces to the right in Celtic sunwise tradition. The hooked mouth makes it – like the bull, the boar and the stag – distinctively male.

The salmon is dominant in Celtic tradition. Dr Ross maintains that it is the most important of all the water creatures and was regarded as the repository of Otherworld wisdom. Its form was adopted by certain gods and it was the symbol of sacred rivers and pools.

In old Celtic mythology, nine sacred hazel trees grew over the springs where rivers rise. Their red nuts fed the salmon and caused pink spots to appear on its skin. Those who ate the flesh of the first salmon of the season received the gift of wisdom and divination. To this day whoever tastes the cooked juice of the first grilse of the year, caught on certain rivers such as the Tay, celebrates with a dram.

Why should the salmon be the symbol of wisdom?

You have only to look at its life cycle to know the answer. Lorraine MacDonald suggests that when it struggles upstream against roaring rapids and tumbling falls to breed, it reflects the path of the warrior as he struggles to overcome the battles of life in his journey to the Otherworld. It represents the struggle of the soul for survival. The salmon dies after it has spawned, thus life is born out of death and the whole great cycle begins again. Like the salmon we

Glamis Manse (back)

must face death before we can grow wise. The salmon possesses the knowledge of eternal life.

Unlike man, it can exist in three elements – air, fresh and salt water. Thus the salmon is magic.

It appears quartered on the heraldic arms of McNeill of Barra, the Macleans of Duart, the Maclachlans of that Ilk, the Macgillivrays of Dunmaglass, the MacDonalds of Sleat and of Clanranald.

THE SNAKE

The snake also appears fourteen times on class I stones, although on seven of these occasions it is crossed with a Z-rod. The snake is the only creature to be crossed by a rod and, as Carola Hicks points out, the only example of animal and geometric symbols superimposed.

The snake is also considered to be a symbol of wisdom. In Ireland, where there were no snakes, its place was taken by the salmon. F. Marian McNeill tells us that it is a recognized folk-practice to substitute some object that is locally feasible for

[89]

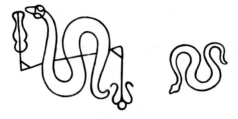

one that is not. In Pictland, where adders and salmon were plentiful, both symbols exist.

One of the mystical beasts of Scotland, the snake is a creature of the earth both wise and dangerous, a symbol not only of healing and fertility but also of death and rebirth. Its spiralling body represents the journey to the Otherworld where it sleeps until it emerges in early spring from its hole in the ground and sheds its old skin to appear new-born.

It is also associated with Bride, the goddess of marriage, childbirth and the hearth, whose festival was Imbolc in February, one of the four great seasons of the Celts.

> Today is the day of Bride
> The serpent shall come from the hole,
> I will not molest the serpent
> Nor will the serpent molest me
>
> *Carmina Gaedelica*, Alexander Carmichael

Pliny (*Natural History* XXXIX 52) described the Serpent Stone formed by secretions and spittle from a tangle of hissing snakes. They were highly prized not only by Gallic druids as healing charms but also throughout the Highlands and Islands. These adder-stones are still occasionally found in the heather. Greatly treasured, they were used in childbirth, for healing in general and protection from evil.

Miranda Green comments on the association between snakes and healing springs and between the snake and the solar wheel. The sun cult was closely involved with fertility.

Thus the snake and its association with the earth, fertility, healing and immortality was well suited to become a powerful Pictish symbol. The Z-rod may have added extra prestige. Generally considered to be a broken arrow symbolizing death, the rod may have represented – in Jackson's view – the protection of dead warrior ancestors.

THE EAGLE

The eagle makes ten appearances on the class I stones and is one of two representatives of the bird species.

Comparisons between the Pictish eagle and the carved bird that appears on the ivory handle of the king's purse at Sutton Hoo and the symbol of St John in various Gospel manuscripts point to a wide sharing of this symbol.

In design it resembles the Roman eagle with its carefully carved wing feathers, but it was also the most important symbolic bird of the Gael and has always been associated with chieftainship.

Frank Adam writes, 'In full dress, the Highlander is covered with heraldry, from cap-badge and eagle plumes, to kilt pin . . . The three pinion feathers of the native eagle are the distinguishing badge of a Highland chief; two are the badge of a chieftain; and one the badge of a gentleman.' So it was and so it still is.

The Eagle stone – Clach 'n Tuidean, which means the Stone of the Turning – now in Strathpeffer (p. 74) was allegedly re-sited to commemorate a battle fought in 1411 by the Mackays, Mackenzies and Munros who 'turned' away the MacDonalds from taking part in the famous Battle of Harlaw, where the Vikings were finally driven out of Scotland (but not Orkney). The Munros may have taken their heraldic totem of the eagle at that time, but the stone was standing long before the battle. It is fanciful but possible that the Munros were descended from the Eagle lineage and that the stone first stood in their territory.

Other clans to adopt the eagle as part of their arms are MacDonald of MacDonald and MacDonald of Ardnamurchan, but the arms, crest and supporters of Munro of Foulis display no less than four eagles.

Lorraine McDonald reminds us that another name for the eagle is 'fireun', from an Irish root word which translates as truth, integrity, a just man. In other words, a suitable candidate for kingship.

Like so many stones, Clach 'n Tuindeain has gathered its share of legends. The Brahan Seer allegedly predicted that when it fell a third time, the Strathpeffer valley would be flooded. It is now firmly cemented into its present site.

[91]

One of six Burghead
Bull slabs, Elgin
Museum

THE BULLS OF BURGHEAD

The bull appears nine times on class I stones, never paired with another symbol, and on six occasions comes from the same site – the great Pictish fortress of Burghead in Moray. One of the four primary symbolic beasts of the Gael associated with the element of earth, it has always been a totem of power, potency and the raw energy of nature. (In Christian terms, the bull or calf was symbolic of the evangelist St Luke.)

To a farming community such as the Picts – and indeed all other Celtic societies – cattle were of supreme importance. They indicated a man's wealth, and no doubt brides were paid for in bulls and heifers as well as gifts of a more personal kind. Cattle were to continue to be essential to the economy of Scotland at least up to the Highland Clearances. Even today you have only to go to the agricultural shows to see how important cattle-breeding still is to the economy of Scotland.

At one time records show that there were twenty-five to thirty carvings of bulls in Burghead. There may have been many more. Only six remain. These were found during the destruction of the fortress in preparation for the building of the village and the harbour. One is in the British Museum, one in Scotland's Royal Museum in Edinburgh, two in Elgin Museum, and two in Burghead Library.

They are masterpieces. Similar to each other but not identical, with swishing tails, heads lowered to charge, and solid muscular bodies, they are among the most realistic of all the animal symbols. Perhaps they symbolized the great defensive site of Burghead itself.

The fortress was immense, three times as large as any other building of the period. Sailors approaching the headland would first have seen a great wall of stone and earth stretched across the neck of the promontory. Behind were two further immense ramparts. The mighty entrance that led into the fort was lined with bull-stones. Within this royal fortress for four hundred years lived the Bull kings, their warriors, priests, craftsmen and servants. It is thought to have been destroyed by fire by Norse invaders in the early ninth century.

On the other hand the bull may not have been used as a lineage symbol but as a votive tablet for some annual festival. Bull sacrifice may have been practised by the Picts as a spring fertility festival. It was also practised as late as the seventeenth century on Isle Maree when one was slaughtered by four sons to cure their mad mother.

Traces of a winter fire festival can be found in a rite still performed in Burghead annually on 11 January and known as 'The Burning of the Clavie'. The history of this fire festival is said to go back fifteen hundred years to the time when the bull-stones were being carved.

The word 'clavie' is thought to be connected with *cliabh* (pronounced 'cleeav'), the Gaelic name for basket. This is made of a tar-barrel and a herring-barrel and filled with wood saturated with tar. It is lit by a live peat by the Clavie King and carried by the Clavie-Bearer and his team throughout the village, then placed on the Doorie, a stone column on a mound, and allowed to blaze for a while. In the old days it was thrown down the slope of the mound and the burning fragments were eagerly collected as charms to bring good luck to fisherfolk for the subsequent year. In the seventeenth and eighteenth centuries it was banned by the Church as idolatrous and sinful, but it has survived to the present day. At one time most of the Moray coastal fishing villages had similar fire festivals.

The Burghead well discovered in 1809 lies inside the fort, a mysterious ancient place whose history is not known. Carved out of solid rock, it consists of a flight of steps that lead down to a dark chamber into which is sunk a rectangular tank fed by springs.

[93]

The great well at Burghead fortress, Moray

Some suggest that it was used for Early Christian baptism, but it was probably older and may have been used for ritual purposes in pre-Christian times, for example the drowning of prestigious enemies. We know of at least two kings who were drowned by Oengus I.

THE BOAR

The boar appears four times on class I stones according to Carola Hicks, if you count the rock carving at Dal Riatan Dunadd. It always appears alone in male form with its crest raised to emphasize its ferocity.

One of the most important of the Gaelic cult animals, the boar is associated with the element of fire and connected with the sun.

Of all the forest animals the boar was the most highly prized for showing off

The Knocknagael Boar, now in Highland Regional Buildings, Inverness

hunting skills and for feasting. Cultivated or wild, the pig was the symbol of hospitality both in this life and in the Otherworld. The 'champion's portion' – the biggest and best cut – was always offered to the bravest warrior present.

In the Otherworld there was the Island of Fiery Swine where the red pigs were fed on apples and provided the great pork feast which was continually renewed; those who ate the flesh were made immortal. The bristles on the ridge of the great spirit Boar of Formael were sharp and tough enough for each to support a plump wild apple.

The boar features in legends beyond number and must have been a popular subject for the oral tradition. J.G. Campbell recorded the following story of the great Boar of Glen Loyal in his *Popular Tales of the West Highlands*.

The King of Sutherland's land was being ravaged by an exceptionally savage beast, so he promised that he would give his daughter Grainne in marriage to the man who killed it. Along came Diarmid, one of the Fenian warriors, who fell in love with the princess and promised to kill the boar which 'was lying as large and black as a boat when its keel is turned up on the shore'. He shot it with his bow, but the king went back on his word and would allow no wedding until Diarmid strode along the back of the carcass from head to toe. One of its poisonous bristles pierced his ankle and he sickened and died. His grave and the boar's den can still be found in Glen Loyal (as it can also be seen in the parish of Kintail). The story is a good example of an Irish tale of the Fianna transferred to a Scottish background.

The Campbells of Argyll and Breadalbane (among other clans) owe their crest of the boar's head to a version of this legend which was still very much alive in the Highlands in the nineteenth century. Diarmid and Grainne had two sons, one of whom was said to have been the progenitor of Clan Campbell.

'It is common in the west of this country to call the Campbells MacDiarmid,' J.F. Campbell wrote in 1861.

The Knocknagael boar that once stood on a hill above Inverness is now housed in the Highland Regional Office at Inverness. It is linked in that locality to Brude mac Maelcon.

The Ardross Wolf, Ross & Cromarty, now in Inverness Museum

THE WOLF

Three wolves appear on class I stones. On Keillor and Newbiggin Leslie they accompany other symbols. On Ardross one appears alone, far more skilfully carved than on Newbiggin Leslie although the designs are identical. Dr Henderson suggests that a template must have been used. Very little of the

High Keillor, Perth & Kinross

Keillor wolf remains. Tom Gray sees it as a badger or possibly a wolverine. Both are possible.

The Ardross wolf is one of the wonders of Pictland in that it exudes the essence of 'wolfness' as it slopes stealthily across the stone. The scrolled muscles are exactly right. The original sculptor knew his wolf, how it moved and how it behaved.

In the *Book of Durrow*, the four Evangelists' symbols consist of the man for St Matthew, the lion for St Mark, the bull for St Luke, and the eagle for St John, as in the Book of Revelations. There is a strong likeness between the lion and the Pictish wolf. The rampant lions on the Sutton Hoo purse also resemble the wolf. Dr Henderson suggests that the Durrow lion appears to be a painting of the hard-metal-bejewelled lions on the purse. Templates of the Pictish animal designs must have been available by 650 to intrigue the jewellers of Sutton Hoo who in turn may have inspired the artists of Durrow.

Wolves in folklore have always had a mixed press, from Red Riding Hood's false grandmother to Mowgli's foster parents. The Romulus-Remus legend has been a favourite mythic theme throughout the ages and still reappears from time to time in newspaper articles.

The last known Scottish wolf was killed at Lothbeg in Sutherland by a hunter called Polson about 1700. Legend relates that a missing child was traced to a she-wolf's den. During the rescue of the infant the wolf and her cubs were killed. The child, so the story goes, was never like other folk.

But to the Pict, the wolf was a reality, a fierce predator of his livestock and a constant danger to night travellers. It was a suitable name for a warrior clan, or so the Robertsons of Struan must have thought, for the gules on their Arms show three wolf heads, while those of the Skenes of Skene have the three wolf heads impaled on daggers.

THE GOOSE

Two geese appear on class I stones. On Roseisle of Easterton, Moray (now in NMS Edinburgh) the goose is most gracefully carved with its head turned aggressively back over its body, as if aware of danger, while the salmon beneath it stares steadfastly ahead.

To the Celt, the goose was always a symbol of watchful alertness. Miranda Green tells us that it stood for war and protection. Geese were buried with warriors in Iron Age graves where their bones have been found. Celtic gods were often depicted accompanied by geese. A most beautiful Bronze Age container in the shape of a goose was found in Hungary. Caesar tells us that the goose was

Easterton of Roseisle, Moray, now in NMS Edinburgh

sacred to the Britons and its flesh taboo.

All birds – but water-birds in particular – were significant to the Celts. The sun itself was drawn across the sky by a goose. What could be more ominous than a skein of wild geese spread in formation across a January sky? Do we not all look up to watch?

In Highland folklore the goose is wary and wily. A fable from Sutherland recounts how a fox caught a fine fat goose asleep by the side of a loch. As he held her by the wing, he joked with her.

'If you had me in your mouth as I have you, what would you do?'

'Easy!' hissed the goose. 'I would fold my hands and shut my eyes and say a grace before I ate you.'

'Just what I was about to do,' said the fox, folding his paws and closing his eyes.

When the goose spread her wings and flew away, the fox swore in disgust that he would never say grace again until after he had eaten.

It is easy to see why geese were important to the Picts. They were useful for meat and eggs – that is if they were eaten, and not taboo as they had been in south Britain. They were fierce protectors of their territory and were no doubt bred for their belligerence.

The goose may have represented a farming family but was much more likely to have been symbolic of a warrior lineage.

THE HORSE

Though the horse appears only once on a stone in a graveyard at Inverurie, it appears many times on the class II stones bearing warriors or huntsmen, thus indicating its importance to the Pictish aristocracy.

Whether it was a lineage symbol in the same way as some of the other animals are thought to be is doubtful, but it was probably a cult animal to the Picts. The Epidii, the tribe named by Ptolemy, translates as we have seen as the Horse Folk.

To the Iron Age Celt, the horse was the embodiment of majesty and nobility. Epona, whose name means 'great mare', was one of the few goddesses to be worshipped by both the continental and insular Celts. Before and after the Roman conquest, Britons and Gauls worshipped her as the 'Lady of the Foals'. She was particularly dear to warriors, and her cult must have been known to the Picts. She may even be depicted on the Hilton of Cadboll class II stone.

Lorraine MacDonald tells us that as a totem animal the horse was closely connected to Macha, the Irish horse goddess and warrior queen who had the gift of prophecy. The phrase 'straight from the horse's mouth' is said to be connected to Macha. Cu Chulain's horse was known as the Grey of Macha.

One relic of old horse ritual magic may have survived in the farms of Pictland up to the early twentieth century. The society of the Horseman's Word or Horse

Horse in Inverurie Cemetery, Gordon

Whisperers gave power to ploughmen over horses and women. Initiation took place in the barn where the young farmer was blindfolded and led before a court of older men to an altar formed by inverting a bushel measure over a sack of corn. After certain secret ceremonies, he was given the magic word thought to be 'Both in One', which may have indicated harmony between man and beast. The Word also gave him power over women. He had only to touch a girl and she would do as asked.

Here in the graveyard at Inverurie against the background of a Norman motte, a horse steps across a phallic stump of granite. Some doubt exists as to whether this carving is genuinely Pictish. Whatever its origin, it emphasizes the importance and endurance of the horse cult in north-eastern Scotland.

Grantown Stag, now in NMS Edinburgh

THE STAG

The symbol of the full stag makes only one appearance on a stone excavated near Grantown on Spey which is kept in NMS. With a full spread of antlers it appears incised above the symbol known as the 'rectangle'.

As a totem the stag is of great antiquity, to be found carved in caves and rocks throughout Europe. He represented the spirit of the forest, the Horned One, sometimes known as Cernunnos of the Groves, who bore the antlers on his brow. His power was essentially peaceful and his symbolism represented fertility and prosperity. He also stood for chieftainship.

Ancient Highland beliefs recorded by the Reverend James Kirkwood in the seventeenth century state that if the enemy of a hunter hid the bone of a deer in a tree he would never have success with that animal. Also, if the deer hunter passed a woman on his left, he would have no success that day, or if he found his venison too quickly he was considered 'fey' and close to death.

The Davidsons of Tulloch in Dingwall and the Frasers of Lovat took the stag's head for their crests. Two splendid roe bucks support the Arms of MacNaughten of Dundarve, but the symbol is mostly associated with the great Clan Mackenzie of Kintail whose Arms bear the stag's head and whose chief is still known as *Caberfeidh* (stag's antlers).

Ardross Deer

Rhynie 5

Mortlach

THREE FABULOUS HEADS

The first of these heads, the Ardross deer, was found in a wall close to the wolf-stone in Easter Ross. There is a similarity of style between them that suggests they may have been carved by the same artist. Both are to be seen in Inverness Museum and Art Gallery with replicas in Groam House Museum in Rosemarkie.

Many believe the head to be that of a horse, and indeed it may be, although I don't think so. Look at its face. Grace and gentleness flow from those simple yet exquisite lines. From the tear (or scent gland) beneath the eye to the budding horns, the carving is embued with the essence of 'deerness'. Children have called it a unicorn. Certainly it displays a mythical quality that fits in well with this interpretation.

In Highland tradition, the deer or 'dun hummel cows' were thought to be the cattle of the *sithean* – the fairy folk.

The Dunachton head from the Spey Valley which was discovered as a lintel

Ardross Deer, Ross &
Cromarty, now in
Inverness Museum

over the door of an old steading in 1870 is also thought to be a deer.

The third head on Rhynie No. 5 would seem to be that of a seal with flippers
and a dog-like profile. It was discovered in the foundations of the old church at
Rhynie in Aberdeenshire. Similar beasts are found on the silver plaques among
the Norrie's Law treasure.

Romilly Allen catalogues the above heads together, and Carola Hicks too
believes they should be treated as if interchangeable. They may have been local
variations on the same theme.

The seal – if the flippered creature is indeed that – is a Highland cult animal
capable of shape-shifting into man or more often woman. In the Hebrides certain
families such as the MacCodrums of North Uist are said to have descended from
seals.

Carola Hicks believes this curved figure found on a stone at Mortlach in Banff
in the 1920s may also represent a seal, but Dr Thomas sees it as a Dragonesque
Brooch in that it resembles a well-known North British type of ornament
common in the first and second centuries AD. Niall Robertson refers to it as a
'double hook'. There is no way of knowing what it represents.

THE SEAHORSE OR HIPPOCAMP

There are no examples of this creature on class I stones, and R.B.K. Stevenson argues that it is not strictly a symbol in the same sense as the others. It appears some dozen times on class IIs. Half-fish, half-horse in appearance, its magical properties lie in the fact that it can live in both fresh and salt water.

On the Rodney stone, on the drive to Brodie Castle, the two creatures with their filed teeth and scaled bodies are more mythical than real, while on Aberlemno 2 they are lovingly carved and as gentle as Rodney's are aggressive.

Perhaps they represent power over sea-lochs that mingle fresh with salt waters, while the Pictish beast represents power over fresh-water lochs and the salmon power over the rivers that flow into the sea. We don't know.

It is intriguing to think that these and the geometric/abstract symbols we are now about to look at were well known to all Picts throughout Pictland, including travelling clerics like St Adamnan himself. It is a pity that he never thought to explain them in one of his books.

OBJECT, ABSTRACT AND GEOMETRIC SYMBOLS

THE CRESCENT AND V-ROD

The crescent and V-rod symbol is clearly one of the most important of all the geometric symbols as it appears incised about thirty-five times on class I stones distributed throughout Scotland, but mainly in the northern areas from Orkney to Inverness and in Aberdeenshire. It also appears carved on the wall of the Sculptor's Cave at Covesea, on bone and on metalwork. (On class II stones it appears carved in relief some twenty times.)

The crescent can appear without its rod but there are only about three examples in each class.

R.B.K. Stevenson has given a great deal of thought to the patterns within the crescent symbol and divides them into three classes: those with two spirals, those with a central pelta design, and those with a central dome and wing shapes at the sides. But the classes merge into each other, which suggests to Stevenson a common origin that might be traced back to the designs on the hanging bowls at Sutton Hoo.

Broomend of Crichie, Gordon

Miranda Green states that Celtic images are based upon deliberate ambiguity and double interpretation. In Iron Age metalwork, faces were often depicted as geometric patterns – circles, crescents and other curvilinear forms, with the emphasis on the pattern. She thinks there is an intentional 'see what you want to see' element in interpretation.

Bearing in mind that each generation will 'see what it wants to see', this symbol today is generally associated with the moon. In old Highland tradition the first Monday of the Quarter was dedicated to the Moon, a day of good omen, a time for augury. The crescent moon was believed to encourage growth, a time for sowing and planting, for starting a journey.

In Western mythology the moon is lord of the tides and the dew and of the life-creating rhythms of the womb. The moon presides over the mysteries of life and death. The moon is the lord of time, the symbol of immortality.

Thomas sees the V-rod as resembling a broken arrow signifying the death of a person from the family represented by the crescent, probably a provincial or sub-king. Where the crescent is shown without the V-rod it represents a living king, perhaps the person who commissioned the stone.

In the *Sculptured Stones of Scotland* (1867), John Stuart called the rods sceptres. Stevenson points out a detail from the letter M in the *Book of Kells* (folio 12r) where the man's head is painted in front of two crossed sceptres.

Anthony Jackson sees the V-rod as a divining rod symbolic of weather magic. St Adamnan records in his *Life of St Columba* that Brude's magician proclaimed that he could 'make the winds unfavourable' to Columba's voyage. Perhaps the crescent and V-rod represented the family or profession of a magus.

THE DOUBLE DISC AND Z-ROD

In common with the other geometric symbols, the double disc with or without its rod, incised on some twenty-five stones and carved in relief on a further twenty-three is another enigma. Second in frequency of appearance to the crescent and V-rod (with the Pictish beast as third), it resembles nothing real to us.

Usually – but not always – presented horizontally, the double disc is generally thought to be a symbol for the sun and perhaps represents high-kingship.

The cult of the sun dates from the North European Bronze Age. The wheel was its symbol. It is possible that the double disc originated from the two linked wheels in a chariot or other vehicle that might symbolize the dual existence of the sun.

Druidism was a form of sun worship based upon the doctrine of the sun's duality, one in the visible world of day, the other in the Otherworld at night. The relationship between light and darkness, male and female, life and death as

Aberlemno 1, Angus   Logie Elphinstone 1, Gordon

symbolized by the sun was at the root of druidic mysteries.

But the sun also had a dual earthly existence: the one benign and indulgent that caused the crops to grow, the other malicious that shone in winter without warmth and withered the vegetation. Thus the two discs could be seen as representing the two faces of the sun.

As descendants of the old stone-circle magicians whose cult was most likely to have been connected with solar movement, the Pictish druids perhaps saw the double disc as the most powerful and ancient of all the symbols connected to the cup and ring marks and concerned with the worship of the sun.

Inveravon 2. Mounted outside south wall of church, Moray

THE TRIPLE DISC AND CROSS-BAR

Allen identifies seven occurrences of the above symbol. Here you see it in its simplest form on Inveravon 2 between a crescent and V-rod and the mirror-and-comb symbol.

Of all the geometric symbols this would seem to be the least obscure. It would appear to represent a bronze or iron cauldron as seen from above.

Cooking pots were not always so simple as the one incised on Inveravon 2. The great silver-gilt ceremonial cauldron found in Gundestrup, North Jutland, is exquisitely decorated with designs that bear comparison with Pictish motifs and remind us of Pictish sacrificial acts, such as drowning and bull sacrifice.

Cauldron on Glamis Manse stone

A cauldron with two pairs of legs protruding is depicted in realistic form on the class II Glamis Manse stone. Here it might represent the Cauldron of Regeneration in which warriors wounded in battle were healed.

But the cauldron was of significance throughout Western mythology. The Celtic gods – the Tuatha de Danaan – when they first appeared in Ireland borne on a ship of mist from four mythical cities beyond the skies, brought with them four treasures: the Invincible Sword, the Lance of Lug, the Stone of Destiny, and the Cauldron of Dagda the Good that would feed a host and never be emptied.

Keridwen, the British goddess of nature, possessed a cauldron with three properties – inexhaustibility, inspiration and regeneration – which represent the reproductive powers of the earth.

In the *Book of Taliesen*, King Arthur journeyed to the Otherworld to bring back the cauldron that was the fount of poetry and prophecy. With the coming of Christianity, the search for the Celtic Cauldron became fused with the quest for the Holy Grail, the Chalice of Christ.

In Pictland it may have represented a powerful family with the practical ability to provide sustenance and the mystical power to give or destroy life.

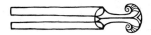

THE NOTCHED RECTANGLE WITH CURVED END

Among the eight appearances of this symbol, there seem to be three separate objects which have become confused with each other – the tongs, broken sword and tuning fork.

Where it appears between a hammer and anvil as on Dunfallandy (p. 194), it must surely be tongs or pincers representing the smith's craft. We have already seen how Gobniu was the most important of the Irish god artificers. But on Abernethy 1 it appears between a hammer and an anvil, and here it must surely be a broken sword.

Iron was always a magical substance in Scotland. Martin Martin recorded thirteen generations of smiths in Skye, all with healing powers derived from the ability to handle it. Some believe that most of the symbols can be traced to objects made of bronze or iron.

One would expect to see a sword among the symbols of a warrior-dominated society. Swords such as these with their curved hilts are thought by Thomas to have entered Scotland in the first century AD. A broken sword might symbolize the death of a sword-making craftsman or possibly a sword-using warrior in the same way as the Z-rod symbolizes the death of the person whose profession is represented by the symbol it covers.

As for a tuning fork, why not? The Picts like all Celts had their bards and musicians. It might indeed have been symbolic of the harpist's profession.

[111]

Ackergill (note part of fish at top and Ogam script), Caithness

THE RECTANGULAR FIGURE

The rectangle appears ten times on class I stones, most to be found from Aberdeen northwards. These are beautifully decorated and could have represented several prestigious objects – a kist, wooden box or chest, perhaps. I.F. Grant, in *Highland Folk Ways*, tells us that kists were an important part of the scant furnishings of croft houses in the Highlands up until recent times. These kists contained not only the family treasures but also their shrouds. It seems reasonable to suppose that Pictish houses also used kists for their belongings.

Thus the rectangle may have been symbolic of wealth, treasure and the spoils of battle.

Charles Thomas suggests that the rectangle represents a container. Just such a box dated between the eighth and tenth centuries, about twelve inches long and carved with scrolls, was found in Orkney. The tools it contained are thought to have belonged to a leather worker.

It might represent a satchel, which must have been part of every Pictish traveller's equipment. On several class II stones, monks are depicted with just such an article slung across their shoulders for carrying their Gospel books.

The rectangle has been linked by Anthony Jackson and others to a shield. The Picts, according to the stones, wore round wooden or leather targes rimmed with metal and with sharp protruding bosses for gouging the enemy in single combat. Square shields, ornately decorated, were also carried, but for battle the rectangular shield provided better protection. The naked warrior known as Collessie Man (p. 174), incised on a stone in Fife, wears a rectangular shield.

NOTCHED RECTANGLE AND Z-ROD

This appears seven times on class I and twice on class II stones. Always crossed by a Z-rod on stone, it appears without the rod on the fastening of the Whitecleuch silver chain. Although this complicated symbol does not look like any recognizable object, Charles Thomas, while admitting that the idea is far-fetched, believes it to be a war chariot drawn by two ponies, perhaps standing for a dead war leader.

'Chariots were part of the common inheritance of the Indo-European warrior élite,' according to Alfred Smyth. Tacitus describes them in the forefront of the Caledonian army at Mons Graupius. Dio Cassius writes of their use in battle by the Caledonians and Maeatae in about AD 200. Iron chariot wheels have been found in wells in the Borders, Strathclyde and at the Roman camp at Raedykes near Stonehaven.

Chariots were made of wood or wickerwork with bronze fittings. The Roman historian Florus describes one entirely plated with silver. Knowing the Pictish love of designs and ornamentation, there is no reason to suppose their models to have been inferior to those of their Celtic cousins elsewhere.

Although their use had died out in Pictland by the time the stones were carved, charioteers and their deeds of daring must surely have lived on in the oral tradition.

Meigle 10 – sadly lost – actually depicted a chariot drawn by a pair of horses and carrying three men.

Some see not the likeness of a chariot but rather that of a fortress. This interpretation is equally tenuous but also equally appropriate to a warrior society.

CIRCULAR DISC AND RECTANGLE WITH INDENTATION
CIRCULAR DISC AND RECTANGLE

The above symbol of the disc and notched rectangle is so similar to the disc and rectangle (not represented here) that it seems logical to look at them together. Between them there are about twelve incised examples and two carved on class II stones.

Jackson sees these as houses.

The great burial monuments of an earlier age were mostly circular. No longer in use as tombs, these great cairns with their low dark passages leading into eerie burial chambers were no doubt considered by the Picts to be haunted.

It would take a magus of formidable power to protect a community from such forces. Perhaps these symbols represented a lineage or profession with the power to dominate the dead.

But Charles Thomas suggests the symbols might represent the solar wheel or sun-disc held up by a human figure. The notch and patterning in the above rectangle would represent the figure and the gap between his legs.

THE ARCH

There are eleven stones identified by Romilly Allen incised with the arch and each one is slightly different from the others.

In folklore the arch is likened to a rainbow, as the following passage from J.F. Campbell's *Popular Tales of the West Highlands Vol. I* indicates:

'When they fled, they came to a great cataract and there was no way of getting over it unless they could walk on two hairs that were a bridge across the cataract and *Maol a Mhoibean* ran with ease over the two hairs; but her sisters could not walk on the two hairs and *Maol a Mhoibean* had to turn back and carry her sisters, one after one, over the cataract on the two-hair bridge.'

The two-haired bridge, according to Campbell, was a double rainbow which spirits but not mortals could cross. Norse gods rode over such a bridge from earth to heaven, and the Moslem bridge to Paradise is as fine as a hair. God's pledge to Noah was sealed by a rainbow.

To the Pict who practised weather magic the rainbow must have been of as great a mystical significance as it was to Noah linking the earth with the sky, heralding the sun.

The arch has also been likened to the horseshoe – still a symbol of good luck in Scotland. It looks like a horseshoe on the Strathpeffer Eagle Stone (p. 74). Although horseshoes with six countersunk nail-heads arranged in the modern manner were unearthed in Colchester and date from pre-Roman times, none have so far been excavated in Pictland. Thus there is no evidence that Pictish horses were shod in iron.

Others see the arch as a torc – a prestigious neck adornment worn by the élite.

THREE DISCS IN A CIRCLE

About six examples of the above symbol can be found on class I stones.

Anthony Jackson sees these as three pots in a circular kiln, representing community skills. As we have seen, pots were of enormous ritual importance in Bronze Age graves, and also for containing the ashes after a cremation, buried in the ground.

Although the period of distinctive finely ornamented pots as prestige items had probably passed, jugs and bowls were still necessary utensils in Pictish households. Potters no doubt retained their trade secrets and rituals which would give them an important place in Pictish society. It is an imaginative interpretation.

Others have suggested that the symbol might represent the Christian Trinity or the Celtic triple-headed goddess who is wise mother, innocent virgin and ruthless warmonger.

More convincingly, it may represent horse ornaments or a circular brooch set with precious stones, again symbolic of wealth and status.

THE TRIPLE OVAL

Another enigmatic symbol, the triple oval appears some three or four times on class I stones, including the Covesea Cave in Moray, and on the class II stone at Skinnet in Caithness.

It most resembles the snake-shaped bronze armlet found in the Culbin Sands in Morayshire and the pair found at Castle Newe in Aberdeenshire, among others.

We know that the European Celts loved finery of every sort. As Strabo wrote:
'To the frankness and high-spiritedness of their [the Gauls'] temperament must be added the traits of childish boastfulness and love of decoration. They wear ornaments of gold, torques on their necks and bracelets on their arms and wrists, while people of high rank wear dyed garments be sprinkled with gold.'

The Picts enjoyed jewellery and fine objects as much as their Celtic cousins elsewhere.

An exquisite arm bracelet made from a spiral band of undecorated beaten silver was one of the treasures found at Gaulcross. It seems that the coiled armlet was a popular piece of jewellery in those days as it is today.

Perhaps this symbol represents body adornment dating again from the Bronze or Iron Ages. Would it be too fanciful to connect it to all body adornment including the tattooist's art? Probably it was a status symbol worn by the élite and representing a warrior family.

THE FLOWER AND S-SHAPED FIGURES

The 'flower' symbol appears incised on three stones and carved in relief on four others. It vaguely resembles a plant, hence its name, given by Romilly Allen. But it has also been likened by Charles Thomas to a bronze harness brooch.

As revealed by archaeology, chariots and the ponies bred to draw them were elaborately furnished with decorated bronze fittings. The Pictish warrior no doubt adorned his horse with as much care as he dressed himself.

Horse decoration reached a peak of sophistication before the age of tractors and even today there is no more splendid sight than the great Clydesdale or Shire horses dressed in gleaming brass furnishings for display at the annual farming shows.

Thus the flower might represent bronze-workers and their god Creidhne.

The S-shaped figure is thought by some to be another bronze horse ornament. Charles Thomas suggests tentatively that it might be a swath of material bound at the centre. These two symbols must be among the hardest to identify.

FOUR RARE SYMBOLS

The Stepped Rectangle

There appears to be only one example of this symbol on a very worn class I stone at Rosskeen in Ross-shire, although it occurs twice on class IIs. On Rosskeen it is paired with the tongs, so might represent an anvil, or maybe – as Jackson suggests – the forge itself. It resembles the L-shaped rectangle to be seen in the Covesea caves, and on class II stones.

The Double Crescent

This appears twice and is thought to be a variation of the single crescent. Charles Thomas remarks that it slightly resembles the older Eurasiatic design of the double lotus.

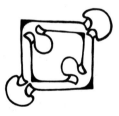

The Bow and Arrow

This is found once at Congash near Inverness and is now more or less invisible owing to the sinking of the stone. It might also represent a helmet.

Square with Corner Scrolls

This may be seen on Kintore 4 in Inverurie Museum (Grampian). The second new symbol to be uncovered since Romilly Allen wrote ECMS, it is impossible to decipher. Discovered in 1974, it is seen by Ian Shepherd, Grampian Regional Archaeologist, as possibly an applied bronze plate.

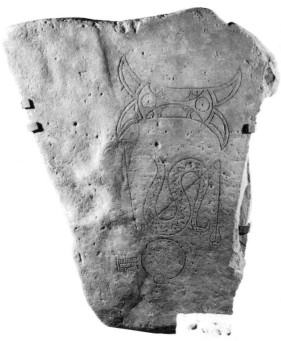

Dunrobin 2, Dunrobin Castle
Museum, Sutherland

THE MIRROR AND COMB

The mirror – with or without a comb – is (apart from the realistic animals) the
only easily recognizable symbol in Pictland. It appears about thirty times on class
I stones with a further dozen appearances on class IIs.

A mirror of the kind seen on the stones with an embossed trilobated plate of
thin bronze connecting the handle was found at Balmaclellan in Kirkcudbright-
shire. Another extremely heavy one made of massive bronze plate and
handsomely decorated was found at Birdlip near Gloucester. Iron Age bronze
decorated mirrors were being made in southern Britain from the first century BC.
The British Museum has a wonderful collection.

An article published in Arch. Camb. (1948) by Sir Cyril Fox suggested that the
Picts imported their bronze mirrors from Brigantia in North England and that
the 'Pictish symbolism was initiated before the use and knowledge of these forms
died out'.

What was that symbolism?

It is generally thought to be representative of high-born women, and there are
three valid interpretative suggestions. When it appears under (usually) two other
symbols it may quite simply suggest the death of a queen or noblewoman of the

tribe or family represented by the other symbols.

Thomas believes the mirror and comb might refer to the commemorator. Thus Aberlemno 1 might read 'To a dead king of the snake family remembered by a woman', presumably his wife.

Or, as Jackson suggests, it may stand for bridal gifts in the marriage settlement suggested by the other symbols above.

Mirrors with or without combs seem to have been a customary gift to offer a woman in those days, just as it was usual to give a silver brush and comb set to a young Victorian woman on a special occasion. Mirrors and combs belong to every age and fashion.

Bede records a letter written by Pope Boniface to Queen Ethelburga in the early seventh century, asking her to encourage her husband King Edwin to become a Christian. The Pope ends by writing '... we send you a silver mirror, together with a gold and ivory comb, asking your Majesty to accept these gifts with the same goodwill as that with which we send them'.

Combs had their ritual uses too. Dr Anderson tells us that one of the rubrics of the ordination of a bishop in the tenth century involved the use of a comb. St Cuthbert's comb was buried with him and is still kept at Durham Cathedral, while Queen Theodolinda's comb was preserved in AD 590 in the Basilica of St John, Monza.

In Highland folklore, mirrors and combs were magic. Men contended with giants for gold and silver combs. An enchanted prince combed silver from one side of his head and gold from the other. Warriors laid their heads on the laps of fair princesses who dressed their hair. Mirrors could turn into lochs and combs into forests.

Mirrors reflect the soul. After a death in the family some people still turn their glasses to the wall for fear that the lingering ghost of the departed may seize their vulnerable souls. During a thunderstorm some folk still cover their mirrors.

Society today associates the mirror and comb with women. In Pictish times this need not necessarily have been so. Classical writers repeatedly mention that the Celts had an abundance of hair worn braided or loose and held with combs and other ornaments. On some of the Pictish stones male figures are shown with elaborately curled hair. (See the leading king on the Birsay Stone from Orkney, p. 65). They must certainly have needed combs.

Look at any mirror and comb on a stone in Pictland. The image is as clear as when it was first carved over a thousand years ago. But for us the reflection remains dark. All we can safely say is that the looking-glass and comb were symbols of prestige, rooted in wealth and magic and dating from long before the Pictish era.

The same can be said for most if not all of the other Pictish symbols.

PART FOUR

CHRISTIANITY AND THE STONES

THE SIGNIFICANCE OF THE CROSS SLABS

W E have now looked at the symbols incised on class I stones. How much more do we know about the Picts?

Precious little. The truth is we may never find a Rosetta Stone with all the answers laid out like the letters of the alphabet. All that we have discovered so far is guesswork.

Professor Alcock and other devoted scholars in the Pictish field insist on the importance of de-mythologizing the Picts. Agreed. The Pictish people may not have been any more 'mysterious' than their neighbours but their stones display a multitude of mysteries.

The most we can deduce is that their symbols were important to them not as pieces of art but for their message.

The best analogy is the Christian Cross which conceals within two simple beams not only the whole doctrine of Christianity but the person of Christ himself.

Suppose we had never heard of Christianity and saw a cross incised with great simplicity on one of Dr Henderson's class IV stones. We could never begin to guess at the depths and breadth of its symbolism.

So it may well be with Pictish totems. Without access to Pictish minds, how can we ever hope to decipher their code?

Joseph Anderson in ECMS classified the class II monuments as having symbols and Celtic ornament carved in relief, including in most cases a cross on a carefully dressed background.

Class III stones are similar to Class II but omit the Pictish symbols.

These cross slabs, as they are called, carved on local stone, are unique in Dark Age art in that the artists did not use the outline crosses of Wales, Ireland and Northumbria but carved them on dressed slabs and crammed every inch of the spaces between and on the reverse side with a marvellous wealth of (usually) eclectic carvings. Both Christian and secular, these illustrations include warriors,

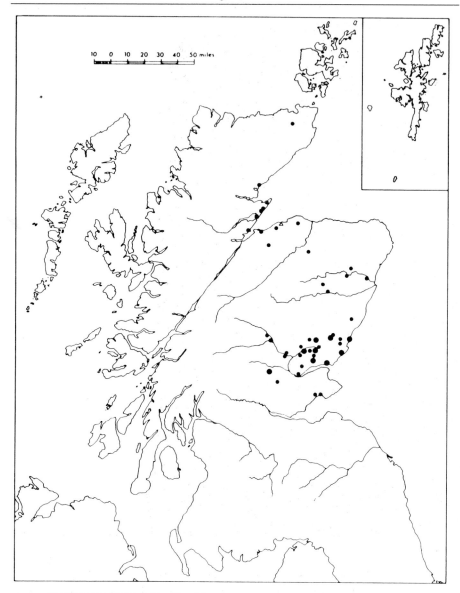

Symbol-bearing cross-slabs sculptured in relief

• Single slab

● Two or more slabs

Class II stones

Rossie Priory, Perth

monks, musicians and monsters, hunting parties, battles and Bible scenes.

The reason why the sculptors and their patrons chose the cross slab rather than the outline crosses of Ireland, Northumberland and Wales can only be guessed at. There are a few cross slabs in Northumberland, so the idea may have been brought north by sculptors in Abbot Ceolfrid's party, sent at King Nechtan mac Derile's request for instruction in the new Church usages from Rome. Maybe the king was making a political statement. He banished the Columban monks behind

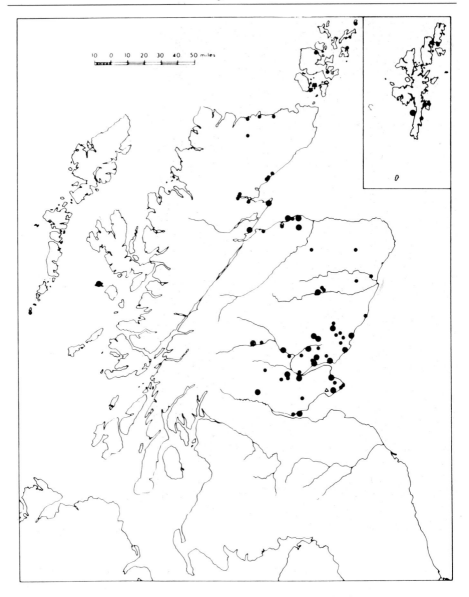

Non-symbol-bearing cross-slabs and recumbents and fragments of sculpture in the Pictish area

• Single sculpture

● Two or more sculptures

Class III stones

Hilton of Cadboll,
Ross & Cromarty, now
in NMS Edinburgh

the mountains of Drumalban, so may have decided against the Scottic style of cross at Iona. Perhaps the cross slabs were another way of proclaiming a reformed Pictish Church.

Or having had so much previous experience of stonework, the Pictish sculptors and their patrons may have chosen the slab as being the better medium for their messages.

Another possibility: the Pictish Christians might not have seen it as appropriate to carve figures and scenes within the cross itself, and hence preferred to place them on the reverse side of the stone.

Whatever the reason, the dressed cross slab was a great step forward artistically from the class I undressed boulder. From a practical point of view the slab provided greater scope for the inclusion of symbols, further decoration and other messages. Cross slabs did not appear until after Nechtan's historic invitation to Ceolfrid. Thereafter the Pictish Church looked to St Peter rather than St Columba as its founder.

Under King Nechtan, Christianity was formally established in Pictland with the king as head of the Church. The first class II stones were erected sometime after 710, a long time after according to Stevenson, who dates their first appearance to the second half of the eighth century.

Dr Henderson does not see the Northumbrian masons as particularly influencing the Pictish carvers or their motifs. The heavy plastic classical style of the outline Northumbrian crosses at Ruthwell and Bewcastle, which date from around AD 710, are carved very differently from the shallow delicate relief style of the earliest Pictish models, such as those at Glamis, Rossie Priory, Eassie and, perhaps the finest of all, Aberlemno churchyard, and the superb stones at Meigle.

When you come to look at the magnificent stones in Easter Ross, you can see that the sculptors of the cross slabs have borrowed from all the cults of the day and made them their own.

Remember, though, that class I stones continued to be carved within the Christian era. This might suggest that the reasons for erecting the two types of stones were different. That difference might be that the class II stones were raised firstly to proclaim the glory of God and secondly to honour some dead aristocrat, or to announce that the stone was commissioned by such and such a family. The emphasis had shifted.

The forty-four or so class II cross slabs are for the most part attached to Christian sites. Most of them have strong Christian messages behind what might appear to be secular themes. Each one of them tells us that the Picts were not just nominal or political Christians but truly dedicated whole-hearted enthusiasts for Christ.

Look at the class III Aldbar stone. With the help of Derek Bryce, let us try to interpret its message.

It was found in the site of a chapel at Aldbar Castle near Brechin. The chapel itself was built on the site of a much older church and the stone is reckoned to have stood in its kirkyard. You can see it today in Brechin Cathedral.

Every cross slab had a message or layers of messages for Christians to learn or preach from. The cross itself in all its many forms represented Christ – not on Good Friday, but in glory.

The Aldbar stone in Brechin Cathedral (front)

Here on Aldbar the shaft of the cross with its key-work decoration may have represented the axis that links a square earth to a round heaven whose centre is Christ.

The cross might also represent the Tree of Life. Two birds perch in its branches. One may have been the dove of the Holy Spirit, the other the cock, ancient symbol of dawn, of Christ as the Light of the World and of Peter's denial of Christ; a warning perhaps to the faithless. Or possibly it was the eagle symbolizing St John the Evangelist.

The Aldbar stone (back)

The cross could also be compared to a saint with the shaft as his back, and his head encircled with the halo of a holy man.

Again the symbolism could refer to the inward spiritual journey of the two monks shown either side of the shaft towards eternal life in heaven.

Every interpretation is a theme for meditation.

On the other side, two important priests are seated side by side on a throne. They may be bishops, abbots or the founding fathers of the original monastery. Here they are symbolic of the Church itself.

Below you can see one of the heroes of Pictish kingship, David rending the lion's jaws, with his harp, sheep and staff. Here he represents kingship. Below, a warrior on horseback represents the nation while the beast with many legs could stand for the animal world.

Thus we see the order of life through Pictish eyes: God and his Church, the king, the nation and the beasts.

So let us too start at the beginning by looking at the Pictish Church, its monks, monasteries and organization. Perhaps we shall find out more about the Picts from their Christian stones.

THE FOUNDERS OF THE PICTISH CHURCH

St Ninian, a Cumbrian Christian, is thought by many to have been the first missionary to have brought Christ to the Picts. Bede records that 'he was a most reverend and holy man of British race', a bishop who worked from Candida Casa at Whithorn in Wigtownshire in the fifth century and who converted the southern Picts.

As to the true extent of Ninian's mission, controversy reigns as to whether he was the first to evangelize Pictland or whether it was Columba.

Those in the Ninian camp trace church sites thought to be his actual foundations northwards through Ayrshire, Glasgow, Stirling, Coupar-Angus, Aberdeenshire, Fochabers in Moray, Loch Ness, the original Fearn community at Edderton in Ross-shire, Navidale in Sutherland, Wick, North Ronaldsay in Orkney, and St Ninan's Isle in Shetland, but does this mean that Ninian planted these churches himself, or were they much later dedications?

Very early churches took their names from their founders, whereas later churches were dedicated to their memories. The Celts did not dedicate their churches until the eighth century when the Roman reforms began. The Pictish Church as such did not dedicate at all until the Roman reforms, and thereafter the dedications were largely made to the great universal saints such as St Peter, St Mary and St Andrew.

There is one small piece of evidence to support the Ninianites. About AD 450 St Patrick wrote a letter to the Britons of Strathclyde in which he condemned their warriors for taking part in a massacre of Christians during a raid on Ireland. Associated with these warriors were 'the most unworthy, most evil and apostate Picts'. The word apostate describes people who had once been Christian and had reverted to paganism.

In the early part of the King List, two Drusts are recorded as reigning between 510 and c. 530. One of them allegedly sent his daughter Dusticc to be educated by Mugint, the abbot of Whithorn.

The reference, if valid, might point to the continued importance of the Ninian influence and Whithorn at least as a college for Christian students, retaining as such a connection with Pictish royalty.

So there are those like the Reverend Archibald Scott who passionately believed that Ninian was the first to organize churches throughout Pictland. Perhaps – if they existed at all – these tiny oases of Christianity were seen by the majority of Picts as oddities in the same way as twentieth-century mainstream Christians regard the back-street sects of today as strange but harmless.

But there are others in the Columban camp who believe that Ninian converted only the southern Picts on the edge of the Strathclyde border, as suggested by Bede.

As for the list of Ninian dedications, these do not prove that St Ninian founded the churches himself. Most of them would seem to belong to a revival of the Ninian cult in the twelfth century, when Ailred wrote his biography of Ninian largely based on old hagiographical legends.

The truth is that there is no real proof that Ninian's mission extended far beyond the southern borders of Pictland. Sadly, all the missing information would have existed in a much earlier *Life of St Ninian* which has been lost.

Dr Henderson suggests that Bede may have obtained his scant information from the first Anglian bishop of Whithorn who had access to the lost manuscript.

ST COLUMBA

If Ninian can be said to have first brought Christianity at least as far as southern Pictland, Columba of Ireland and Iona introduced it to the north and west while his followers took it throughout Pictland.

The Columban or Celtic Church was entirely monastic. All its clergy including bishops were subject to monastic rule. A bishop's main function was to continue the apostolic succession by the laying on of hands in the consecration of priests and other bishops.

Skene assures us that there was nothing derogatory in the functions of a Celtic bishop. His powers were purely spiritual. The exercise of jurisdiction lay in the monastery and was performed by the abbot.

So there were no diocesan or monarchic bishops in the Pictish Church except for a period of thirty years when southern Pictland as far as the Mounth was subject to Northumbria. This period ended in 685 when Brude mac Bili defeated the Northumbrians and killed their king. The Northumbrian bishop Trumwine made a hasty exit south of the Forth.

Thus the Celtic Church and what was to become the Pictish Church were organized in small clans in which the abbot was chief. To begin with these clans consisted of twelve members in emulation of the Apostolic band, but later abbots presided over monasteries that numbered hundreds of monks engaged in writing, illuminating the Gospels, teaching and evangelizing far afield.

We know a great deal about St Columba thanks to St Adamnan who wrote about his life in Scotland. Born in Donegal in about 521, he himself, through the Irish laws of inheritance, could have been elected king of Tara. As we have already seen, he was well educated, charismatic and hot-headed, a typical Celt. Over-involved in politics and largely responsible for the Battle of Cul Dreibne in which three thousand were killed, he was obliged at the age of forty-two to leave Ireland. With twelve companions he set out for Dal Riata to become 'a pilgrim for Christ'.

As we have already seen, he visited King Brude mac Maelcon for permission to set up his monastery on Iona, thus paving the way for his followers to spread the gospel within Pictland.

But Columba was not the only missionary from Ireland. The great monastery at Bangor continued to send evangelists to the Picts until at least the eighth century.

It would be stupid to think that all was smooth going for the infant Pictish Church as a result of Columba's friendship with King Brude. There was no mass conversion, and although tiny pockets of Christianity tucked themselves into the glens here and there, Smyth tells us that territory north of Skye did not become Christian for at least a century after Columba.

This was not for lack of zeal.

St Donnan, a younger contemporary of Columba, set up a community on the island of Eigg. The Annals of Ulster record that he and 150 martyrs were slaughtered after Mass on Sunday, 17 April 617. This is thought to have been arranged by a minor Pictish queen who objected to sharing her sheep pasture with the intrusive monks. Donnan place-names abound in Wester Ross, including that most famous of all, Eilean Donnan (Donnan's Island), which later supported the famous castle.

Adamnan tells us that Columba himself encountered hostility from pagan Picts.

St Maelrubha was another Irishman trained at the famous monastery at Bangor who in 671 established his community at Abercrossan (Applecross in Wester Ross). His influence was particularly powerful in Skye and Wester Ross.

Gradually Pictland became supplied with small but efficient Columban-based but Pict-manned monastic communities throughout the kingdom, probably starting in the Moray Firth area. Columba may not personally have converted many Picts, but it was his original leadership and spirituality which directly inspired his followers.

THE SYNOD OF WHITBY

Why, then, should this zealous Pictish monastic Church have been challenged by an Anglian-based denomination that recognized the Church of Rome as its master?

The main cause was probably the Synod of Whitby.

We have referred to Eanfrid, one of the sons of the Northumbrian King Ethelfrid exiled to Pictland during the reign of Edwin, who married a Pictish princess and fathered the Pictish king Talorgen. When Eanfrid succeeded to his Northumbrian throne he was immediately killed in battle and his younger brothers Oswald and later Oswiu inherited his kingdom. They had both shared Eanfrid's exile to Pictland where they had converted to Christianity.

During Oswald's reign, the king sent for St Aidan from Iona to preach Christianity to his subjects. After Oswald's death in battle in 641, Oswiu succeeded him, and he too looked to Iona for guidance. Then in 651 Aidan died and his successors at Lindisfarne, Finan and Colman, found themselves mixed up with what is now known as the Easter Controversy.

This dispute was not only to do with calculating the correct date for Easter. New baptismal rites and changes in the way of consecrating a bishop were also important, as was the way monks cut their hair. Celtic monks used the ancient frontal tonsure which was anathema to Roman-taught Christians who saw it as pagan because the druids had used it. The approved tonsure was coronal (as it still is), where only the crown of the head is shaved.

Thus the Celtic Church had fallen behind the European Churches in several ways. One faction led by Wilfrid, the powerful Bishop of York, argued for uniformity throughout Christendom, the other, headed by Colman of Lindisfarne, was for keeping the old Celtic customs.

How modern it all sounds.

The climax came in 664 when a synod was called at Whitby. All the leading churchmen and royalty of the day attended. In the end Oswiu made the decision to vote for the Roman faction. Though sympathetic to the Celtic Church that had been his cradle, he was no doubt encouraged by Wilfrid to believe that his best interests lay with Rome.

But Colman rejected the changes and Iona refused to accept the reforms and stood out strongly against them.

During this time the south and east of Pictland as far as the Mounth were, as we have seen, under Northumbrian rule, and the Pictish Church in that area was subject to Bishop Trumwine, who himself was assistant to the powerful Bishop Wilfrid.

ADAMNAN AND NECHTAN MAC DERILE

Meanwhile Adamnan, already in his fifties, succeeded to the abbacy of Iona in 679. Of noble birth and related to Columba's family, Adamnan was a good man, scholarly and diplomatic, biographer of Columba and author of *The Holy Places*, a fascinating travel book dictated to him by Bishop Arculf of Gaul. This book was not just about the Holy Land but included a description of the Nile and its crocodiles. Perhaps some of the creatures on the class II and III stones can be traced to this source.

Under Adamnan, Iona became a place of high learning with an important library and artists with superb skills. Not long after his death in 704 the *Book of Kells* itself – or part of it – is thought to have been written in his monastery.

During his period as abbot, Adamnan spent time in Northumberland and there came to the conclusion that the Synod of Whitby had made the right decision. He was never able to convince the Iona community of this belief, but it is quite possible that he had enough influence to persuade King Nechtan.

Adamnan was the friend of kings. He was able to persuade King Aldfrid (successor to Ecgfrid, who was killed by the Picts at Nechtansmere) to return sixty Irish captives. He mourned by the corpse of King Brude mac Bili. He may have educated King Nechtan.

Nechtan IV succeeded his brother Brude mac Derile to the high-kingship in 706. His territory is thought to have included Angus, Stormont, Atholl as far as the western frontier of Drumalban, Badenoch, and north to both sides of the Inverness Firth. He may have held a fortress in Strathspey near Loch Insh whose ruins you can still find. He may even have lived there. A monastery or bangor was established probably by him near his Strathspey fortress on the River Calder near Newtonmore. The locality is still known as Banchor.

Bede tells us that Nechtan was a man of education who 'meditated on ecclesiastical writings'. He was a king who took a strong interest in all matters pertaining to the Church. Where did he receive his interest and education? Scott suggests that he was probably a pupil of Adamnan himself, either in Iona or one of the other Pictish monasteries. He may have been a hostage among the Scots in pledge of the long peace that subsisted between the Picts of Atholl and Badenoch and the Scots of Lorne.

I would think it equally possible that he had been fostered in the Celtic custom with a family who knew and was sympathetic to Adamnan's point of view. Nechtan may have been educated at Iona.

Thus Nechtan from his early years came under the influence of Adamnan. He would have known the reasons for Adamnan's choosing to adopt the decisions of Whitby. He must have thought hard and prayerfully about the whole matter. He must have guessed that it would not be easy to reform the Pictish Church.

No wonder he took his time about making the momentous decision to write to Abbot Ceolfrid for further instruction and to instruct masons and architects to build him a stone church in the Roman fashion. In his reply Ceolfrid refers to Adamnan as one already known to Nechtan.

It seems to us such a simple reformation – but to the Pictish clerics it must have been a blow to the soul. To be told that they had been celebrating the greatest Christian festival in the calendar on the wrong date must have hurt. The change in tonsure would have caused as much distress to the older clerics as it did to twentieth century nuns when they were obliged to exchange their formal habits for skirts.

As soon as Ceolfrid's reply arrived in 710, Nechtan summoned a synod composed of the Pictish clergy, provincial kings, chiefs and, according to Bede, 'many learned men'. After the letter was read, Bede tells us that Nechtan knelt and gave thanks to God 'that he had been found worthy to receive such a blessing from the land of the English'.

You can imagine the feeling of the kings and warriors assembled, whose grandfathers had fought and destroyed the English just over twenty-five years previously. You can hear the distressed murmurings of the abbots, the angry muttering of chiefs, see the thunderous looks as fingers felt for sword-hilts.

Then Nechtan declared that he would observe the new Pascal dates and decreed that his clerics would be tonsured in the Roman fashion. Bede tells us that this decree was sent to 'all the provinces' of the Picts.

Nechtan was not a popular king. A year after Ceolfrid's letter, in 711, a Northumbrian overlord sent a raiding army into the Lothians and as far north as Clackmannanshire. The warriors of Fortrenn defeated them on the Moor of Mannan but many Picts, including a leading warrior, were killed. That can have done no good at all to Nechtan's cause.

In 713, his kinsman Kenneth was mysteriously murdered. Thereafter, although the events of this time are very muddled, Talorg of Atholl was invited to Nechtan's court as adviser.

Four years later, in 717, Bede tells us that all the Iona clergy in Pictland were expelled back to their own territory. Scott (who gives no references) reckons this was not necessarily a national movement. Owing to a misinterpretation of Ptolemy's map – which Bede might have used – the northern Picts on the map represented the western Picts of today. Scott therefore interprets Bede's northern Picts as those living on the border with the Scots, particularly the strong communities at Dull on Loch Tay planted by Adamnan. Scott also emphasizes that before the ninth century, no Iona Scot controlled any religious community in Pictland except for those few on the Dal Riatan frontier line.

In other words, there were no Columban abbots to expel.

Some have said that Nechtan expelled the Scottic clergy because they would not conform to Roman usages. This can't have been true because Bede records that in 710–16 'the man of God, Egbert brought the monks of Hi [Iona] to observe the Catholic Easter and the ecclesiastical tonsure'. Iona and the Columban clergy had already conformed.

The strange *Legend of Triduana* tells us that Nechtan became her lover and chased her from Rescobie in Angus to Dunfallandy in Atholl. This sounds like spiteful gossip which may have come from a non-conforming community.

Triduana's name means 'lady of the three days' fast'. She is thought to have been one of two abbesses belonging to the party sent north by Ceolfrid. (Other sources associate her with St Regulus and the cult of St Andrew.) She has a number of dedications including healing wells at Rescobie, Restalrig in Edinburgh and one at Kintradwell in Brora (where incised stones were found).

This does not seem to accord with the holy Nechtan who was soon to abdicate and go into Christian retreat. But the story might symbolize some event in his private or political life to account for his retreat into religion.

Where he made his retreat is not known, but it may have been Easter Ross. A cave in the cliffs between the North Sutor of Cromarty and the seaboard village of Shandwick is still called the King's Cave and is considered to be the legendary site.

This would have been a likely spot within his kingdom, close to his Northumbrian foundation at Rosemarkie, and the monasteries at Edderton and Tarbat.

Although he was succeeded by Drust VI and Alpin mac Ferath, he still kept an eye on his kingdom and attempted a return. In 726 he was arrested but recovered his throne for a short period until he was finally defeated by Oengus I in the Battle of Monith Carno (the Battle of the Cairn), thought to have been somewhere in central Pictland.

Thereafter he may have retired to his fortress in Strathspey until his death in 732. In spite of his zeal he left only four monastic communities founded by the leader of the evangelizing party who had been sent north by Ceolfrid. His name is thought to have been Curadan or Boniface or both.

CURADAN-BONIFACE

Curadan (Kiritinus) is a shadowy figure often confused with Pope Boniface and the legend associated with his visit to Pictland.

Aidan MacDonald suggests he was the 'chief clerical agent' sent by Ceolfrid to

Restenneth Priory, Angus

The Invergowrie Panel, now in NMS Edinburgh. Possibly connected to St Curadan-Boniface

instruct Nechtan in the new Roman usages. He may have taken the surname of Boniface in honour of Pope Boniface V (619–695) and to mark his allegiance to Roman policies. But this is only guesswork. Certainly he was not the only cleric to take on the name of Boniface, a Latin word that means 'do-gooder'.

It is thought he sailed north with a company of fellow evangelists who may have been called Benedictus and Benevolus; perhaps Servandus and Pensandus, and the two women Crescentia and Triduana. Boniface (Curadan) himself was paired with a Bonifandus.

Curadan was especially associated with four churches dedicated to St Peter.

[137]

Rosemarkie cross slab (front)

The church at Restenneth in Angus is thought to be the original 'stone church built in the Roman fashion' promised by Nechtan in his request to Ceolfrid. It was once known as Egglespether, a name of Pictish origin.

The church at Invergowrie or Dargie with a stone depicting three monks is also associated with Curadan Boniface. Tealing church in Angus has St Peter's Well nearby. The fourth site was established with a monastery at Rosemarkie in the Black Isle.

Rosemarkie may possibly have been part of Nechtan's personal clan territory and an ideal site for preaching the new innovations to the monasteries in the north. That Rosemarkie was by 750 to become an important monastic site is proved by the wealth of class III stones found in the old churchyard and the magnificent class II cross slab found in the floor of the original church during rebuilding in the eighteenth or nineteenth century.

This stone may well have been raised by the local king at that time in memory of St Boniface himself. It bears the regal symbols of the crescent and V-rod (three of them), the double disc and Z-rod with two mirrors and a comb. But this can only be speculation. The cross slab is one of the finest in Pictland.

Place-names such as Kincurdie and Kilcurdie have survived both in Rosemarkie itself and near Invergowrie while his fellow labourer in the mission field, Benedictus, one of his companions or relatives, is remembered by St Bennet's Chapel and Well near Cromarty and Bennetsfield and its well in the parish of Avoch, both in the Black Isle.

Bishop Leslie wrote in the sixteenth century that 'the toun is ancient and of gret antiquities called Rosmarkine, throuch the Reliques of St Boniface; and decored thouch the Sepulchres and monunmentis of alde of his fatheris'.

Here one supposes that Boniface did not bring his natural parents to Rosemarkie (though he might have done) but rather that family in Christ of whom he was abbot.

The quotation comes from a translation of Bishop Leslie's original *Historie of Scotland* by Father Dalrymple in 1596. In the next reformation of the Pictish Church in the twelfth century Rosemarkie was to become the centre of the Diocese of Ross, of which John Leslie was for a short while bishop.

For the hundred years after Nechtan's death, the Picto/Celtic Church with its Roman innovations must have flourished. This was the era of the cross slabs which show forth with shining integrity the spiritual depths of its conviction.

THE CHRISTIAN CROSS

'Stones are holy places where the Picts encountered God.'

So said Stephen Driscoll at the Second International Conference on Insular Art in Edinburgh in 1991.

It was for me one of the most memorable statements to come out of a most instructive weekend.

Today so much emphasis is put on the artistry of the Pictish cross slabs that sometimes their original purpose is lost in a maze of argument and connoisseurship. Unfortunately, bringing the stones into museums encourages us to see them merely as works of art, isolated from the cult and landscape to which they belonged.

The cross slabs grew out of fairly settled and orderly communities ruled by wealthy warrior kings recently converted to Christianity. The larger, more prosperous settlements supported monasteries whose abbots and monks were related to these kings. Smaller settlements governed by lesser lords also had churches evangelized from the monasteries and patronized by local lords.

The stones were commissioned, carved and erected in the heart of these communities not just as monuments of prestige or commemoration. They were of far deeper significance than the village war memorial of today. As Dr Driscoll says, the cross slab was not just a place where things happened, it was an object that made things happen. Just as the stone in Groam House Museum is known as the Soul of Rosemarkie, so these cross slabs symbolized the spiritual centre of the communities they graced.

The old magic that the class I stones represented – good luck in battle, fertility, power over animals and the elements – was, in the cross slabs, retained but widened and transformed into the greater wonder that was Christ, the high-king of heaven, the god above all lesser gods, the source of all good things.

Their symbolism was astonishingly elaborate, multi-layered and deliberately difficult, made to be taught from, and translatable today only by the art and ecclesiastical historians.

Like the great cathedrals of a later age, the cross slabs were – and still are – witnesses of Pictish man's zeal and devotion to the Christian God.

GREEK AND LATIN CROSSES

Of all the symbols on Pictish class II and III stones, it goes without saying that the cross is of paramount importance. It symbolizes not only the death and resurrection but Christ in glory.

The basic designs suggest that there may have been templates. The crosses follow about thirty varieties of pattern, but no two crosses are alike in their decoration.

Isabel Henderson tells us that the cross itself was first introduced by the Irish and British missionaries. For a people so symbol-minded as the Picts it would be easy for them to assimilate the cross into their code.

The first inspiration probably came from Dr Henderson's class IV stones, the simple grave-markers of the Iona monks later to be found in Pictland also. These were usually shaped like the Latin cross with straight arms and rounded arm-pits, and were often ringed.

Another appropriate model for the cross slab comes from Monkwearmouth – where else when you consider the significance of King Nechtan's request to

Eassie cross slab, Angus

Ceolfrid? – and is a dressed slab with a Latin cross projecting in relief on one side. There are several of these slabs at Jarrow which date from the eighth century.

Shafted equal-armed Greek crosses also appear on stones in Jarrow.

The basic design of the cross on most Pictish stones incorporates the Columban Latin cross with rounded arm-pits combined with the Northumbrian idea of the Greek cross set on a pedestal.

Anderson suggests that the hollowing of the arm-pits was a device to soften the harsh outlines of the basic cross. Many of the rounded arm-pits are segments of a circle.

Dr Henderson believes that Eassie in Angus is a good example of the earliest cross slabs.

[141]

The Peter stone, Whithorn,
Dumfries & Galloway

THE RING CROSS

Some believe that the ring cross developed from the Chi-Rho (the first two letters of Christ's name in Greek) which, when twisted and enlarged, looked like a cross within a circle. Thus it resembled the ancient eastern totem of the sun, which was also a symbol of Christ.

The ring cross was not connected to the Crucifixion but rather represented Christ in Majesty, the Light of the World.

The ring also resembles the Roman laurel wreath presented to generals victorious in battle. The Emperor Constantine is said to have ordered the Chi-Rho monogram to be placed within the wreath that crowned his standard. Thus the ring cross is also thought to represent Christ in Victory.

The commonest interpretation is that the ring represents the halo or nimbus behind the head of Christ.

The small indentations in the centre and in the arms of the equal-armed cross

[142]

Aberlemno Kirkyard cross
slab (front), Angus

on the front of the Rosemarkie cross slab may have contained precious gems including perhaps a reliquary attached on special occasions.

The ringed cross may have entered southern Pictland by way of St Ninian. This simple ringed cross found at Whithorn may have developed from the Chi-Rho.

THE DECORATED CROSS

Within the varied outlines of the cross and elsewhere, the types of ornamentation include plaitwork, knotwork, key-patterns, spiral designs and snake bosses, each with its own particular symbolism. It is probably fair to say that everything the Picts carved, from the simple triquetra knot to the most complicated interlace, was of symbolic importance.

One of the most glorious of all the cross slabs is the Aberlemno kirkyard stone.

Though a cast is kept in NMS, it still stands in the open air, a tribute not only to the artistic talent of one sculptor but to the culture and beliefs of a whole nation. Let's look at the front.

The central motif of spirals is said to represent the 'motionless mover', God Himself, around whom all life revolves.

The triangular knotwork within the upper and lower arms of the cross might be seen as representing the soul inextricably and eternally bound to its maker.

The knotwork on the lower shaft of the cross set within saltires and circles may be symbolic of the ties that bind the soul to this world and which must be cut before the spirit can transcend the flesh.

The key-patterns on the left and right arms of the cross are similar to Greek fretwork turned though an angle of forty-five degrees. They represent interlacing in straight lines.

Interlacing has been likened to weaving. Derek Bryce suggests that 'the basic symbolism is that of the great cosmic loom of the universe . . . there are no loose ends, and the symbol is also one of continuity of the Spirit throughout existence'.

The marvellous entwined creatures that surround the cross may be interpreted as symbols of protection from the Devil's wiles. Note the perfectly executed triquetra above the adjacent tails of the sea-horses on the right. The triquetra symbol appears on other stones and is said to represent the Eternity of the Unity of the Trinity.

Dr Anderson was quick to point out that these interlacing and key-designs were not exclusively Celtic. The same meanderings occur on Babylonian, Mycenaean, Alexandrian, Ethiopian and Pompeian ornaments or manuscripts. They were common forms of decoration throughout the world. But interlace reached a peak of perfection in Ireland and in Pictland. 'It never gave a distinctive character to any art but Celtic art.'

Quoting J.M. Kemple, Dr Anderson continues, 'There is nothing like it in Etruscan art; there is nothing like it in German or Slavonic art. There is little like it in Gaulish or Helvetian art; it is indigenous – the art of those Celtic tribes which forced their way into these islands, and, somewhat isolated, here developed a peculiar, but not less admirable, system of their own.'

THE BIBLE STONES

Farnell cross slab, Montrose
Museum, Angus

ADAM AND EVE

The woman saw how beautiful the tree was and how good its fruit would be to
eat, and she thought how wonderful it would be to become wise.

Genesis 3, Good News Bible

It is a pity that so much of the Farnell stone has been effaced, for perhaps we
would have seen more of the story of Adam and Eve.

Two serpents frame the small figures of a fully clothed Adam and Eve who

Inchbrayoch cross slab
(front), Montrose
Museum, Angus

stand beneath the Tree of Knowledge. You can clearly see the apple in Eve's
hand. Anderson suggests that two serpents rather than the conventional one
were carved to give the picture symmetry.

Immediately above, the cross symbolizes the Tree of Life, whose fruit is now
available to mankind through the death and resurrection of Christ.

At the top of the stone you can just make out the head and possibly wing of one
of the cherubim who guard the gateway to Eden. The theme would seem to be
the fall of man and his ultimate redemption and salvation through the Cross of
Christ.

The Farnell stone is in Montrose Museum.

[146]

Inchbrayoch (back)

SAMSON AND DELILAH

There is an endearing clumsiness about Inchbrayock 1 which tells the story of Samson on both sides. Here on the back, the extraordinary figure in the lower right corner has been likened to Samson's mother, pregnant as divinely foretold, but is much more likely to be, as Romilly Allen suggests, a fallen Philistine warrior.

In the left corner Samson appears again in full vigour with long prominent hair, smiting one of the Philistines with the jawbone of a donkey. Note however that the teeth have been carved on the wrong side of the jaw!

[147]

Above, the hunting scene is full of symbolism. One interpretation could be the analogy of the Christian warrior's journey through life. The soul, represented by the fallen hart, is beset by evil in the form of hounds, but finds shelter and safety beneath the Tree of Life.

The two circles that seem to be suspended from the Tree have been compared to the Pictish double disc, although this does not seem at all likely. Perhaps they represent the fruits of the Tree of Life and the Tree of Knowledge.

Norman Atkinson, curator of Angus Museums, believes that 'its size and generally debased carving fit in well with the overall style of monuments after the Viking invasions, and a date in the latter half of the ninth century or some time during the tenth century has been suggested by most scholars'.

Here in the lower right corner of the back of Inchbrayock 1, Samson appears to be reclining with one arm behind his head. The tall beast-headed creature is associated with Delilah in the act of cutting off his hair.

The animal in the left corner may be intended for the lion which Samson 'tore apart with his bare hands'. That same lion whose carcass housed a swarm of bees led to the riddle that Delilah betrayed to the Philistines.

Samson's betrayal by Delilah brings to mind Christ's betrayal by Judas and warns the Christian to be on guard. The hero is seen as a prefiguration of Christ both in the matter of his miraculous birth and in his eventual victory over evil.

St Brioc, whose name has been given to the three Inchbrayock stones, two of which may be seen in Montrose Museum (the third is lost), was allegedly born in Wales and became a follower of St Germanus of Auxerre near Paris in 429. He founded monasteries in Brittany and died there in his nineties in 502. His tomb became a place of pilgrimage. Norman Atkinson suggests that when the Vikings raided Brittany, his relics were removed. One may have been taken to Angus and a chapel founded there in his name.

THE DAVID STONES

Of all the Old Testament heroes who prefigured Christ in Early Christian art, David was the greatest. Dr Henderson has identified and described six stones where there can be no doubt as to the iconography, and a further half-dozen or so that may or may not be associated with David as harpist or musician.

These are to be found on Nigg in Easter Ross, Kinnedar in Elgin Museum, Aberlemno 3, Aldbar in Brechin Cathedral, Dupplin in Perthshire, and the sarcophagus in St Andrews Cathedral Museum in Fife.

Undoubtedly the finest of these is the last. Thought to date from the tenth century, this altar-tomb or box-shrine could fairly be called one of the finest

The St Andrews Sarcophagus, Fife

examples of Dark Age art in Europe.

Set within two superb panels of deer-headed serpents to the left and intertwining snakes to the right, David – symbolic here of the Good Shepherd – rends the jaws of the lion with his bare hands. Note the regal folds of his garment, how the draw-string of his shirt is neatly tied in a bow and his hair elaborately curled. Above his left shoulder a horned sheep looks on with curiosity. Over his right shoulder a monkey, possibly meant to be a demon, turns its back.

The central mounted figure is David as royal hunter with a falcon on his wrist, about to defend himself with drawn sword as a lion springs up at him from the branches of the tree.

The tree may be the vine presented in the form of a thicket, the Tree of Life symbolic of communion with the Creator, in which a variety of animals are caught. These creatures may represent all created life.

Below, a griffin (part lion and part eagle) pounces on what might be a mule. The griffin at one time was seen as an evil beast that preyed on human souls.

To its left, David appears again as the warrior/hunter with his hound and spear at the ready. Notice that he wears a plaid over his shoulder and that his tunic would almost appear to be kilted. His shield has a central boss with four rounded corners unlike the shields on earlier stones. The David on this marvellous stone is clearly a Scot rather than a Pict.

'Surely', Dr Henderson writes, 'the sculptor must have intended these images

[149]

to convey a meaning at least as intricate and coherent as his artistic conception.'
She suggests that the panel may show David exhorting the whole of creation to
praise God and thus bring peace and harmony to earth.

THE DANIEL STONE (BACK)

Above, a troop of four spirited hunters with two hounds canter across the stone
while at the top a more imposing figure, perhaps a king, appears to be led by a
spirit symbolizing his guardian angel or perhaps his soul.

The central figure is thought to be a bearded Daniel in flared and pleated robe.
His arms are outstretched in prayer as if to bless the four affectionate lions and
their cubs which you can clearly identify above the tails of the upper pair of lions.
Daniel is shown in a Christ-like attitude and the whole scene is symbolic of the
Resurrection. The den of lions could not destroy Daniel nor the sealed tomb hold
the Saviour.

Below is Chiron the centaur with an axe in each hand and the centaury branch
(cummel or mugwort) under his arm. Here is a Classical pagan figure who
because he gave the healing branch to Aesculapius, the god of healing, is shown
here probably as a prefiguration of Christ the Healer.

Below Chiron is a strange scene where a dragon appears to be devouring the
head of a bull, overlooked by a man with a club or possibly wearing a yoke. This
probably illustrates a tale from the Pictish oral tradition lost to us today, or it
might symbolize the punishment of pagan man and the bull he worships in the
jaws of hell.

What a marvellous collection of eclectic themes, the first purely Pictish, the
second resembling the pictures of Daniel in the Roman catacombs, while the
centaur, says Allen, would not seem out of place on an Etruscan vase.

JONAH AND THE WHALE

Two cross slabs bear the Jonah image – Dunfallandy (possibly) and here
(thought to be the earlier of the two) at Fowlis Wester church.

At the top of the front of the stone, either side of the upper arm of the cross,
there are two images of Jonah. On the left the whale has swallowed him. All that
remains is his sword and shield. On the right the whale is disgorging him.

Jonah is a symbol for the resurrected Christ. The creature represents the tomb
from which Christ rose after three days. The message is undoubtedly salvation
through Christ.

top Meigle 2, Meigle Museum, showing Daniel surrounded by lions

bottom Detail of Jonah on Fowlis Wester cross slab, Perth & Kinross

Mourning angels. Aberlemno roadside, Angus

Bede tells us in his book on the lives of the Northumbrian abbots that John, abbot of St Martin's, not only taught the monks to sing the services, but left at Monkwearmouth a great number of pictures, both from the Bible and from ecclesiastical history, which were mounted on boards and fixed across the nave from side to side. Thus everyone who entered the church, whether or not he was able to read, could dwell upon the blessings of the Incarnation and the perils of the Last Judgement and examine his heart accordingly.

The cross slabs served much the same purpose for the Picts.

NEW TESTAMENT STONES

THE ANGEL CROSS

And behold, angels came and ministered unto him.

Matthew 4 v.11: Mark 1 v.13

Here on the roadside at Aberlemno, mourning angels are placed at either side of the cross. Apart from the Biblical reference, which in fact applies to Christ in the wilderness, the image conveys the same message and more.

Dr Henderson sees the mourning angels as deeply significant in that the interlace cross which essentially symbolizes Christ in Glory is now given its historic meaning. It becomes a reminder of Christ on Good Friday. In other words the cross has become a crucifix.

Judging by the number of angels to be seen on the cross slabs, the Pictish Christians took their existence seriously. Apart from philosophical justification – Plato believed that every created thing had its spiritual counterpart – the life of Christ, according to the Evangelists, was attended by angels from the Annunciation to the Ascension.

Here on Aberlemno 3 they are depicted holding books in a pose of reverent mourning at the foot of a crucified Christ, the scene so delicately carved, so redolent of grief, that it brings to mind the 22nd Psalm, which begins:

'My God, my God, look upon me; why hast thou forsaken me; and art so far from my health, and from the words of my complaint?'

The four indistinct creatures at the foot of the cross seem to represent the symbols of the Evangelists in the *Book of Kells*. These symbols appear and re-appear on the cross slabs.

A solemn stone indeed.

Virgin and Child in Brechin Cathedral

VIRGIN AND CHILD

He [Bede] speaks in terms of the highest respect of the Virgin Mary, as blessed above all women. But he goes no further than that. His manner of speaking of her may be gathered from a remark which he makes in preaching on one of the festivals in her honour. A most excellent and salutary practice, he says, has long been established in the Church, that her hymn [Magnificat] is sung every day at vespers.

The Venerable Bede, Reverend G.F. Browne, 1887

[154]

The Apostles' stone in
Dunkeld Cathedral

Although the *Book of Kells* has a representation of the Virgin and Child surrounded by four angels, there is only one architectural fragment, which cannot truly be said to belong to the Pictish era, but to a later date.

Brechin 1 is so worn that it is almost impossible without Romilly Allen's help to make out the figures. The equal-armed cross, he tells us, is divided into four panels. The central circular medallion surrounded by a pelleted frame shows the Virgin and Child with an inscription in Hiberno-Saxon minuscules that translates as 'Saint Mary, the Mother of Christ'.

[155]

Camus outline cross
by Monikie, Angus

The bird in the top arm of the cross represents the Holy Dove. The angels in the right and left arms of the cross support the circular aureole that surrounds the Virgin. Below, you can see two haloed saints. One has his palms raised in prayer while the other seems to be holding a key and is probably St Peter. Below them you can see the eagle of St John and the lion of St Mark.

THE APOSTLES' STONE

There seems to be doubt about the subject-matter of this exceedingly worn stone in Dunkeld Cathedral. On the front you can just about make out a representation of Daniel in the lions' den. The other side is a little clearer.

The back is divided into three panels. At the top are about sixteen heads with a circular disc. Below, a panel consists of six men, and the third panel also shows six men.

Dr Anderson thought the scene represented the destruction of Pharaoh's host in pursuit of the Israelites crossing the Red Sea, and that the disc is intended for a chariot wheel. Below, the twelve men represent the twelve tribes of Israel.

But Romilly Allen believed that the top scene might have represented the Feeding of the Five Thousand with the disc representing one of the loaves on a platter. Below are the twelve Apostles.

THE JESUS STONE

The Camus outline cross stands sheltered by trees in the grounds of Panmure House four miles north of Carnoustie. About six and a quarter feet tall, it is made of old red sandstone and depicts the Crucifixion on one side and Christ in Glory on the other.

Although badly worn, the front divides into three panels with Christ crucified between the spear and sponge-bearers in the upper scene. In the second panel you can just make out a sagittarius, another aspect of the centaur. As a creature from the Divine Bestiary it may represent the conquest of the spirit over the flesh.

Scrolls of foliage fill the third panel.

On the back, Christ is depicted in glory with a halo round his head, holding perhaps the Book of Remembrance in his left hand and giving a benediction with his right. Angels kneel in adoration either side of him while below the four evangelists – each with a nimbus round his head – hold their gospels.

[157]

top St Vigean's 7, St Vigean's
Museum, Angus

bottom A bull sacrifice? Detail from
St Vigean's 7

STONES WITH EARLY CHRISTIAN SYMBOLISM

THE SORCERER OF SAMARIA

There have been many interpretations of the scene on the left of the cross shaft from St Vigean's 7. The traditional method of execution among the Picts may have been ceremonial drowning. We know of at least two kings who suffered this fate at the hand of King Oengus in the 730s.

It is far-fetched but tempting to trace this motif back to the Smertae – the Blood-Smeared tribe on Ptolemy's map – who drowned their enemies in a vat of blood.

However, at the Second International Conference on Insular Art held in Edinburgh in 1991, John Higgitt suggested that the motif might illustrate the death of Simon Magus, Nero's wizard and the founder of Gnosticism, who was brought crashing to the ground by the prayers of Peter and Paul. The story goes that while the Apostles laid hands on Christian converts who then received the Holy Spirit, Simon offered or received money (hence the term simony). By AD 150 he was regarded by the theologian Justin Martyr as the father of Christian heresy. Incidentally, the Celtic tonsure practised by the Columban monks was known to the Romanists as the 'tonsure of Simon Magus'.

Notice the monks' elaborate vestments and their neatly shod feet. Higgitt suggests that the two lower figures in the scene may be Peter and Paul, the latter holding his Acts in a book satchel over his arm.

The two seated figures beside the upper right shaft are thought to be the hermits Paul and Anthony in the desert, while the emaciated little man with his long scrolled tongue is kneeling below a bullock or cow and holding a knife directed at the creature's throat.

In keeping with the other Christian images on St Vigean's 7, this scene might possibly represent the saying from Hebrews 10 v.4: 'For it is not possible that the blood of bulls and of goats should take away sins.' The feeding of the pagan starveling by the blood of a bull contrasts with the feeding of the well-clothed redeemed monks by bread from heaven.

(Blood-letting of cattle for sustenance in winter was common practice in the Highlands up until the nineteenth century.)

Fowlis Wester cross slab, Perth & Kinross

THE DESERT FATHERS (I)

... for a hundred and thirteen years the Blessed Paul lived the life of heaven upon earth, while in another part of the desert Antony abode, an old man of ninety years. And as Antony himself would tell, there came suddenly into his mind the thought that no better monk than he had his dwelling in the desert. But as he lay quiet that night it was revealed to him that there was deep in the desert another better by far than he, and that he must make haste to visit him.'

The Life of St Paul the First Hermit, St Jerome, fourth century
The Desert Fathers, trans. Helen Waddel, 1936

Perhaps it is not surprising that at least four cross slabs are illustrated with scenes from the lives of St Paul and St Antony, the first hermits. Their lives must have been read and meditated upon not only by those in Pictish monasteries but throughout Christendom.

The story as written by St Jerome tells us that the 115-year-old Paul, forced to flee from Christian persecution in Egypt, found a remote cave in a rocky mountain by a stream with a palm tree which provided him with food and clothing. Here he remained in prayer and solitude until Antony, as the result of a vision, decided to pay him a visit.

Antony's journey was eventful. First he met a centaur. 'Ho there,' said Antony, 'in what part of the country hath this servant of God his abode?' The creature 'gnashed out some barbarous speech' and pointed across the open plains. Then Antony met a monstrous creature with goat's feet, 'its forehead bristling with horns', who offered him dates and asked for God's blessing. Finally he saw a she-wolf disappear into a cave and, following it, found St Paul and pleaded with tears to be let in.

'No man pleads thus, who comes to threaten: no man comes to injure, who comes in tears: and dost thou marvel that I receive thee not, if it is a dying man that comes?' Paul jested and opened the door, whereupon the two embraced and exchanged 'the holy kiss'.

Here on the Fowlis Wester cross slab you can see the two men enthroned and in conversation. The date palm that had fed and clothed Paul for so many years fills in the spaces behind and in front of him, while the figure at the back of Antony is probably the spirit who revealed to him in his sleep that there was another in the desert better than he whom he should visit.

Nigg cross slab pediment. Old parish church, Nigg, Ross & Cromarty

THE DESERT FATHERS (2)

... and as they [Paul and Antony] talked they perceived that a crow had settled on the branch of the tree, and softly flying down, deposited a whole loaf before their wondering eyes. And when he had withdrawn, 'Behold,' said Paul, 'God hath sent us our dinner, God the merciful, God the compassionate. It is now sixty years since I have had each day a half loaf of bread: but at thy coming, Christ has doubled his soldiers' rations.' And when they had given thanks to God they sat down beside the margin of the crystal stream.

> *The Life of St Paul the First Hermit*, St Jerome, fourth century
> *The Desert Fathers*, trans. Helen Waddel, 1936

Then, the story continues, an argument arose as to who should break the bread, each protesting that the other had the better right. Finally they agreed that each should take hold of the loaf, pull it towards himself and eat what remained in his hand. Then they drank some water, holding their mouths to the spring; 'and offering to god the sacrifice of praise, they passed the night in vigil'.

When Paul told Antony that he had not long to live, the latter was so upset that Paul sent him back to fetch his cloak 'which Athanasius the Bishop gave to thee, to wrap around my body'. This he did, not because he needed the cloak but to spare Antony the grief of his dying.

In due course Antony returned with the cloak to find the lifeless body of his friend. He wrapped it in his cloak for burial but he had no spade. At that moment two lions came bounding towards him. 'Roaring mightily', they scratched the ground with their paws and buried the holy man.

On the pediment of the Nigg cross slab you can see the crow with the bread and the kneeling figures of Paul and Antony and the lions under the palm. Isabel Henderson points out that the carving is symbolic of the Eucharist with the two figures as priests with their gospel books. Between them the Holy Dove holds the Bread of Communion over a chalice.

Meigle 26. Detail of recumbent stone showing swastika made of four men, and possibly hyenas eating a corpse

THE DIVINE BESTIARY

This singular treatise [*Liber Bestiarum*] has exerted such a wide-spread influence on the Christian art of Europe, that its traces are found pervading the ecclesiastic manuscripts and sculptures of every country from Iceland to the Mediterranean. The date of its compilation is unknown, but it seems that its original source was in Alexandria. It is distinctly specified by its name of *Liber Physiologus* in a decree attributed to Pope Gelasius (AD 469) which denounced it as having been written by heretics. But Gregory the Great (AD 590–604) makes use of its allegories in his Homilies, and it subsequently became the favourite repertory of Middle Age Natural History and a popular treatise of

Meigle 26. Man with Manticora?

religious allegories. Before that it was known to Bede as the treatise *De Naturis Bestiarum*.

ECMS, J.R. Allen, 1903 Introduction, Rhind Lectures,
Joseph Anderson, 1893

Isabel Henderson refers also to an illustrated Anglo-Saxon version of the *Marvels of the East* which may also have been available to the Picts.

Whatever the source, there is no doubt that the Picts were obsessed by monsters, and much of that ancient bestiary still survives in the folklore of Europe. Few have not heard of the salamander that lives in flame, the pelican that gorges its young on its own blood, the phoenix that rises from its own ashes.

That fascination still persists. What child today is not thrilled or frightened by the thought of dinosaurs and dragons? How many people still believe in the Loch Ness Monster?

The allegories connected to these often horrific animals supplied the early Christian teachers with ideas in the same way as a book of sermon notes might do

Rossie Priory. Detail of beasts and interlace

today. The very fact of their proximity to the Christian cross points to a Christian symbolism.

The trouble is that the symbolism is hard to uncover because we – like the sculptors before us – have no idea what the monsters actually looked like.

Romilly Allen believes this creature on Meigle 26 might be a manticora. This particular monster is described as a tall quadruped with a human head and face on a long vertical neck. It delights in human flesh and its name means man-eater.

BEASTS AND DRAGONS

Rossie Priory stone has a marvellous selection of these fantasy creatures which came from the spiritual allegories under the title of *Divine Bestiary*, to be found in various forms and languages on the Continent.

The texts are in Latin or French but the illustrations bear a striking resemblance to the beasts on the Pictish stones. They were written, according to the Bishop of Beauvais (1175–1217), because '... all the creatures which god has created in the earth, he created for the benefit of man, and to give him instruction in the faith through them'.

Forteviot 1, Perth & Kinross. A unicorn perhaps?

Fantasy beasts like the manticora, the basilisk with its death-dealing eyes, siren, griffin and cockatrice were described as if they were living creatures. The unicorn had a body like a horse and a head like a stag with a single horn curved backwards.

Actual animals were also described in detail. The tiger had wings and a tail like a dragon, while the crocodile was a quadruped with no reptilian features, and the hyena was a bear in everything but colour and fed on the dead.

The *Divine Bestiary*, ascribed to Pope Gregory, taught that the sea-eagle was symbolic of a good man who feeds on the Son of God. The fish on which the eagle feeds represented the soul adrift in the sea of the world to be caught up and rescued by Christ.

The stag represented Christ in that it pursued and trampled on the Devil as a serpent, while the hind stood for the human soul pursued by evil and driven to find shelter in the Church. The whale, dragon and fox were all symbolic of the Devil.

[166]

Dunfallandy cross slab, Pitlochry,
Perth & Kinross

The lion had three powers. Firstly, it could smell hunters on its track and
obliterate its footprints with its tail. Secondly, it never slept, so Christ in his
human form slept the sleep of death, while his divine nature kept watch over the
world. Thirdly, cubs were still-born until the third day when the lion breathed
life into them. So God on the third day brought his son to life again.

You can see what might be the lion above the top right arm of the cross on
Dunfallandy. There too is the centaur, the lion as symbol of St Mark, two angels
with two unrecognizable creatures, the stag above the dragon which has a pair of
legs protruding from its mouth (symbolic perhaps of Jonah), and in the bottom
right corner a beast eating its own tail, which might mean evil destroying itself.

These creatures with their deep symbolic meanings were the stuff of sermons,
homilies and meditation.

St Vigean's 1, detail

SHEILA-NA-GIG?

Benjamin Walker, in a paper on *Phallic Symbolism*, tells us that until fairly recently in Ireland there were carvings of females with exaggerated sex organs called sheila-na-gigs. These were often found on church doors or arches. Most were removed in the nineteenth century, and some are in museums. Such figures were also found in English churches.

Tom Gray suggests that the weird little figure in the top left corner of St Vigeans 1 (The Drosten Stone) is perhaps a sheila-na-gig.

In the distant past, according to Benjamin Walker, sexual images were mainly magic in character. They were not intended to be pornographic or even for marital encouragement. They were there to encourage nature or God himself to shower abundance on the land, the community, the harvest, the weather and the cattle.

This is a relic of imitative magic to induce God to respond in the manner suggested by the symbol, to shower fertility on the land.

Such creatures were there also to ward off the Evil Eye, or imps and demons that might otherwise harm the place they are there to defend, a church perhaps, or in this case a sacred stone.

This little sprite may simply be symbolic of Christ as the giver of all good things and is thus in no way intended to be disrespectful.

[168]

PART FIVE

IMPORTANT PICTISH PEOPLE

WARLORDS, HUNTERS AND MONKS

F ROM Nechtan's reign onwards, Christianity became officially established in Pictland.

How did the Pictish Christian aristocrat see Christ? As a supreme warrior perhaps. We can only guess that he may have taken his model from St Paul's *Letter to the Ephesians*, Chapter 6, where the Christian is exhorted to 'put on the whole armour of God' including the breastplate of righteousness, the shield of faith, the helmet of salvation and the sword of the Spirit, in order to 'stand against the wiles of the devil'. St Patrick's breastplate hymn comes from the same source.

Probably it is true to say that he saw Christianity as a glorious battle against the forces of evil, with Christ as chief and captain of his soul.

Some Picts abandoned the life of the warrior to become monks or abbots. We know that in Northumbria there was some concern that the army might be too depleted if any more warriors turned from the physical battlefield to the spiritual one.

The Pictish Church was probably served largely by the aristocracy. Brothers and sons of kings and warriors became abbots and evangelists. As we have seen, the monasteries were run like clans with the abbot as chief and his friends and relations as members.

This would seem to be evident from the prestigious stones, most of which were cross slabs, for they teem with warriors and monks, each with his own battle to fight against spiritual or physical foes.

The warrior's reward at the great festive gatherings was to be toasted in ale or mead, praised by the bards in words or music and recompensed by a grateful king in cattle, treasure or land. Death took him not to the physical pleasures of the Otherworld but to eternal life with Christ and his angels in Paradise.

Let us now look at the warriors for ourselves. Battles, weapons and methods of fighting which match up to the scanty literary accounts are all to be found on the stones. They tell us next to nothing about the ordinary Pict but reveal a great deal about the aristocratic way of life.

Dupplin Cross, Perth
& Kinross. Detail of
foot soldiers

Meigle 3

THE MOUNTED WARRIOR

So dexterously, so gracefully,
Intrepidly, audaciously,
So actively, so haughtily,
All-wrathfully, so yellingly,
So hurtfully, so dreadfully,
Trustworthily, honourably,
So zealously, so grave-pit-ly,
Superiorly, cheerfully,
So readily, so jewelled,
Well-mailedly, high-breastedly,
Preparedly, authoriatively,
Pushingly, all-seeingly,
Bustlingly, right-trimmedly,
Well-strikingly, well-mowingly,
Eloquently, dexterously, all-powerfully,
To win the field of battle.

Old War Song, *Popular Tales of the West Highlands*

[171]

Glamis Manse. Detail of two warriors in single combat

Look at this typical mounted warrior who dominates the back of Meigle 3. From his sleek hair curled at the ends to his splendid beard and moustaches, his erect back and prancing horse, he is every inch a warrior. He wears fine leather bootees and a short tunic, perhaps covered with a cloak, from the folds of which his sword with a chaped end protrudes. You can also see his spear, which he holds in his right hand.

With no stirrups and no saddle for support he holds his horse with one hand on a tight rein. Notice the elaborate pattern on his saddle blanket.

SINGLE COMBAT

An important feature of Celtic warfare was the custom of fighting in single combat. Strict rules surrounded the practice. One of these was known as 'fir fer' which translates as fair play and ensured that a man engaged in single combat should be opposed by one enemy at a time. Between kings or warlords on opposing sides it could be the deciding factor in an argument over disputed territory.

But single combat did not apply only to battle.

If two warriors had quarrelled or believed themselves to have been insulted they would begin by taunting and reviling each other while boasting of their own heroism and skill in the martial arts. Egged on by eager onlookers, they chose their weapons and challenged each other to the death.

This detail on the Stone at Glamis Manse shows two Picts in single combat with axes. Their long hair, prominent noses and beards would seem to indicate that they were of the warrior élite.

The axe must have been one of the most important of all Pictish tools, used by all classes of Picts from the humblest labourer to the proudest warrior. Tim Newark believes that it was during the early clashes with the Vikings that the Irish and Picts adopted the axe as their principal weapon. This may have developed into the long-handled battle axe of many a later skirmish in the Highlands.

Collessie Man, Fife

THE NAKED WARRIOR

This standing monolith at Collessie in Fife is some 2.7m tall and probably dates back to the late Neolithic or early Bronze Age. No one knows exactly when the figure of a naked warrior with a long rectangular shield, holding a spear with a

[174]

round butt, was incised on it. The carvings probably date from the time of the earliest class I stones because there are faint traces of other symbols at the side of the stone, one of which may be an arch.

The interesting hairstyle worn by this apparently beardless young warrior may correspond to a description in Tacitus *Germania* 38 of the 'Suebian knot' worn by the Celto/Germanic tribe of the Suebi. 'It is a special characteristic of this nation to comb the hair sideways and tie it in a knot,' wrote Tacitus, and he goes on to say that other tribes copied the fashion but abandoned it when they became grey-headed, whereas the Suebi practised it into old age. 'The hair is twisted back so that it stands erect and is often knotted on the very crown of the head.' Tacitus amusingly adds that this hairstyle was not meant to please the ladies but to give tribesmen extra height with which to frighten their enemies.

Cassius Dio, writing in 230, states that the Caledonians and the Maeatae ancestors of the historical Picts were armed with spears that had short bronze knobs at the end of the shaft. Naked warriors armed with rectangular shields appear on slabs along the Antonine Wall.

Traditionally, the first line of battle against the Romans consisted of naked, tattooed or painted warriors whose task it was to taunt and flaunt themselves fearlessly before the enemy.

Apart from the freedom acquired by wearing no clothes in battle, the main reason for nakedness may have been to show off elaborate body decorations to the enemy. Campaigning was usually a summer occupation, so the cold would not have been too much of a problem.

Tattooing or painting the body or face was fairly common practice among the peoples north and north-east of the uncivilized world. Thomas thinks it likely that the Celts first learned the custom in the late Hallstatt or early La Tène time from the Scythians living to their east. The custom may have lapsed during Roman times elsewhere in Europe but was retained by the Picts owing to what Thomas calls their 'isolated conservatism'.

Isidore of Seville, writing in the seventh century but using earlier sources, tells us how the tattooing was done: 'a needle working with tiny punctures, together with the squeezed-out juice of a native herb, is wrought, so that each bears designs proper to him'.

The skin was pricked by bone or iron pins and rubbed with soot or herbal dyes to give it colour. Perhaps it was done with needles drawing threads under the skin to raise the flesh. It must have been an extremely painful undertaking and may possibly have been combined with initiation rites.

The primary reason for tattooing was probably to distinguish one tribal group from another in battle, as with the standards carried by soldiers in another age. Personal pride and prestige would also have been important.

St Orland's stone, Cossans, Angus. Detail of ship

SEA WARRIORS

Two ships appear incised on a stone in Shetland and the wall of Jonathan's cave in East Wemyss. These may be Viking, but the boat on St Orlando's stone in Angus is undoubtedly Pictish.

You can just make out four oarsmen while the large object in the prow may be a passenger or a piece of cargo. Bearing in mind that where the figures are concerned big is best, and the possibility of Christian symbolism, the larger passenger may represent Christ preaching on the sea of Galilee, with his four evangelists.

Wainwright tells us that the Picts possessed a fleet of considerable size manned by sea warriors who had the necessary skills to navigate in difficult waters. The fleet was able to dominate the Orkneys and raid the Northumbrian coast at its peak of military strength.

Like the Irish, they probably made three types of boat. The plank-built long ship with its broad bottom and high stern was used for war. Irish ships were said to be large enough to be crewed by sixteen pairs of oars, a helmsman and a master. Sails were made of leather hoisted by chains.

For raiding, narrow-beamed oak-clinkered rowing boats were popular while curachs of wicker covered with hide, water-proofed with grease and propelled with oars or sails, were the most usual.

Gildas, writing of the Picts and Scots, recorded that they used these curachs to raid southern Britain while the old annals mention fleets of fifty. No doubt the more important kings possessed their own fleets to protect their territory and savage the shores of their enemies.

THE VICTORY STONE

This marvellous scene on the back of Aberlemno 2 is thought to depict the Battle of Nechtansmere or Dunnichen Moss fought in 685. The victor, Brude mac Bili, finally drove the invading Northumbrians under King Ecgfrid south of the Forth forever. Although the stone was carved long after the event, the battle was no doubt remembered and repeated in the oral tradition for centuries to come.

Let us look at the stone in detail. The top symbols could – following Charles Thomas – translate as 'To a dead-war leader remembered by a member of the magician clan.'

The battle scene reads like a cartoon. Top left is an unhelmeted Pictish warrior, sword at the ready as he chases his Anglian foe (recognizable by the long-nosed guard on his helmet), who has already cast away his sword and shield. Judging by his large saddle blanket and the undocked tail of his horse, he may represent Ecgfrid himself.

Below, three foot-soldiers in battle formation with shields and weapons at the ready stand up to a mounted Anglian warrior on a horse with a docked tail. Note his huge nose-guard.

In the bottom left scene, a mounted Pict with spear and shield raised directs his horse with his knees as he charges his enemy whose horse is tightly reined back. In the bottom right corner an Anglian in a divided tunic (probably made of padded ox-hide), who may be King Ecgfrid himself, lies dead, food for the symbolic raven.

Brude had planned this battle well. He split his army and left the best part of it hidden on the south side of Dunnichen fortress. The weaker half on the north side of the hill went down to confront the enemy.

[177]

Replica carynx

Imagine the noise, the screams of the wounded, the whinnying of horses, the clash of weapons, the sinister roar of the carnyx as the battle progressed. Feigning fear, the weaker Picts turned heel and retreated back over the hill chased by the Angles who, scenting victory, broke ranks to follow.

This was what Brude had been hoping for. The bulk of the Pictish forces who were waiting on the far side of the hill caught the Anglians by surprise. There was no escape. If they eluded the Picts, they drowned in the marshy loch at the foot of the hill.

Ecgfrid and his bodyguard were killed. Indeed, few if any Northumbrians returned from that bloody battle.

Had the Anglians won, there might never have been a Scotland – a sobering thought.

Aberlemno 2. A battle scene

Part of Aberlemno 3. A hunting scene with centaur

HUNTERS, HOUNDS AND HAWKERS

When Pictish warriors were not fighting, they were engaged in the princely pastime of the hunt, or so the stones would seem to indicate.

John Gilbert tells us that there were basically two ways of playing the hunting game – the drive and the chase. Both methods must have been current in Pictland to judge from the carvings.

The drive involved large numbers of beaters whose task was to enter the forest and make enough noise to drive the game towards the king and his chosen companions.

An old Gaelic poem called *The Enchanted Stag* describes a drive in which 120 of the Fianna with 1,000 hounds and 1,000 men in attendance killed 100 deer and 100 stags. An exaggeration no doubt, but the story indicates the numbers required for a successful drive.

Gilbert believes that royal hunting reserves were not established and controlled by the kings until the twelfth century. Pictish lords no doubt had their own favourite forests forbidden to ordinary people for felling and poaching.

Horns were sounded either to drive the game to the point of slaughter or to herald the chase. They were also blown to indicate various stages of the hunt. Pictish hunters may have possessed their own horns to pin-point their position on the field. In a later age, Robert the Bruce was always recognized by the sound of his horn. Today the horn is still an important part of full Highland dress.

Hunting then as today would seem to have depended upon the hound. Many of the scenes on the stones suggest coursing, since the hounds are unleashed and biting the beast while the hunter follows with his spear. Deer- or wolf-hounds as big as calves hunted by sight rather than smell and could pull down a heavy stag by running close to its flank and springing up at its throat.

Here on Aberlemno 3 (which stands on the roadside close to the kirk) you can see beneath the symbols a lively hunting scene with four men on horseback, three on foot, two of whom are blowing long hunting horns, three stags and three hounds.

Although it was once thought that hawking was brought into Scotland by the Normans, it is evident from the cross slab in Elgin Cathedral and the St Andrews sarcophagus that it was practised by the Pictish élite in the eighth century.

The two commonest species of bird used were the long-winged hawks such as the peregrine, the kestrel and the merlin. The other group consisted of the short-tailed goshawk, sparrowhawk and buzzard. These used different methods of approach. The long-winged birds flew in wide open spaces and exhausted their prey in the air while the short-winged hawks flew in woodlands and hunted by stealth.

[181]

Elgin Cathedral hawker, Moray

In medieval times you could tell the rank of a warrior by the bird he used, from the eagle which symbolized the king down to the sparrowhawk of the humbler knight. In practice, the peregrine was preferred for sport while the goshawk was used to provide food.

Stalking was another method of hunting depicted on the stones. Stalkers could either trail the game with a scenting dog until near enough to shoot, or wait close to a lair or drinking pool until the beast appeared. John Gilbert tells us that because this method of hunting was so ideally suited to poaching, James I banned it in 1424.

Short and crossbows were both used by the Picts. Of the three stones showing

St Vigean's 1. 'The Drosten stone'

the crossbow, St Vigeans 1 (the Drosten stone) is clearest. Here the stalker wears an animal skin for disguise as he crouches with his bow drawn and resting on the ground. One hand holds the string while the other grips the end of the stock. When the string is released the arrow is fired. The stock was used to enable both hands to be kept close to the body.

The crossbow was first recorded in China in about 1500 BC and was used in Europe since Roman times. The Pictish way of firing the bow by releasing the string by hand rather than by the use of a revolving nut is strange. However, one nut and two heads of crossbow bolts have been excavated at Urquhart Castle on Loch Ness, and another in Buston crannog in Ayrshire. These would seem to prove that the crossbow, however elementary, was used by Pictish hunters.

Shandwick cross slab, Easter Ross. Detail of hunting panel

THE RITUAL HUNT

Miranda Green, in *The Gods of the Celts*, suggests that healing, death and hunting could all be associated in Celtic religion. The Christian divine hunt is, as we shall see, shown on Hilton of Cadboll.

At first glance this panel on the back of the great Shandwick cross slab appears to be a straightforward hunting scene with all the forest animals represented together with their hunters. Look again.

The two dominant figures in the top corners of the panel would seem to be the

[184]

king-hunter on the left and the quarry on the extreme right. The stag carries his antlers – totems of fertility and rebirth – with pride. Symbolic of Cernunnos of the Grove, lord of the beasts, he may represent the king-god of the forest.

In the lower left corner of the panel the mystical element of the hunt is further emphasized by the two men who appear to be fighting over a docile calf. It has been suggested by an anthropologist on a visit to Groam House that these men are performing a ritual dance carrying small square flags and swords prior to the sacrifice of the creature in order to bring success to the hunt.

This is achieved when stag and hunter face each other in the right corner of the panel. The bond between hunter and hunted is emphasized by the hooded deerskin disguise worn by the hunter and the extraordinary eye contact between them. The beast appears fearless; the hunter on bended knee has a respectful attitude. Through the kill, stag and hunter become symbolically linked, thus bringing prosperity and well-being to all.

Between the four corners of the panel most of the animals follow the path of the sun across the sky, acknowledging perhaps its role as the father of creation. Two wolves, a lynx, boar, goat, fox and hare can all be identified. Among the birds the eagle dominates in size, signifying perhaps the hunter in another element.

The bird attached to the archer's back has been identified as the Greater Spotted Woodpecker, one of the commonest of the old Caledonian forest birds, now rare. Perhaps it also represents the hunter's tutelary spirit, summoned to bring him strength and protection. Similarly the huge capercailzie-like bird may be the guardian spirit of the pedestrian hunter who appears to be carrying a carcass over his shoulder.

THE DIVINE HUNT

Who can she be, this lady from the Hilton of Cadboll stone? Many have asked that question and there have been almost as many interpretations.

There are very few women depicted on the stones and some of them might not be female at all, but this mounted figure is undoubtedly an important aristocrat and she appears to be holding something on her lap.

Does she perhaps represent a princess from East Ross leading her warrior nobles in the chase? The large mirror-and-comb symbol close to the head of her horse, her richly pleated gown and the fact that she is facing to the front all point to her singular prestige.

Note that she is seated sideways without a saddle or pommel for support. Any

Hilton of Cadboll, Easter Ross, now in NMS Edinburgh. Hunting scene detail rider will tell you that her position is untenable for more than a moment. This is a strange mistake for the sculptor to make considering his accuracy in carving male riders. Probably Pictish women rode astride and her position is symbolic rather than realistic.

Look carefully and you can see the profile of another horse and rider with prominent nose and beard riding parallel but behind her.

Who are they all and what is she holding in her lap?

R. B. K. Stevenson saw the object as a large penannular brooch, and this has until recently been the unquestioned explanation.

Catriona Black in PAS Journal 1993 sees her as an important bride wearing a torc with her groom behind her.

R. Trench-Jellicoe in PAS 1994 sees her with a hunting bird.

I think that these suggestions miss the point of the class II cross slabs – that they were essentially symbolic in their interpretation and that the symbolism in most cases was Christian. It was not usual for a nation that practised such sophisticated symbolism to portray contemporary people. Isabel Henderson suggests she might represent Epona the Gaulish horse-goddess, symbolic of motherhood, fertility and prosperity, who appears in a similar position on several stones in Europe.

But this is a highly Christian stone as we shall see. It was Professor Alcock who first offered me the suggestion that the lady might represent Mary in the Flight into Egypt.

Far-fetched? I don't think so. Look at the lady again. I see her as hallowing a small round object in her hands which could just as easily be an infant head representing the Christ Child as a brooch. Joseph profiled behind her is the least important figure in the scene. Her prestige is further emphasized by the mirror and comb.

The King List has told us that their were no queens in their own right. What Dark Age woman in a country without inheriting queens could have been so demonstrably superior to her husband? The answer must be Mary, the Mother of Christ. A further relevant point: the ancient church associated with the stone at Cadboll in Easter Ross was dedicated to St Mary.

With regard to the hunt, notice that the hunters are all in battle-dress with spears and shields. Shields are not usually carried when hunting. Thus the rest of the scene might demonstrate the medieval Divine Hunt where the hind symbolizes the human soul pursued by the hounds and forces of evil.

The wonderful inhabited vine-scrolling that borders the stone shows the bird as the human soul feeding on the grapes of the Tree of Life, thus symbolizing salvation through the blood of Christ.

The message of the stone would seem to be flight from evil to sanctuary in the church.

[187]

The Papil stone, Shetland
(now in NMS Edinburgh)
with lion of St Mark and
birdmen holding a human
head

HOLY MEN AND WOMEN

According to Romilly Allen there are some forty stones depicting monks and
holy men as opposed to over twice that number which show warriors and
hunters.

Life in a Columban monastery was not easy. Obedient to the rules of poverty,
chastity and obedience as ordained by St Benedict of Nursia in about 530, the
monks sang the daily offices and lived a life of prayer and hard physical labour.
They slept in single isolated stone beehive cells or in communal timber-built
dormitories. The monastic settlements included refectories, hospitals, small
stone or wooden churches and graveyards enclosed within a circular wall known
as a rath.

It was within these early Christian monasteries throughout Pictland that the

Monks on St Vigean's 11
(front). Note the Triquetra
symbols above them

cross slabs were to be erected as far north as Shetland.

When not employed in the laborious day-to-day chores of monastic life, many went on missionary journeys, 'a'wandering for Christ'.

These worker-priests entered the surrounding farming settlements where gradually they gained the confidence perhaps of a local leader, introduced him and his family to Christ, built small churches and laboured alongside the community. These must have been strong men physically and spiritually, not afraid to dirty their hands, so convinced of their calling that they were able to influence the hardest of hearts. Many lived to great ages even by today's standards. Always they looked to the mother house for guidance and assistance.

It is thought that these small Christian settlements so painstakingly established were later to become the parishes that made up the dioceses of the established Catholic Church of the eleventh and twelfth centuries. In spite of today's changes

St Vigean's 11 (back). Monks
with flabellums

and amalgamations, most of them still retain virtually the same boundaries.

Within the monasteries they sang the offices, learned or taught Latin,
illuminated manuscripts, studied the Bible and other available literature. Iona
had one of the finest libraries of the day, and the Iona monks were respected
throughout Europe for their zeal and education.

They wore long wool habits with hooded mantles for warmth. On some of the
stones the monks are wearing priestly vestments with embroidered hems, and
some seem to be carrying the crozier of a bishop.

On the back of St Vigeans 11 you can see two enthroned priests wearing
decorated vestments beneath a cope (or a cloak) each carrying a Gospel book and
a liturgical fan known as a flabellum or *rhipidion.*

Hilary Richardson tells us that these feathered or decorated metal fans had their special use during the liturgy to protect the altar and sacred elements from contamination by flies, dust and the forces of evil.

Their symbolism was deep and multi-layered. The feathers represented the adoration of the winged seraphim and therefore stood for fidelity. The eyes in the feathers represented vigilance. At the same time the peacock itself stood for immortality, from the ancient belief that its flesh never corrupted. The use of a flabellum was particularly important in hot countries and may have been brought to Iona by visiting clerics. Columba is thought to have possessed one and the stone is proof that they were used in the Pictish Church.

The little figure below the two enthroned monks on St Vigeans 11 is interesting because he seems to be wearing short trousers. Maybe he was a working saint.

In the Dark Ages, the word 'saint' was usually applied to most Celtic missionaries. It had the same meaning as the Greek word 'hagios', which could be translated as 'holy' but also retained its primary meaning of 'different' or 'separated' upwards from the great body of believers.

Are the monks that we see on the stones in any way connected with the early Celtic saints? Who indeed were they? There are many names so shrouded in later hagiographic legend that we know next to no absolute facts.

Apart from SS Columba, Maelrubha and Adamnan, whom Dr Smyth calls 'one of the last of the great holy men of the Dark Ages', there was St Moluag, who was a contemporary of Columba who founded his great community at Lismore.

Legend associates Moluag with the founding of monasteries in Rosemarkie in the Black Isle long before Curadan-Boniface arrived, at Mortlach in Banffshire, and at Clatt in Aberdeenshire, but none of this can be proved, and there are thought to have been several evangelizing Moluags.

Very little is known of St Drosten, whose name seems to appear on St Vigeans 1. The *Book of Deer* (now in the University Library at Cambridge), a ninth-century Scottish Gospel manuscript, has an account written in the margins some two hundred years later of the founding of the great monastery at Deer in Aberdeenshire by Columba, who gave it to his nephew Drosten. The story is thought to be legend.

St Vigeans Museum, which now holds an important collection of cross slabs and other Pictish fragments, takes it name from another little-known saint who is said to have been known as Fechin of Fore in West Meath, and who died of the plague in 665 or 668. According to Professor Watson, Vigean is said to be the Latin form of Fechin.

St Fergus is thought to have been a Pict from the north of Scotland where he founded churches in the Caithness area. Later he visited Glamis where his cave

Three nuns from
Abernethy 4, now in
NMS Edinburgh

can still be seen. His healing well is still used by the local minister for baptisms. It
is tempting to associate the cross slab in the grounds of Glamis Manse with
Fergus the healer. The centaur in the top right corner symbolized Christ the
Healer while the cauldron with the legs protruding may also have symbolized
healing and regeneration.

Abernethy 4, now in Edinburgh, shows three women dressed as nuns below a
crucified Christ. They may well symbolize the three Marys at the foot of the cross.
The interesting connection is that there were nuns of the order of St Bridget of
Kildare established in Abernethy in the early seventh century.

It is impossible to prove a link between the saints of Pictland and the monks
carved on the stones, but as you admire the cross slabs there is no harm in bearing
them in mind.

THE LEGEND OF ST ANDREW

History never turns out as you expect. St Columba you would think, should have become the patron saint of Scotland rather than the apostle St Andrew, but that did not happen.

According to the famous old legend, it was Oengus mac Fergus (d. 761) who was responsible for the foundation of Kilrimont or St Andrews.

According to the *Register of St Andrews*, during his campaign against the Saxons, Oengus was camped near the mouth of the Tyne when St Andrew visited him in a dream and promised him victory if he dedicated the tenth part of his inheritance to God and St Andrew. Three days later he divided his army into seven parts – note the use of the symbolic number seven – won the battle and returned with the Saxon king's head to fulfil his vow.

Meanwhile St Regulus arrived at Kilrimont with the relics of St Andrew which he had brought over from Constantinople. He and his party set out to find the king at his royal seat at Forteviot. There they found Oengus's three sons worried because their father was again campaigning and in danger of his life. In exchange for his safety, the sons dedicated to God and St Andrew the tenth part of Forteviot.

Regulus then visited Monichi in Forfarshire where Finche, Oengus's queen, bore a son and gave her palace to God and St Andrew for the protection of her husband. Finally Regulus crossed the Mounth and met Oengus, who honoured the relics and built a church. They all returned to Monichi and Forteviot where Regulus established more churches, and finally to Kilrimont, which then became known as St Andrews, the principal church in Pictland, where the relics were held.

The legend is of course what one might call holy fiction to account for the adoption of St Andrew as special protector of Pictland. Just as Nechtan mac Derile disposed of Columba for largely political reasons in favour of St Peter and the Roman reformations, so Oengus abandoned St Peter, whose connections were Anglian, in favour of St Andrew.

The legend, Skene suggests, emerged from the new church at St Andrews in order to claim an antiquity superior to Iona. It was in keeping with what we know of Oengus's power-crazy character that he should want to place the Pictish Church under his direct influence.

Dunfallandy (back), Pitlochry

THE PRIEST'S STONE

The Dunfallandy cross slab, which was always known locally as the 'Priest's Stone', once stood in the ruins of an old chapel near Killiecrankie before it was removed to the present site near Pitlochry.

The two figures enthroned either side of the small cross on the back of the cross slab are sometimes associated with the Trinity. God the Father, the larger figure, is shown with a rod over his shoulder which symbolizes creative power.

Romilly Allen saw the group as possibly SS Paul and Anthony in the wilderness.

More sensibly, in my opinion, the group has been associated with the Transfiguration. Moses with his rod and Elias – smaller thus less important – appear either side of the cross which symbolizes Christ. You can clearly see the cloud that enveloped them.

The central mounted monk seems to be the subject of the stone, which could be his memorial. The story might tell us that he had been elevated to a higher plane or 'transfigured' through death into spirit as represented by the elevated head held between the tongues of the two protective fish-tailed serpents that frame the motifs. In Celtic tradition the head is considered to be the seat of the soul.

The symbols of hammer, anvil and tongs might tell us that the stone had been raised by a craftsman or that this had been the priest's family trade.

Niall Robertson, editor of the PAS Journal, has come up with a unique reading of the stone. He sees the enthroned couple as a man and wife united in Christian marriage, as evidenced by the cross that links them.

The central figure with the cowled hood could be their son, an important churchman, an abbot perhaps. His symbols are carved beside the horse's head and would appear to be inherited from both his parents, the crescent from his father and the beast from his mother.

It is possible in a multi-layered symbolism that both the latter interpretations are valid. The design could well represent the family, their commemorator and their lineage, while at a deeper level the Transfiguration is intended.

Fowlis Wester. Detail of cow in ritual scene

MAGICIAN OR PRIEST

Although the class II and III stones are Christian through and through, every now and again you come across a stone which would seem to have pagan imagery that might refer to older but not forgotten beliefs.

One of these stones is in the church of Fowlis Wester in Perthshire. Although it is badly worn, you can clearly make out a cow with a bell round its neck led by a figure in a long tunic and followed by six men wearing long tunics with decorated hems. Two are carrying what look like square shields but which might be receptacles, buckets perhaps. The figures do not appear to be monks or warriors.

Romilly Allen suggests that the procession might refer to the Old Testament story of the worship of the Golden Calf, or to a legend relating to a local saint.

There is always the possibility that it indicates a Pictish pagan ceremony led by a pagan priest which has been used to symbolize some aspect of Christianity.

Stuart Piggot, in his definitive book on the druids, writes that their lore would have included the beliefs and rites of a pre-farming people surviving in elements of shamanism (which we have already discussed), and also in the cult of the dead and other obscure religions of the Neolithic farmers, not forgetting the rites and traditions of an Indo-European past. 'A pedigree', he writes, 'which could be a good 20,000 years old.'

Ward Rutherford, who has also made a comprehensive study of druidism, suggests that the roles of magician and priest were different. The magician had a clientele while the priest had a congregation. Both roles could be combined in the same person, and so it may have been with the Pictish druids, or magicians as they are usually called.

In the role of magician they had certain powers over the weather, as we have already seen. Irish and Welsh sources also record their ability to raise mists and fog. It was believed that they could change their shape at will, read signs and omens, predict the future, while in the role of priest they would have made sacrifices to propitiate the gods of war, health, or fertility, depending upon the occasion or request. This may be what is happening on the Fowlis Wester stone.

Golspie 1, Dunrobin Castle Museum

PAGAN MAN

This splendid eight-foot cross slab once stood in the churchyard at Golspie in Sutherland. It became the tombstone of a certain Robert Gordon, and was removed in that capacity to the churchyard of Craighton two miles south of Golspie. In 1868 it was taken to the museum at Dunrobin Castle, where it is now handsomely restored and displayed.

The back is decorated with a wonderful selection of Pictish symbols, including the rectangle, the beast, flower and V-rodded crescent, double disc, and two entwined snakes that look like adders. You can also see a fearsome man holding an axe in his right hand and a knife in his left who seems to be confronting a lion and a fish.

An ingenious interpretation on the part of Joanna Close-Brooks suggests that here is pagan man holding an axe and dirk in the act of confronting Christianity as represented by the lion of St Mark and the fish (not the salmon) of Christ. He appears to be surrounded by the symbols of his people.

Bearing in mind Dr Henderson's belief that the designs on class II stones are for the most part eclectic and do not necessarily have a 'cumulative significance', the above theory may be fanciful, but it makes sense to twentieth-century students.

Along the top edge and one side of the back there are some Ogam letters which, reading upwards from the bottom right, spell out the letters ALLH-HALLO R R E? DDME Q Q NI?V?V?H R? R E R? R?. Dr Close-Brooks suggests that the only recognizable element here is the MEQQ or possibly MAQQ meaning 'son of – '. The whole inscription might therefore read 'Here lies X son of Y'. More of the Ogam script when we look at the Pictish language.

PART SIX

PICTISH LANGUAGE
AND THE ARTS

THE PICTISH LANGUAGE

Every aspect of the Picts, it seems, is controversial, and none more so than the problem of their language. With Professor K. H. Jackson's help, let us try to make this complicated subject as simple as possible.

The parent language of the Celts was Indo-European. At some stage it became divided into two branches, Q-Celtic and P-Celtic. The main and simplest difference between the two was that Q-Celtic retained the original Indo-European 'qu' sound whereas P-Celtic turned the 'qu' into a 'p' sound.

The Q-group included the Goidelic language as spoken by the Irish, Scottish Gaels and Manx peoples.

The P-group covered a number of dialects including Gaulish and the British spoken by the people of Roman Britain and their ancestors for as far back as Classical sources go. Some of the later dialects of British were Welsh, Cornish and Breton. All these particular dialects were sub-groups of P-Celtic and are known as Brythonic or Brittonic.

Jackson points out there must have been a period in the history of the Celtic language before it split into the two branches of Q and P. This language he calls Gallo-Brythonic.

British (P-Celtic), therefore, was the language spoken generally by the people living south of the Antonine Wall.

As for the Picts, Jackson presents some of the possibilities. If they spoke a Celtic language, was it P or Q or was it an earlier offshoot of Gallo-Brythonic before the split? If Goidelic, it must have been a separate dialect from Irish, for Columba, who spoke Goidelic, required an interpreter at the Pictish court of King Brude. Some scholars in the past thought it was not Celtic at all, but Iberian allied to Basque.

All these theories have had their advocates at one time. The opinion generally held by Celtic scholars from the beginning of the twentieth century was that the Picts spoke a P-Celtic language. Professor Watson argued that Pictish was a northern offshoot of British while Stokes and Macbain both held that it was a separate language allied both to Gaulish and to British but distinct from both. T. F. O'Rahilly restated this opinion in 1946.

What sort of evidence is there apart from Columba and King Brude's need of an interpreter? Bede again comes to our assistance. His *Ecclesiastical History* was finished in 731, towards the end of the Pictish period. He tells us that Pictish was a fourth language distinct from Gaelic, Brythonic and English. He was in a position to know from his contacts with Iona, King Nechtan and other Christians north of Jarrow. He also mentions (Bede 1.12) that Kinneil at the eastern end of the Antonine Wall was known as Peanfahel in the Pictish language.

Place-names give evidence too. If you remember, Pythias, who travelled round Britain as early as 325 BC, called our nation the Pretanic Islands and the cape facing Orkney Cape Orcas. The Pretani are thought to be one of the earliest Celtic tribes to reach Britain, although later they were identified solely with the Picts. The word Orc exists only in medieval Irish, not in medieval Brythonic, but this is no proof that it was exclusively Goidelic. Other Celtic words known in early Brythonic did not survive into the medieval period in Britain, although they survived in ancient Irish. What it does prove is that Celts were living in the north of Scotland possibly as early as the fourth century BC.

Interestingly enough, Jackson points out that although Calgacus, hero of the Caledonians in the Battle of Mons Graupius (AD 84), had a Celtic name, the word Caledonia still traceable in Perthshire place-names, can't be proved to be Celtic and may be possibly pre-Celtic.

Looking at Ptolemy's map, Jackson reckons that out of thirty-eight names, sixteen of them are probably Celtic but the rest are not. Of these non-Celtic names, most are to be found in the Pictish heartland between the Moray Firth and the Forth.

So far, then, Classical sources tell us that there were Celtic-speaking people in the far north probably as early as the fourth century BC. By the first century AD there was an assortment of Celtic peoples in Scotland which judging by their place-names were of Gallo-Brythonic descent, and none of whom were Goidelic. A number of names are not Celtic at all so could be pre-Celtic.

The Pictish King List is another source for the Pictish language. As we have seen, there were two major editions of the List, and only List 1 can be used as evidence of the Pictish language. Some names – such as Brude, Derile and others – are not Celtic at all, so may be pre-Celtic. Others, like Talorgen, are Celtic, while some, like Drosten, Uuen, Taran and Onuist (Oengas), are P-Celtic.

Then of course there are the Pit names – Pit was a P-Celtic word which Jackson suggests was part of the vocabulary of P-Celtic people, and distinct from the Brittonic people living south of the Antonine Wall.

Jackson therefore concludes that the Picts spoke a language that was P-Celtic and Gallo-Brythonic, akin to Gaulish and to the language of the Britons further south. But it was not identical to Gaulish or Brythonic. It retained a strong pre-Celtic element owing to the survival of a pre-Celtic population in northern and eastern Scotland into early medieval times.

However, Dr Smyth does not believe that Jackson's theory of a pre-Celtic survival can necessarily be proved. He concludes from Ptolemy's map that the Pictish area included several tribes with Celtic names which can be related to other Celtic names elsewhere in Britain and in Gaul, and that all of Pictland and the Isles north of the Antonine Wall were thoroughly Celtic before the end of the first century AD. The aristocracy of the Caledonians were certainly Celtic, as Tacitus suggested when he wrote in *Agricola* that their red hair and large limbs made them no different from the rest of the Britons and their Gaulish ancestors in language, ritual and religion.

Because a name is not obviously Celtic it does not necessarily mean that it must be pre-Celtic. Names can be transmitted carelessly and changed to be almost unrecognizable in any language. Some names can support a case for a Gallo-Brythonic origin. 'Taran' is one of many examples. This king's name can be found in the historic and prehistoric sections of the King List. Taranis was the Gaulish thunder-god, so the name has a Gallo-Brythonic origin.

So is there any trustworthy evidence for the survival of a pre-Celtic language? We should give the etymologist, Professor Nicolaisen, the last word. He tells us that there are a sizeable number of names of geographical features, particularly of rivers, that might be pre-Celtic. Rivers and water-courses drew the first settlers to their banks because of the rich soil, easier means of travel and therefore of communication, and their use in marking boundaries. They were also regarded as objects of religious significance. Their names were generally known to more people than those who used them. These names therefore tended to survive, transmitted from language to language and from generation to generation. Here is perhaps where proof may be found of a pre-Celtic language.

Up until the time of Professor Jackson's erudite paper it was taken for granted that pre-Celtic must have been non-Indo-European, for example the language spoken by the Phoenicians, Berbers or Basques. The weakness of this theory lay in a scarcity of suitable linguistic material and ignorance of what to look for. Could these seemingly pre-Celtic names also be non-European?

One of the examples Nicolaisen gives is the river-name 'Farrar', which with the river Glass forms the Beauly in Inverness-shire.

The name is mentioned as Varar by Ptolemy (AD 150). Thus it excludes a

Germanic derivation, also Pictish (c. AD 300) or Scottish Gaelic (c. AD 500). Therefore it could be non-Pictish P-Celtic, or pre-Celtic Indo-European, or pre-Celtic non-Indo-European in derivation. After reasoned discussion on the interpretations of other etymologists, Nicolaisen claims there is hardly any way in which 'Var' can be considered to be Celtic. Farrar can't be explained through any of the individual western Indo-European languages, yet it has an undeniable Indo-European aspect. It must therefore come under the heading of pre- or non-Celtic Indo-European in origin. 'Varar' was derived from the word 'moisten' and has its counterparts in Europe.

If there is one river-name which can be traced to a pre-Celtic Indo-European origin there are others. 'Adder' is one of these, to be found in the Blackadder and Whiteadder rivers in the Lammermuirs. Nicolaisen suggests that the Loch and River Ness may also be of pre-Celtic derivation.

What Nicolaisen is telling us is that when the Celts first arrived in Scotland, there were immigrants from Europe already living here who had brought with them their own Indo-European language.

So there may have been Indo-Europeans in Scotland – indeed throughout Britain – some three thousand years ago whose language has survived at least in river-names, not just into Pictish times but up to the present day – an awe-inspiring thought.

To sum up briefly, some of our Scottish river-names can't be described as Celtic but are likely to be Indo-European. It would seem, then, that the Picts spoke a form of P- or Brythonic Celtic allied to Welsh that contained elements of Gallo-Brythonic and probably retained traces of a pre- or non-Celtic Indo-European language that still survives in a few river-names today.

Alas, nothing can be proved.

WRITING AND INSCRIPTIONS

It used to be thought that the Picts had no written language and that the symbols were their only way of communication.

However, according to ECMS there are some thirteen Pictish stones bearing Ogam letters, with five of them coming from Orkney and Shetland and about one each fairly evenly distributed between the other provinces of Pictland.

Two stones have Anglo-Saxon capitals at Tarbat 10 in Ross-shire and Lethnott in Forfarshire. Three have Hiberno-Saxon minuscules at St Vigeans, Fordoun and Papa Stronsay in Orkney, and one from Newton of Garioch also has a statement written in an unknown script, which K. H. Jackson suggests might be

[203]

St Vigean's 1. Detail of panel which reads 'Drosten Ipe Voret ett Forcus'

an eighteenth century forgery. Finally, on the Drosten stone there is an inscription in Hiberno-Saxon minuscules which reads *Drosten ipe Uoret ett Forcus* – three names, it would seem, written in Latin.

What are these all about? Do they mean that the Picts had a written langauge after all?

Traditionally, Celtic was a non- or pre-literate language. The creators of Celtic myths were the druids who for their own reasons were strong advocates of the oral tradition. Caesar records that they refused to commit their teachings to writing and suggests that this may have been to prevent their pupils from neglecting their memories!

James Dillon and Nora Chadwick tell us that in the fourth century, very soon after Christianity had come to Ireland, there appeared a script credited to the Gaulish god Ogmios (Ogma the Honey-mouthed in Irish). Its key is given in the *Book of Ballymote*, a 1391 compilation of various ancient manuscripts from Ballymote in County Sligo.

The book contained a treatise on the alphabets of ancient Ireland which it ascribes to Ogma son of Elathan who 'being a man much skilled in dialects and poetry invented the system of Ogam writing for signs of secret speech known only to the learned'. In the complicated and copious explanation of the alphabet, no fewer than sixty varieties of the writing are explained and illustrated.

Damian McManus in his *Guide to Ogam* tells us that the Ogam alphabet (known in Old Irish as *in Beithe-luis*) was based on the Latin alphabet. It was divided into four groups of five letters, each called after the first letter of that group. The letters were called *feda*, the plural of *fid*, which means wood or tree. Each individual stroke was a *flesc* or twig with the upright stem a *druim*, the edge or spine.

Most of the letters took their names from a plant or a tree as follows:

Beithe is birch		*hUath* is fear or horror	
Luis	herb (or flame)	*Dair*	oak
Fern	alder	*Tinne*	metal ingot
Sail	willow	*Coll*	hazel
Nin	fork or loft	*Cert*	bush or rag
Muin	neck	*Ailm*	pine-tree
Gort	field	*Onn*	ash tree
nGetel	slaying	*Ur*	earth or clay
Straif	sulphur	*Edad*	?
Ruis	redness	*Idad*	?

With regard to the two meanings of *cert*, the word was originally related to the

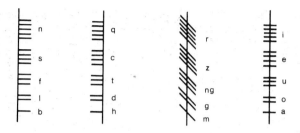

Welsh *perth* meaning bush but by the time Ogam was invented the 'kw' of Primitive Irish had fallen together with the soft 'C' so the name *cert* was confused with the word *ceirt* meaning a rag. In modern Gaelic there is no soft 'C'.

Edad and *Idad* don't seem to be words in their own right. They suggest an artificial pairing.

Niall Robertson suggests that when the Picts wrote their Ogam inscriptions in P-Celtic they might have used the *fid* for 'q' to represent 'p', so that inscriptions including MEQQ or MAQQ (mac) (Golspie in Dunrobin Museum is a good example) would have been read as MAPP or MAP, similar to old Welsh. A certain Talorggan Maphan mentioned in the *Annals of Ulster* in 726 might therefore have been 'Talorggan map Han'.

Ogam inscriptions in the other P-Celtic areas such as Wales and the old district of Dumnonia used the *Cert* for 'q' if they used it at all, but these inscriptions are written in Irish and don't attempt to represent the local language as the Pictish Ogams seem to do.

Dillon and Chadwick reckon there are about three hundred known inscriptions, mostly found in southern Ireland, with some forty in Wales, a few in the Isle of Man and southern Scotland (Dumnonia), with the remaining thirteen or so in Pictland.

Ogam is thought to have been invented as a ceremonial script, for it occurs only on memorial stones or as cryptic messages on knife handles from the Hebrides and Orkney and a stone spindle whorl from Buckquoy, Orkney. Perhaps here it was used as a good-luck charm, or possibly it bore the name of the owner.

It is thought that the alphabet was first introduced to the Picts by the Dal Riatic Scots. Ogam evolved over the years and most of the examples found in Pictland were of the later type known as 'scholastic Ogams', which date from the eighth or ninth centuries. Jackson suggests that at least half of the inscribed stones were

Logie Elphinstone 2 with circle of Ogams at the top, Gordon District

erected during the last one hundred and fifty years of Pictish existence.

There is a possibility that the Picts used the script not as writing but as an extension of their use of symbolism, representing certain secret powers.

This is unlikely as the inscriptions often (but not always) appear on class II or III Christian monuments. Dr Dransart, in her useful papers on the Bennachie stones, suggests that they were meant to be read by at least some of the Picts trained to understand them who would thus mediate between the script and the rest of society.

Let us look at the Ogams on the otherwise unornamented stone known as Newton-in-the-Garioch, which reads as follows:

I D D A I Q N N N V O R R E N N I x U A I O S R R

Interpretation would seem to be impossible and has defeated scholars to the present day. It is generally thought to commemorate some important personage. Could, as a recent interpretation suggests, the name have been EDDARRNONN?

Found in 1803, Newton probably dates from the eighth century. An unshaped pillar of dark blue granite, it originally stood on the moor of Pitmachie a couple of miles from its present site, and Anderson records that a cluster of graves was found in the vicinity. The connection of graves would help to point to the Ogams being of a commemorative nature.

But what about the other writing on the stone? The more you look at it the weirder it becomes. There are six lines of forty-four characters. In the middle of the fourth line there seems to be a cross with the extremities bent over to the right, possibly a swastika. To those who would see this as a pagan symbol, Anderson says that the 'fylfot' was not always and everywhere pagan. It was used as a Christian symbol in the catacombs from the third and fourth centuries and it appears in a variety of forms on other Pictish Christian stones.

Dr Anderson sees this writing as debased Roman minuscules carrying an inscription, and although Newton is unique in Scotland for bearing bilingual inscriptions it is not unknown in the Celtic world. There are at least eleven in Wales, one in Ireland and two in Cornwall.

There have been many interpretations of this strange script over the years. Lloyd Laing suggests that the likeliest explanation is that the letters were carved in imitation of Irish majuscules by an illiterate sculptor.

Newton stone with Ogams and inscription near Insch, Gordon District

Musicians on Lethendy Tower
panel near Blairgowrie, Perth &
Kinross

MUSIC AND THE HARP

The only evidence we have for the existence of Pictish music is once again to be found on the stones.

Several show harps, pipes, drums, horns, cymbals and trumpets. Most of these stones are directly or indirectly connected with the symbolism attached to King David as a harpist. *Aldbar*, *Nigg*, *Aberlemno 3*, the *St Andrews Fragment*, *Dupplin*, *Monifieth* are all examples of David iconography. Here on *Lethendy*, Dr Henderson suggests that the players might represent David's musicians.

The Lethendy stone is built into the tower of that name in Perthshire. The figure playing an unsupported triangular harp faces a musician playing a triple-pipe. The rectangular object in the middle may be a barrel-drum. An animal, possibly a dog or cat, wearing a collar can be seen below the drum. The two figures above the musicians are holding horns while an angel looks down.

The presence of instruments and players, whether or not they are intended to represent David, points to the importance of musicians (particularly harpists) and consequently of their music to the Picts. The harpist was one of the élite.

How was music perceived by the Picts? When did its importance originate?

James Porter suggests that it may have been with the shamans who probably used chanting, humming or drumming to invoke the trance state.

No doubt children played tunes through blades of grass, men whistled through their fingers or made simple pipes, while mothers crooned their infants to sleep just as they have always done, until gradually music became an increasingly important part of their lives.

One of the functions of the Celtic druids was to teach the children of the warrior élite as Cathbad taught Cu Chulain. The teacher intoned the information while the children chanted it in chorus in much the same way as multiplication tables were taught in any village school of the recent past. The old Irish word for teach was *forcain*, which means literally 'to sing over'.

Diodorus Siculus mentioned that as well as being eulogists and satirists the Celtic bards used instruments similar to lyres. He also referred to the warriors as 'striking up a paean and singing a song of victory' on the battlefield.

Scottish folklore and ballads are full of stories about harpers and the magic qualities of their music, which could induce sleep, seduce women, call up the fairies, or raise the dead.

Early Christian Celts were great musicians. Pagan priests dreaded the powers of music as evidenced in a story of St Patrick at Guth-ard where his mighty voice paralysed pagan worshippers and overthrew their idol.

Early missionary monks are said to have carried the *cruit* or small lyre to help in worship. An Ulster bard, when he heard of Columba's death in 597, proclaimed, 'A *cruit* without a *ceis* [tuning pin] – A church without an abbot.'

Harps began to appear on Pictish stones in the eighth and ninth centuries. These, as Sanger and Kinnaird point out, are triangular-framed harps, 'that is harps with fore-pillars bracing the frame between string-carrier and box'. These particular harps were first found on the Pictish stones along the east coast of Scotland before they appeared on the Gaelic crosses of the West Highlands and Islands, and they predate the triangular-framed crosses in Ireland by several centuries. On the SS Oran and Martin's crosses in Iona the harper is playing a quadrangular harp. These two at Iona are the only instance of quadrangular harps in Scotland. The rest are all triangular.

The earliest stone thought to depict the Pictish harp is at Nigg in East Ross, a replica of which can be played to great effect in Groam House Museum. This is simply a three-cornered harp with a rounded curve between the neck and the soundbox, and a straight forepillar.

Lethendy is thought to date from the tenth century. The design of the harp is still triangular with a straight forepillar.

The earliest examples of triangular-framed harps appear on stones that are furthest away from the great Christian centres of Iona and Ireland and closest to native Pictish culture. Sanger and Kinnaird make the interesting deduction that the sculptors were representing not an imported Christian accessory but an instrument already in existence among the Picts before they had any close contact with Christianity.

A stone like Lethendy, which has the Pictish harp side by side with the Irish pipes, points to the fusion of Pictish and Scottish culture which was well established by the tenth century.

There is a noticeable difference in size between the small triangular-framed harp shown on Lethendy and the massive instruments on Dupplin and Monifieth. Sanger suggests that they must have been strung with horsehair or gut. The tension required using metal as in the Irish clarsachs, would have been impossible.

Anglo-Saxons used gut for their strings while the Welsh used horsehair, which produced an extraordinary buzzing sound altogether different from wire- or gut-strung instruments. Perhaps the Picts used horsehair too. The Eriskay ponies researched by Dr Robert Beck, who believes them to be the breed shown on the stones, have dense coats, with long thick manes and tails. Some of the tail hairs measure forty inches. Experiments by Robert Evans show that one method of twisting the strands gives a pleasing note that sounds more like clear humming than angry buzzing.

As to how the tunes and rhythms sounded, we can never know. Perhaps they

Dupplin Cross detail

Monifieth harpist, NMS Edinburgh

resembled the interlacing patterns on the stones which have been compared to Scottish country dancing, which is in essence a moving form of interlace in circles and chains. If the same pattern is to be found in stone and in dance, why not in music?

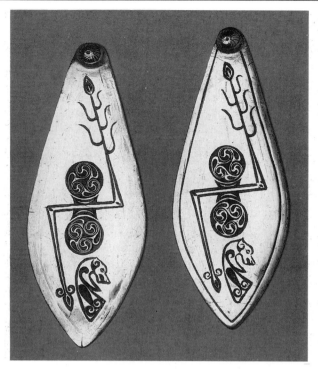

Silver plaques from Norrie's Law Hoard, Largo, Fife

PICTISH TREASURES

All Celts liked to look good and the Picts, judging by what has been found hidden in the ground or in excavated sites, were no exception.

The Caledonian School of Celtic art developed between the first and third centuries AD. Great bronze armlets and bracelets such as those from Castle Newe in the Grampian area were probably created around this period.

Pictish silverwork is typified by the hoard found at Norrie's Law in Largo, Fife. The date is debated by the experts, with Lloyd Laing placing it in the late fourth and early fifth centuries and James Graham-Campbell suggesting that a significant quantity dates to the seventh century while some of it was of late Roman manufacture. He sees it as a single hoard hidden between 655 and 685 when Fife was under Northumbrian rule to prevent it from being seized by an Anglian overlord.

Part of St Ninian's Isle treasure, now in NMS Edinburgh

No one knows who found it, but the silver items turned up in the hands of a hawker who sold some of them for scrap to a jeweller in Cupar, some to other locals, and a larger amount to an unknown person in Edinburgh. Gradually the pieces were gathered together and are now in the care of NMS.

Found about 1819, the hoard was described in 1839 as weighing some 400oz (12.5kg). Twenty years later a total of 153 silver objects and fragments weighing about 28oz (750g) were described. What survives therefore is only a seventeenth of the original treasure by weight. This includes two handsome penannular brooches, two oval plaques displaying the Pictish symbols of the double disc and Z-rod and the beast's head, originally enamelled in red, as well as finger rings, discs and fragments of knife handles, arm-bands, chains and possibly parts of a shield or dish.

The greatest treasure of Pictland was discovered in 1958 on a small green island reached by a tombola of sand and called after St Ninian. You can see the spot under the chancel arch of the ruins of a small pre-Norse church where the

Part of St Ninian's Isle treasure

hoard was found. It was buried in about 800 and is considered to be the finest collection of Celtic metalwork ever discovered, the counterpart of Sutton Hoo.

It consists of a collection of silver items including penannular brooches, a series of bowls, a sword pommel, a pair of scabbard chapes with inscriptions in Irish lettering bearing the Pictish name of 'Resad son of Spussico' (or possibly 'the Son of the Holy Spirit') on one side and a Latin Christian inscription on the other. There are also two thimble-like mounts probably meant for a sword harness.

The fact that so many Pictish treasures, such as Norrie's Law, St Ninian's hoard, Rogart and Croy in the Highlands, and Gaulcross, hidden in a stone circle in Banff, have been found buried points to the fact that Pictish people were constantly under threat of battle or invasion. How many more, one wonders, remain to be found.

The Monymusk Reliquary, which Anderson describes as the most beautiful of all the ecclesiastical relics, is a small wooden box with a cottage-shaped lid enclosed in a bronze framework and covered with plates of silver decorated with

Monymusk Reliquary, NMS Edinburgh

superb zoomorphic interlace and raised bejewelled and enamelled panels. At the ends there are appliances to hold a strap so that it could be worn round the neck. Known as the 'Brecbennoch of St Columba', it was carried at the head of the Scottish army at the Battle of Bannockburn in 1314.

Jewellers and craftsmen had workshops attached to the royal courts and later to the monasteries. Some of these 'men of art', as the Irish called them, probably travelled from place to place with templates and samples to tempt the wealthy.

We tend sometimes to think romantically that Celtic artists drew their designs freehand, but evidence from excavated sites shows that this was not the case. The patterns were carefully controlled according to geometric rules. Trial pieces were found in Irish sites showing how the craftsmen worked. Grids and compasses were used for interlace and linear patterns.

Once the design was determined, a mould had to be made by setting a wax model in clay then heating it to get rid of the wax. For simpler objects, two-piece moulds were made, used once then thrown away.

Hundreds of fragments of moulds have been found in important sites such as

Dunadd, Dundurn, Birsay in Orkney and Clatchard's Craig in Fife.

On stone, sculptors also sketched out the pattern first then blocked it out in rough relief. A stonemason visiting Groam House Museum told me that the setting out of the pattern alone on the Rosemarkie cross slab would have taken at least two years to accomplish. One of the box-shrine stones in the museum demonstrates clearly the use of sparrow-quirking. The pattern is punched out in a series of small holes which are then linked to complete the key-work design.

The sculptors of class II and III stones are thought to have travelled from schools attached to the larger royal households and monasteries to fulfill commissions on the site. Their pattern books would have given the patrons an idea of what they could do, and no doubt as artists they had their own ideas to present.

Lloyd Laing believes that most modern Celtic art consists of blundered patterns or slavish copies. The Celtic cult of today is symbolic of a past that is thought of as being wild and free. The opposite is true. Celtic art was highly controlled, the product of reason and discipline rather than wild imagination.

Nowhere is this more true than on the great Gospel manuscripts of the early Christian era. The earliest insular manuscript is thought to have been the *Cathach of St Columba*, now in the Royal Irish Academy, which may have been written by Columba himself. There are sixty-four pages, fifty-eight of them containing initials decorated in red and brown ink. It is the earliest-known Celtic manuscript.

Apart from a Celtic-style manuscript made in an Italian monastery at Bobbio that was founded by an Irish monk, there are a series of scripts that were probably produced in Northumbria. One of these – the famous *Book of Durrow* – probably dates to the second half of the seventh century. This is the first book to have whole pages of decoration – carpet pages, as they are called – and pages of decorated initials or the evangelists' symbols.

The *Lindisfarne Gospels*, designed in Hiberno-Saxon style by the artist-scribe Eadfrid, were created in a Northumbrian scriptorium, while the *Book of Echternach* from Luxembourg has Celtic influence and the *Lichfield Gospels* of St Chad are probably Northumbrian. But the *Book of Kells* is the crowning achievement of scriptorium art. Professor Julian Brown believed it to have come straight from a Pictish monastery some time towards the end of the eighth century, but a monastery influenced from Northumbria rather than Iona.

This brings us back to Nechtan and his request to Abbot Ceolfrid for Northumbrian architects and teachers. Could that party have included a writer and illuminator? Books were obviously of the greatest importance to Pictish monks. Many of them carved on the stones are carrying books or book satchels.

Several court monasteries must have existed among the Picts, Professor

Brown argues, capable of producing *Kells*. If we don't exactly know where they were, the groups of stones from St Andrews, Meigle, Aberlemno, St Vigeans, Tarbat in Easter Ross, not forgetting St Ninian's Isle, show where they may have been and at the same time demonstrate the quality of work the Picts were capable of doing.

Brown does not think it was written in the monastery at Kells in Ireland because this was an insignificant place until taken over by the displaced Iona Community between 807 and 814.

Dr Henderson sees the famous stones in Easter Ross, particularly at Tarbat, Nigg and Hilton of Cadboll, as nearest in style to *Kells*, with the vine-scrolling there better than any in Ireland.

But the question has not been resolved and no Irishman will believe that it was written anywhere else than in Iona and finished by the Iona monks at Kells Monastery in Ireland. One theory is that it was started in Iona, taken to Tarbat in Easter Ross for completion, and later returned to Kells for safe keeping.

As in the class II and III stones, the symbolism in the picture pages of the Gospel books is dense and multi-layered. Those early scribes knew and understood the Gospels in a way that is not found in modern preaching and only fully understood by theologians today.

All we can say is that with its wonderful sense of colour, superb overall decoration, tender and often humorous details, magnificent portraits of Christ and the evangelists, and learned symbolism, it is Celtic to the tip of the tiniest scroll and undoubtedly one of the world's greatest treasures of all time.

Meigle 27. A slave perhaps?

PART SEVEN

DAILY LIFE IN A PICTISH SETTLEMENT

An Icelandic writer in the twelfth century described the Picts as little men who 'did wonders in the mornings and the evenings but at mid-day lost their strength and hid in holes in the ground' – an amusing piece of mythology with perhaps a grain of truth based on the existence of souterrains.

So far the stones have told us a certain amount about aristocratic life in fort and monastic circles, but very little about how ordinary people passed their time.

Crop marks in southern Pictland show a quantity of unenclosed ring ditch-houses arranged in small settlements with souterrains attached. Gordon Maxwell describes crop mark evidence at Wellton near Blairgowrie pointing to a more varied settlement. Here, beside a bi-vallate fort, you can find a palisaded homestead, several unenclosed ring ditch-houses, at least one souterrain, and a cluster of round and square ditched burial barrows.

So let us suppose that here at Wellton we have a small Pictish community, with a warrior landowner and his immediate family occupying the fort, surrounded by his relatives and dependents, their landless labourers and slaves. All, with the possible exception of the lordling, would take a hand in cultivating the land, keep a portion of the harvest for their own use, and provide their lord with the necessary wealth in cattle and kind to enable him to pay his dues to his local overlord, take his place with the warrior élite and drink mead at the king's table.

Here he may be on the Bullion stone, an elderly man by now who has survived many campaigns. Perhaps he is on his way home from just such a festival, drunk and as exhausted as his horse.

If there was ever any doubt that the Picts had a sense of humour, Bullion dispels it at a glance. As Davin Hood suggests in PAS Newsletter No. 6, this is 'one of the most extraordinary ancient works of art in western Europe'.

Look at the rider. His warrior days are over. Bald, with jowls and a paunch, an untrimmed beard, bulbous nose and bibulous lips, he is the antithesis of the noble horsemen who swagger across the other stones.

The Bullion stone from Invergowrie, now in NMS Edinburgh

The pony too is a sorry creature as it plods uphill exhausted by its overweight burden. Davin Hood describes it as a 'richt jaud, tied in below the knee, sicle-hocked, weak in the quarters, the tail set too low, narrow-chested, hammer-headed, shallow in the girth with no heartroom and extremely tucked in at the loins'. The lowered head, drooping eyes and resigned mouth all betray its age and weariness.

The bird-head terminal of the drinking horn is also full of expression – superior, sarcastic, amused.

Bearing in mind the time and skill needed to carve a stone of this nature, who would want to commission such a memorial?

There have been many suggestions, but Dr I. L. Gordon has come up with one of the best. She suggests that Bullion could be an insult stone. According to the Icelandic saga of Gisli Sursson dating from the late tenth century, an incident took place in Norway when Gisli was a youth. When Skeggi challenges a certain Kolbjorn, whose seconder is Gisli, to a duel, Kolbjorn loses his nerve. Skeggi orders his carpenter to set up wooden effigies of Kolbjorn and Gisli. 'And one shall stand behind the other, and the insult shall stand there forever to shame them.'

One can imagine the old man speaking too freely in his cups and offending some fellow warrior who, being aware that the old man was beyond a physical challenge, commissioned the stone instead.

Ale drinking was part of Celtic culture, and mead, of superior quality, was recorded in the great British poem *Y Goddodin* by the poet/warrior Aneirin as being given to warriors either in part-payment for the use of their swords or to exhort them in battle.

Pictish wives must have been used to husbands with sore heads, and not just the warriors. No doubt the villagers brewed their own kind of strong drink, as suggested by Robert Louis Stevenson whose tongue-in-cheek poem about the lost recipe for heather ale has persuaded more than one twentieth century enthusiast to search for it.

WIVES AND MARRIAGE

We know little about Pictish marriage, and the whole subject of matrilinear succession is, as we have seen, still a matter of debate.

Julius Caesar, in his *Conquest of Gaul*, mentions the British habit of sharing one woman among groups of ten to twelve men, 'especially among brothers and among brothers and sons'.

Dio Cassio (AD 150–225) recorded a conversation between Julia Domna, the wife of the emperor Severus (AD 193–211), and a Caledonian woman, probably a royal hostage. When the empress challenged the princess about the Celtic custom of the 'freedom of the thighs', the Caledonian had a ready answer. She was proud to give herself openly to the bravest and finest of men, whereas Roman matrons had double standards. They were either taken by rape or forced into secret relationships.

Some cite this conversation as a reason for matrilinear succession. You knew your mother but could never be sure of your father's identity.

Ancient passages in the Old Irish law-tracts copied in the monasteries from the oral tradition date from the seventh century. They may have been in use for hundreds of years before that date according to Dr Binchy, who has pointed out many likenesses between Irish and Indian marriage laws.

There were ten sorts of marriage according to Irish laws, of which nine were explained. Three of these were regular and differed only in the amount of goods brought into a union and by which partner. Four were temporary unions and two describe forced marriages by abduction or seduction and were considered wrong.

These laws included the right to divorce. A marriage could always be ended by common consent. This custom seemed to persist in spite of Christianity into the fourteenth century, when the *Annals of Ulster* record that a king of Connaught married the wife of an Ulster nobleman and put away his own wife. If these laws of marriage had, as Binchy claims, an Indian or Indo-European origin, then it would seem likely that the Picts too would have practised at least some of them.

The system of 'hand-fasting' or 'left-hand' marriage, which survived in Scotland into comparatively recent times, perhaps owed its origin to these old laws. A contract was made between two chiefs in which the heir of one lived with the daughter of another for a year and a day. If there were no children or the couple did not agree together, then the contract was ended and he could send her home and try again with someone else. If a child was conceived during the period then the 'right-hand' marriage was solemnized. The custom was recognized by the Church until abolished in the Statutes of Iona in 1616.

Among the labouring folk in Scotland up until fairly recent times, marriage was not considered necessary or economic unless at least one child had been born. Sometimes it was never solemnized. This was called common-law marriage and was as legally binding as any other contract. It still is.

Well-born women were obviously important in Pictish society, although none are mentioned in the King List. The evidence comes from the mirror-and-comb symbol on the stones. What it stood for is, as we have seen, still a matter of speculation, but most are agreed that it was a status symbol to do with important women.

Very few women are mentioned by name in Pictish lore except for the very occasional king's wife or saint, and the princess Drusticc, daughter of one of two kings called Drust who ruled Pictland in the early sixth century. Her story is preserved in the *Book of Leinster* and in the *Liber Hymnorum* as a preface to a hymn allegedly composed by Mugint, the abbot of Whithorn.

Sent to Whithorn to be educated by Abbot Mugint, Drusticc was a contemporary of St Finnian of Moville and, among others, two young men called Rioc and Talmach. Drusticc fell in love with Rioc and begged Finnian to get him for her 'in marriage'. Rioc must have refused because Finnian sent Talmach to her room in disguise. Mugint blamed Finnian and was so angry with him that he tried to get him murdered, so the story goes. Drusticc had a child by Talmach called Lonan who is named as a saint in Galloway. Nora Chadwick saw no good reason for disbelieving the story.

CHILDREN

Up until the nineteenth century there was no such thing as childhood as we understand the word. Childhood is a feature of a leisured society, and there can have been little time for play and schooling in the farms and fields of Pictland. Young adults would have been expected to take their part in the grown-up world as soon as they were able to walk.

One can only imagine Pictish childhood in the villages. The boys no doubt learned how to handle the axe, how to herd livestock, how to groom horses, how to farm, smith, tan leather and all the other necessary skills handed on by their fathers and needed for the community to function. Some may have been singled out by their local lord as likely battle-fodder in warfare, or as raiders in inter-clan strife.

A girl's life in a Pictish village was probably much the same as it was in the Highlands and Islands up to comparatively recent times. Spinning, waulking the tweed, visiting the well, milking, herding the cattle, minding siblings, grinding grain, cooking, slaving. . . the list is endless. Prayers and incantations were learned to protect every part of a life shrouded in superstition and fear, whoever the God. Every inch of the countryside was crowded with whispering stones, polluting water sprites, secret entrances to the Otherworld, fairies and giants.

Rhynie Man, to be seen in Grampian Regional Headquarters in Aberdeen, has every aspect of a giant set up in stone to frighten children or warn the passer-by to keep off the territory he guarded. J. F. Campbell wrote, 'It seems to me that giants are simply the nearest savage race at war with the race who tell the tales.'

Rhynie Man, now in Grampian regional headquarters, Aberdeen

Certainly such a creature has always been prominent in Gaelic story-telling.

At 1.03m (3.4') Rhynie Man is exceptionally tall for an incised figure. His prominent nose suggests he could smell blood. His bared teeth are filed for human flesh. His brooding eyebrows threaten dark deeds while his furrowed brow suggests tattooing.

Giants exist in every culture and mythology from Goliath of Gath to Bunyan's Giant Despair. They speak a strange language – 'Fee-fi-fo-fum' in English, but 'Fiaw, fiaw, foaghrich' in Gaelic. Campbell suggests these sounds may be corruptions of the language of an older race. Could it have been Pictish?

Everyday life must have been uncomfortable and hard, but there would have been good times too. Festivals heralded the seasons with dancing, singing, story-telling and special food. There were wells to be dressed and ceremonies to perform, some of which may have survived to the present day. Courtship and companionship went hand in hand with an appreciation and respect – not unmingled with fear – for the natural world.

With the coming of Christianity, a new feeling of self-respect, a new understanding of what love is all about, a lessening of fear of the occult slowly reshaped the outlook of the poor as the poetry in *Carmina Gadelica* indicates.

Aristocratic childhood included tuition either under a druid or later in a monastery, such as was enjoyed by Drusticc. It also included fosterage, which we have already discussed. Although this was generally a good experience, many Pictish children must have known the same pangs of homesickness as the small girls and boys of today during their first term at public school.

Our lordling at Wellton in his younger days might well have fostered the sons of wealthier relations, thus cementing family bonds within the clan into another generation.

The *Tain Bo Cualnge* gives a delightful portrait of Cu Chulainn as a little boy on his way to visit his uncle, King Conchobar. His toys consisted of a hurley stick of bronze and a silver ball, his small javelin and a toy spear with its end sharpened by fire. When he reaches the king's rath the other boys are playing hurley. He joins in without being asked and they all – 150 in number – range themselves against him. There he stands – the dream of any child today – alone in the goal fielding an avalanche of balls and outplaying everyone.

It is possible that Pictish boys enjoyed a similar game. Shinty or *camanachd* played with hockey-like sticks and twelve players is similar to hurley and still has its league in the Highlands today.

Board games were played sometimes with counters or pegs set into little holes. A stone board was found at Dun Chonallaich in Argyll and three at Buckquoy in Orkney. Gaming boards could also be made of bone. Part of just such a board made of whalebone with perforated intersections was found on Birsay, and two

St Andrew's 24

others near Stromness. Small pieces of incised slate from Jarlshof might be tally sticks, while playing pieces were probably small pebbles, shells or bones.

One of the games for two players resembles an Irish game called *Brandubh* or 'Black Raven'. The king-piece was placed at the centre of the board surrounded by his warriors and the task of the opponent was to prevent the king from reaching the sides or corners.

But a warrior's son would have spent most of his childhood learning the skills of horse-riding and practising with his weapons. Isabel Henderson suggests that St Andrews 24 might possibly depict an initiation ceremony where the young lad is being presented with his sword and shield having first accomplished the skills required. The symbolism is not hard to find. The young lad may represent the newly baptised Christian putting on the armour of Christ.

With the coming of Christianity, our little imaginary community might well have been visited by a Christian monk from a nearby monastery – Meigle or Aberlemno perhaps. He might well have found himself accepted into the village through tiny gifts and Bible stories told to the children. By befriending the children, he might have drawn their parents to Christ. It would not be the first time a missionary used such a means to conversion.

But this is fanciful stuff.

Equally likely, the local lordling would have seen social advantages in having a church in the heart of his territory. Indeed, one of his sons, educated at the great monastic school of Iona or Whithorn, might well have planted a community with himself as abbot on a site close to the family fort.

A FARMER'S LIFE

Cattle were of prime importance to the Pictish farmer, not only for the obvious reasons, but also as a means of denoting a king's wealth. They would have consisted mostly of shorthorns of the *bos taurus* breed now extinct but similar to the Highland cattle of today.

According to the bones unearthed by the Alcocks' excavations at Dundurn, the cattle were small and mostly over two years old. Bone-counts in other excavations show that pigs were next in importance, but not just for food. Because of its suppleness, pigskin was probably the most popular choice for making those tunics worn by the warriors on the stones.

Sheep were raised on the St Kilda Isles some two thousand years ago. Their bones resemble those of the Soay sheep of today. In the central mainland fewer sheep were raised than pigs and they were slaughtered young, suggesting that they were more important for their meat than their wool.

Goats were useful for milk and cheese and also for ridding the cultivated fields of unwelcome larger weeds like thistles. Their hides were tough and useful for sheltering purposes.

Horses were élitist and raised to be ridden rather than as beasts of burden. The common breed resembled the Highland garrons and ponies of today – sturdy, tough, broad-backed and friendly. The better horses are thought to have come from Islay, but there must have been some cross-breeding for the horses on the stones seem to vary in size.

Wolf-hounds, some as big as calves, were bred by the élite for hunting, but other dogs were used by the farmers for herding. No doubt many roamed the villages and found their way into the hearts and homes of ordinary folk.

Poultry were domesticated, and doves too may have been kept for their eggs, although I can't see them being welcomed by farmers who had crops to raise. Perhaps they were used by the élite as carriers. Pigeons have been domesticated for five thousand years. The Romans may have brought their use to Pictland.

Bees were of utmost importance to all Celtic farming life. Superstitions concerning bees are still part of Scottish folklore, in which they are seen as messengers from the dead while the soul is said to leave the body at death in the form of a bee or butterfly. Honey was not only essential for cooking and for making mead but also for its wax in the casting of metal and probably the making of candles. Any farming settlement would have been alive with the sound of bees.

Wheats known as emmer and spelt, and barley used for bannocks and the brewing of ale were grown in the fields. The Picts probably ate porridge. The contents of the stomach of a Celtic Iron Age aristocrat nicknamed Lindow Man, unearthed from a bog in Cheshire, contained traces of burned bread or porridge.

At Dundurn the Alcocks discovered traces of wild cherry, raspberries and hazelnuts. No doubt apples too were cultivated, while bracken or heather was collected for bedding, and moss perhaps for lavatory paper.

Grain was mostly dried in kilns or on racks and may have been stored in pots and baskets in the souterrains. It was mostly ground in rotary querns, although saddle querns were also used. Tools consisted of flails, reaping hooks, shears, knives, hammers, the foot plough (*cas chrom*) and of course the ubiquitous axe.

Timber was felled for building, fuel and furniture. Wood is thought to have been seasoned in running water, perhaps driven down the rivers from well-timbered areas to coastal settlements and dragged by oxen to the nearest yard.

Serious battles and planned campaigns usually took place in the spring or early summer before the harvest was ripe and no man could be spared from the fields. A bad harvest heralded a merciless winter.

The salmon is one of many carvings in the East Wemyss caves, Fife

CAVE-DWELLERS

There is ample evidence that certain caves were used for temporary shelter, permanent occupation and ritual acts.

Frank Rankin, who is one of those dedicated to saving the Wemyss caves in Fife from sea erosion, records an old legend about the caves:

'They were biggit [built] by the Pechs, short wee men 'wi' red hair and lang airms and feet sae broad that when it rained they turned them ower their heids and they served as umbrellas. Oh aye, they were graund builders the Pechs.'

In fact the caves were formed by the sea about eight to nine thousand years ago. In two land shifts they were raised fifty feet, so that now there are two levels of caves, one above the other.

Of the ten or so remaining caves at Wemyss, all of them contain symbols, markings and doodles that provide a good record of prehistoric and Dark Age history. Here have been found cup and ring marks, Pictish symbols, Ogams, animals, fish, fertility symbols, stick people, a hunting scene, the Viking god Thor with his hammer and other Norse gods, Christian Latin crosses and, in Jonathan's Cave, a boat that may have been Pictish or Viking but which is thought to be the earliest-known drawing of a ship in Scotland.

The Court and Well Caves are now exceedingly dangerous and entry is forbidden. Hard hats are available at the visitors' centre and these should be used for all the other caves. The tragedy is that unless expensive steps are taken, the

Jonathan's cave, East Wemyss

caves will soon be eroded beyond recovery.

About three miles east of Burghead at Covesea (pronounced Cowsie) on the Moray coast, a stretch of golden sandstone cliffs can be found riddled with caves. Hugely impressive and dry, one is known as the Sculptor's cave for obvious reasons. Every inch is carved with initials ancient and modern, indecipherable doodles and a collection of undoubtedly Pictish symbols.

Two excavations have led to the conclusion that it was an important settlement site in the late Bronze Age where a quantity of fine metalwork was either lost or deposited. Roman coins and artifacts were discovered dating from the middle of the fourth century, and there are at least fifteen Pictish symbols carved on the walls and roof of the entrance passages. Some simple Latin crosses (like those at East Wemyss) can also be seen together with a twelfth century Russian cross on the west wall of the east entrance.

We don't know how the Picts used the cave, but an early excavation discovered some two thousand human bones whose dates were not determined. Ian Shepherd suggests there is some evidence for it being a ritual site dating from the late Bronze Age or early Iron Age through the Dark Ages into the Christian era. Shepherd also points out that the Pictish symbols range from the basic to the ornate. This perhaps indicates a continuing use of the cave for religious purposes throughout the Pictish era.

Bearing in mind its closeness to the royal fortress at Burghead, there may have been a ritual connection between the two.

[232]

PART EIGHT

THE END OF PICTLAND

THE VIKINGS

We have seen Pictland evolve into a well-organized society on the whole, increasingly committed to Christianity, appreciative of the arts, troubled occasionally by the Angles but more often by the Scots who were in outlook similar to themselves. Confront them with the savagery of the Viking pirates and imagine the culture shock.

For years the Norsemen have had a good press from those who fail to distinguish between the different phases of their activity in Britain, the three classes of incomers and the motives for their voyages.

During those three hundred years of relative calm in the four kingdoms of Pictland, Dal Riata, Strathclyde and Anglia, the Scandinavians were finding it increasingly difficult to feed their growing population.

Along the 1,600 miles of Norwegian coastline, the country is slashed into deep inlets leaving only the narrowest strips of land suitable for cultivation between the fiords and the mountains. Largely dependent on fish, the Norsemen worked hard to improve the designs of their boats. These reached such a peak of excellence that their crews were not only able to navigate the fearsome currents and dangerous outcrops of their own coastal waters, but also to become the undisputed masters of the wider seas. One of their inventions was the massive oak keel which enabled a ship under sail to hold a steady course.

The three groups included the settlers. These were farming families driven from their own sparse land to find a foothold elsewhere. South Shetland may have been the first place they settled to build their rectangular homesteads, often from the stones of disused brochs. Their descendants intermarried with the Picts and eventually became Christians. They brought new ideas, skills and genes that were eventually to enrich the lives of the Picts and Scots. Orkney and Shetland were to remain part of Norway until the fifteenth century.

Then there were the traders, whose boats were bulkier than the longships and who were a different class again, intent mainly on bartering their goods.

But the Norsemen are remembered chiefly for their warrior pirates, the Vikings. These were a merciless class of men who worshipped the war-god Odin, and gloried in his service. Pirates, pillagers and man-slayers, the dreaded strangers in their swift sea-steeds glided soundlessly into every sea loch, round every island, up every inlet and river to beach where they chose with only a crunch on sand or shingle to give warning of their approach. Grabbing their shields from the boat-sides, protected by iron helmets and chain mail, armed with battle-axes, swords and spears, roaring like bears, they plundered every fort, monastery and settlement they could find and murdered all who could not escape, including old women and children in their beds.

Warfare is never pleasant, but the beserkers disobeyed all the rules of Celtic battle. There was no escape from them and no mercy shown by them. They arrived, slaughtered and stole gold, slaves and cattle, and after a night or two of rape, drink and gluttony were on their way to the next settlement, riding the ocean at ten knots in a good wind. So the sagas say.

The earliest reference to the Vikings is recorded in the *Anglo-Saxon Chronicle*, which mentions the attack on Lindisfarne in 793. The community there was eventually driven to regroup in Durham. The *Annals of Ulster* continue the history of atrocity when they refer starkly to 'the devastation of all the islands by gentiles' in 794. The pillaging of Skye came the following year. Nor was Ireland exempt. By 796 the raiders were on the Connaught coast, mainly after monastic treasures.

Dr Smyth believes that the Viking Age opened in Scotland, Ireland and England with violent and massive attacks as a prelude to colonization. There may have been peaceful trading expeditions prior to these attacks, but colonization came later.

Of all the monasteries that were savaged, Iona suffered most. The first raid was in 795. As we have seen, Iona was the soul itself of Celtic Christianity, and had been enriched over the years by kings, visitors and abbots from all over the Christian world. To the raiders, it was a treasure-house of gold unguarded and unprotected by unarmed men whose god, 'the white Christ', was the antithesis of all that Odin stood for.

They returned to Iona in 802, and in 806, when sixty-eight members of the community were slaughtered. The abbot, Cellach, decided to evacuate Iona for a while, and in 807 began to build a new site for his monks at Kells in County Meath. Luckily, some of its treasures, such as the *Book of Kells*, were saved, some sent to Ireland for protection, and some to Dunkeld. But Iona was not abandoned. A few monks who were not afraid of martyrdom remained.

One of these, called Blathmac, was allegedly 'blood-eagled' or torn limb from limb and his rib-cage ripped apart for refusing to reveal where Columba's shrine was hidden.

In the wake of the warriors, the settlers arrived, and by the tenth and eleventh centuries they had made homes for themselves all over Britain, intermarried locally and adopted both Christianity and the Celtic culture of their neighbours. Their domination of the Western Isles and the Isle of Man was to last for three centuries and end after the Battle of Largs with the Treaty of Perth in 1226.

The first phase is what concerns us here. As we have seen, this started during the last decade of the eighth century and continued well into the ninth. Such unexampled savagery confused and silenced the recorders, destroyed valuable documentation, such as the great library of Iona, and helped to shift the balance of power from the Picts to the Scots.

KENNETH MAC ALPIN – THE FOUNDER OF A DYNASTY

Towards the middle of the ninth century, the Norsemen had begun to change the map not only of Pictland but also of Dal Riata. Their farmers had settled on all the islands from Shetland to the Outer Hebrides and south to the mouth of the Clyde. The whole of the western coastland of Dal Riata and north, to include Caithness and Sutherland and from thence south to the Moray Firth, including the north-eastern Pictish coastline, was being savaged and resettled.

Kenneth, a shrewd Scot with supposedly a Pictish mother, must have realized at some stage that unless he laid strong hands on Pictland, he would have no kingdom at all. The Scots of Dal Riata would be wiped out.

Luck was on his side when so many Pictish and Scottish princes including Eoganan their king were killed in battle against the Vikings in 839.

As we have seen, the King List records two or three further kings, whose dates are very uncertain, the third of whom was Drust IX. He is mentioned as the last king of the Picts killed at Forteviot or perhaps Scone by treachery.

The story of treachery is recorded in several late legends. One states that the Scots came secretly armed to a meeting and slew the unsuspecting King Drust and the chief nobles of the Picts. Giraldus Cambrensis in *De Instructione Principus* elaborates by describing how the Scots invited the Pictish nobility to a great banquet and when the Picts were drunk, removed the bolts from their benches. Trapped in the box-like hollows under the benches, they were murdered to a man.

Part of *The Prophecy of St Berchan*, translated by Skene, says:

A son of the Clan of his son will possess
The kingdom of Alban, by virtue of his strength,
A man who shall feed ravens, break battles,
His name was the Ferbasach [conqueror].

He is the first king who possessed in the east
of the men of Erin in Alban,
It was by the strength of darts and swords,
By violent deaths, by violent fates.

By him are deceived in the east the fierce ones,
He shall dig in the earth, powerful the art,
Dangerous goad blades, death, pillage,
On the middle of Scone of high shields . . .

This was not a prophecy as such but a convention for writing history after the event. It is supposed to describe the legend recorded by Cambrensis and may date from the late twelfth century at the very earliest.

The *Chronicle of Huntington* tells us that Kenneth in the seventh year of his reign attacked and overthrew the Picts when they had been crushed by Danish pirates and secured the whole of Alba. In the twelfth year of his reign he fought successfully against the Picts seven times in one day.

The *Scottish Chronicle*, part of which may date from the tenth century, records that 'Kenneth, son of Alpin, therefore the first of the Scots, ruled this Pictavia happily for 16 years. Now Pictavia has its name from the Picts, whom Kenneth destroyed as we have said.'

In records of a few succeeding reigns, the kingdom is still mentioned as Pictavia but Kenneth and his successors are called Scots. By 900 and the reign of Domnall or Donald II, the kings are referred to as rulers of Alba, which was and still is the name for Scotland in the Gaelic. Thus the old national title disappeared not with Kenneth but with one of his grandsons.

Kenneth's brother Donald I succeeded him and with his fellow Scottish noblemen saw to it that the Dal Riatan laws of Aed were recognized by the Picts. Girig, Donald's son, is said to have freed the Columban Church from Pictish rules and burdens. The Pictish language dropped out of use. No doubt there was a period of bi-lingualism before it ceased to be spoken by the farming community, but it probably disappeared fairly quickly at court.

Nowadays Kenneth is not viewed as a revolutionary who by foul means got rid of the Picts to become ruler of both nations. Dal Riatan kings had held Pictland before he appeared, and Pictish kings had royal fathers from Dal Riata. Eoganan, killed in 839, had reigned as king of both territories.

He was perhaps only the culminating figurehead of a long, slow process of Scottish infiltration into Pictland which began with the Columban monks. Remember how Nechtan expelled them from Pictland in 717? Their power and therefore the power of the Scots was becoming politically unwelcome even then.

Remember too how Oengus I somewhat carelessly lost his kingship over the Dal Riatans and how the Scottish King Aed Find the lawgiver invaded Fortrui in 768? This was perhaps the time when the Scots first began seriously to take over Pictland. Thereafter it appeared for a while that the Pictish kings were in the ascendancy, but Smyth suggests it was the Scots who were in fact taking over from the Picts from the time of Aed Find rather than the other way round.

Smyth points out that Oengus II and his son Eoganan were more Scottish than Pictish in name and in descent from Fergus, who was in the direct line of the Dal Riatan dynasty of Gabran. But both kings were also descended from the Picts. The dynasties by now were deeply intertwined.

The Viking invasion was only the catalyst which forced the immediate and inevitable fusion between the Picts and the Scots. It needed a strong man to take over joint rulership. Kenneth, son of a Scot (as some believe mac Alpin to mean), was that man and the symbol of that unity.

Who exactly was Kenneth's father, the mysterious Alpin? One suggestion is that so many Pictish and Scottish royalty had been killed by the Norsemen that the only person left to take over kingship of Dal Riata in 839 was Alpin, but the *Annals of Ulster* don't mention him.

All that is known of him is that he was the father of Kenneth, who seized power among the Scots in 840.

Smyth suggests that Alpin's reign was probably invented to give more credibility to Kenneth. Alpin was – as the name suggests – merely 'a Scot' whose wife may or may not have had Pictish credentials. Kenneth could easily have been the warrior son of a lesser king whose skills in generalship and courage paved the way for his more illustrious son.

Marjorie Anderson reckons that if Alpin had really been a king of Dal Riata, he would have been the founder of a new dynasty, not Kenneth. And that is what makes Kenneth so important; not his father or his origins, but the fact that he was the progenitor of a new dynasty which was to found a new kingdom that was neither Irish nor Pictish but henceforth to be known as the Kingdom of Scotland.

But Kenneth was not only to establish a new dynasty, he was also to oversee the beginnings of a new Christian era in Pictland. The Columban monks chose to retreat to Kells rather than follow their fellow Dal Riatans eastwards to the great Pictish centres of Christianity at Dunkeld, Scone or St Andrews.

Kenneth saw to it that some of Columba's relics were taken, possibly to

Dunkeld, among them perhaps the Brecbennoch of Columba.

When in 905 the Viking leader Ivar II led his hordes against Fortriu and the rich church at Dunkeld he was defeated by the Scots who carried Columba's *bachall* (crozier) into battle and won. But Iona remained according to the *Scottish Chronicle* as the burial place of the Scottish kings.

Meanwhile the Picts were forced to submit to a growing intolerance of their laws and customs both secular and ecclesiastical. The re-founded church centres were no longer Pictish in their outlook, but altogether Scottish. The *Scottish Chronicle* had no sympathy for them saying they deserved to be treated harshly because they spurned the Mass and precepts of the Scots and 'wished (or refused) to be held equal to others in the law of Justice'.

Reading between the lines, the proud Picts were deeply resentful of any attempt to make them conform to new ideas. This must have been the time when old annals, records and gospel manuscripts kept in the old Pictish monastic sites were thrown away, burned or hidden.

By 900, however, the dynasty of Kenneth was firmly established at Scone and St Andrews and Scottish ways were imposed upon the Pictish Church. The *Scottish Chronicle* tells us that Constantine II, that great and Christian grandson of Kenneth, with the Bishop of St Andrews, 'pledged themselves upon the hill of Faith near the royal city of Scone, that the laws and disciplines of the faith, and the rights in churches and gospels, should be kept in conformity with the Scots'.

So was finally born the first Church of Scotland.

The Dupplin free-standing cross is said to date from the ninth century. Recently recast for the Work of Angels exhibition held in Edinburgh in 1991, it has been carefully studied by Katherine Forsyth and Michael Spearman. Owing to the excellence of the cast, it has been possible to translate the seven lines of Latin writing that you can find on a panel on the west face of the cross: CUSTANTIN SON OF WUIRGUST (Constantine son of Fergus).

The images on the stone may not refer to the life of Kenneth as had been thought but to the life of Constantine I. Dr Spearman suggests that the Dupplin Cross might have been erected by Kenneth or one of his sons as an apt dedication to a Pictish king who like Kenneth himself had not only ruled both nations but had held their best interests at heart.

KENNETH AND THE NORSEMEN

Diplomacy must have been one of Kenneth's outstanding talents. That more than anything else may have won him the Pictish kingdom.

The Dupplin Cross, Perth & Kinross

The shift of Dal Riatan power from the west to the east happened at a time when the Norse raiders and settlers were teeming into the Western Isles, Ireland and the coasts of Dal Riata. Kenneth surely should have been their keenest enemy. Yet his relationship with the Norsemen was always ambivalent.

According to the *Prophecy of St Berchan*, Alpin married a Norse woman as his second wife. The account includes a quick description of Kenneth's reigns as follows:

[239]

> Seventeen years of warding valour
> In the sovereignty of Alban,
> After slaughtering Cruithneach [the Picts],
> after imbittering Galls,
> He dies on the banks of the Earn.

The *prophecy* now switches to Donald mac Alpin.

> It was bad with Alban then,
> Long ere another like him shall come,
> It was a short time till took the kingdom,
> The wanton son of the Gaillsighe [Norse woman].

Thus Kenneth's successor, Donald mac Alpin, was also his half-brother, the son of a Norse princess. Possibly Kenneth grew up in the care of a Norwegian step-mother.

Dr Smyth's scholarship informs us that in 836 a certain Gathfrith Fergusson visited Dal Riata at the request of Kenneth to ask him for support. This Gothfrith, who was a king in the Hebrides, was another leader born of a Norse mother and Scottish father. Smyth points out that Kenneth was already in negotiation with the Norwegians before he moved against the Picts.

Although there was nothing new in such marriage alliances between opposing nations, Alpin's marriage was the first to be recorded between the Vikings and the Scots, and it looks as if Kenneth's policy was built on that connection.

The *Chronicle of Huntingdon* records that Kenneth overcame the Picts at a vulnerable time when they were being attacked by the Vikings. Later Kenneth was to marry one of his daughters to the powerful Olaf the White, Norse king of Dublin. It all fits. Kenneth must have made full use of his friendship with Olaf to consolidate his own position.

In due course, Kenneth's son Constantine of Scotland was to help Olaf of Dublin in his harrying of Strathclyde when the king was killed. Constantine married his other sister to Rhun, the new king of Strathclyde. It was the same when the Danes arrived in Northumberland. The Scots allied themselves to the Norse in Dublin against the incoming Danes.

Meanwhile, what of the Picts? In 866, the Irish annals record that Olaf of Dublin led a force of Irish and Scottish Viking foreigners against Fortriu (Pictland). Here Olaf was not at war against the Scots in Alba but the actual Picts from whom he took hostages and exacted tribute for years to come. Who were these Picts? Probably they were not those under Constantine's rule in the southern areas of Perth and Fife which were now Scottish. They may have been those who lived north of the Mounth in the Pictish kingdom of Fidech, which included Moray and parts of Inverness-shire and Ross.

Moray was still a Pictish region under strong pressure from a son of Olaf of Dublin called Thorstein the Red. He had already conquered Caithness and Sutherland and was harrying the Moray coast. Excavations at the Pictish fortress of Burghead indicate a great fire which may have caused its total destruction by the Norse. But Ian Shepherd suggests that the fort may have been repaired sufficiently to save Moray and beyond from total Norse invasion.

We guess that there must have been a tremendous battle fought in the Moray area because of the presence of Sueno's Stone in Forres, but we know nothing.

In 875 there was another great massacre of the Picts and the Scots together in Dollar by Halfdan, a Dane from York (whose army had been defeated by the Dublin Norwegians). The Scots were fully involved in this battle and Constantine I may even have lost his life in the fighting here or in a subsequent battle in Fife, as Halfdan himself was soon to do. These Danish Vikings who were friends of no one, may have remained for as much as a year in Pictland/ Scotland, leaderless and living a life of pillage and plunder until, with only a few of their crews left, they were firmly outlawed.

Thereafter the Scots continued to subdue the rest of Pictland, operating from the centre of their kingdom in Perth. The period is so poorly documented that little of fact remains.

Strathclyde was ruled by a Scottish sub-king from Constantine's reign onwards. It took well over a century to gather the Lothians into Scottish kingship and still longer to get rid of the Norse earls. By then the Picts had been firmly and forcefully integrated into Scotland.

'If only . . .' is an irritating phrase, but I'm going to use it nevertheless. If only the shadowy Alpin had not married an equally shadowy Norsewoman, Kenneth might have ended up slain by Viking pirates. Scotland or rather Dal Riata might have become a province of Pictland (as it once had been) and Pictland, which had the right to sovereignty from its Iron Age inheritance, might have survived as a nation today.

On such frail hooks the pictures of history hang.

SUENO'S STONE

For the last word on the Picts, let Sueno's Stone in Forres speak.

Dr Anderson calls this stone 'unquestionably the most remarkable monument in Britain', and so it is. I've seen nothing comparable.

Sueno's Stone (now encased in glass) at Forres, Moray

Sueno is a class III cross slab measuring 7 by 1.2m (23' by 4') and is 38cm (15') thick. It weighs some 7,112kg (7 tons). Badly weathered, it is none the less remarkably clear considering that it dates from the ninth or tenth century. This is probably due to the fact that it lay buried for many years before it was re-erected in the eighteenth century on its present site.

Although in 1991 it was enclosed in a glass and steel structure for preservation, it has lost little of its splendour, particularly at night when floodlight adds to its magnificence.

The towering height, elaborate cross and superb decoration inspire so much awe that you feel like sinking to your knees before it. If we can feel that way today, how did the Picts of Moray who saw it new feel? Perhaps its message meant more than its appearance and its beauty was lost on those who knew its meaning.

The story it tells is a sombre one. Let us look in detail at the four panels on the back. Although they are almost indecipherable, Dr Anthony Jackson, who has made a clever and detailed study of the stone, sees at the worn top of the first panel five men dressed in tunic facing us and holding swords at the ready. The central figure may be Kenneth himself, flanked by four sub-kings or his sons and successors.

Below these are three rows of mounted warriors all facing to the left, Kenneth's army perhaps.

The second panel is topped by a similar row of five men holding raised swords and spears. The centre warrior seems a shade larger than his companions and appears to be wearing a kilt – perhaps King Kenneth.

Below is a row of eight warriors. All except two are facing left. The central couple are fighting with swords and shields. The battle has started.

Below again, and still on the second panel, is an execution scene. You can clearly count seven decapitated bodies lying on the left with the seventh torso centre-right of the others. This warrior has just been killed by the man who appears to be holding a sword in one hand and a head in the other. Could these be the seven kings of Pictland, now all dead?

Under the quadrangular Celtic bell (or broch), which appears to have a clapper, you can count five heads, and there appear to be two more heads on the ground below the two fighting couples that you can see beneath the row of torsos. Again, perhaps they are dead Pictish kings. Behind the executioner are three men who look as if they are each blowing a carnyx, that dreaded battle-trumpet. Below, three rows with two mounted warriors in each appear to be leading a pair of archers and six foot-soldiers – Kenneth's army?

The third panel shows a tent-like structure with finials at the top ends – or could it be a bridge? This is sheltering a row of corpses with seven severed heads.

Does this signify the death of lesser lords? The central scene is surrounded by combating couples.

The fourth panel shows two identical rows of eight infantrymen. The first eight are being chased by the second group who have raised swords and shields – defeated Picts fleeing from the victors of the day?

Dr Anthony Jackson's theory is that the cross on the far side of the stone should be facing east, in which case the above scene would be facing west. This would make the riders move from south to north.

Thus he reckons that the stone commemorates a victory of the southerners over the northeners, which might indicate a stunning victory by Kenneth over the Picts. He further suggests that the stone was erected by Kenneth to tell the Picts in Moray that they were done for.

The front of the stone appears to repeat the same message in less bloodthirsty terms. The cross is superb and its message clear. It is not possible to decipher the carvings at the top, but the lowest panel shows a group of five men, two of whom are larger than the others and kneel like acolytes over the smaller central figure possibly seated on the sacred crowning stone. He would appear to represent Kenneth himself at his coronation. Two smaller figures look on.

Jackson see the acolytes as SS Columba and Andrew, the guardian saints of Scotland, presiding over the Christian crowning of the true ruler of a united kingdom.

This of course is only one of many theories. The earliest is that the stone may commemorate a great victory in the early eleventh century won by the Scots under Malcom II over the Scandinavians led by Sueno. During this battle the Vikings were turned out of Burghead.

The scene may or may not commemorate an actual battle, but is more likely to commemorate the outcome of a long war. The *Legend of St Berchan* suggests that Kenneth tricked the Pictish kings to come to Scone where he murdered them all, thus leaving his path to conquest clear.

Kenneth may not have raised the stone himself. That could have been done by one of his sons or his successors, one of whom may even have commissioned the raising of the stone. But the message is still the same.

This, then, as I see it, is the crux of the meaning conveyed by the stone to the far-flung Picts beyond the Mounth.

Your kings are dead, your kingdoms leaderless, your race is finished. Kenneth mac Alpin reigns.

A GOLDEN AGE

Now that we can look back on Pictland, was it that golden age we hoped to find or just another landscape in the vast and aged kingdom of the past?

The greatest obstacle to deeper research when it comes to knowing more about the Picts is the lack of contemporary documentary evidence. So much has to be assumed, guessed at or discarded.

As we have seen, there are the Classical writers who give us glimpses into the world of the proto-Picts. But the annals and chronicles, the legends, prophecies and hagiographies, the tales from the oral tradition and mythologies mostly date, with some notable exceptions such as the Venerable Bede, from a period as much as five hundred years later than the Pictish era.

Therefore everything written or collated at a later date was coloured by the perceptions of a different generation. Nothing can be relied on as absolute fact, little can be taken for granted, still less assumed. These times were justly named the Dark Ages.

As a result, the Picts have – at least until recently – entered the realms of mythology as little dark painted savages with feet as big as umbrellas who lost their strength at noon.

This book has been an attempt to make the Picts a little more accessible, and a little less fantastical ... but a golden age?

We have watched them grow from a loose collection of quarrelling Celtic tribes to become a nation more or less united under a high-king. We have seen them accept the new leaders and teachings of Christianity. We have followed them through numerous celebrations or lamentations of victory or defeat. We have mourned for them in the final loss of their kingdom to the Scots.

It all looks very like a microcosm of the world today, only the tribes have become countries, the battles wars, and the priests politicians. There can be no such thing as a golden age. Each generation repeats in one way or another the mistakes of the past and suffers accordingly.

Raasay cross slab stands in a rockery near Raasay House on the island of Raasay

And yet ... and yet ... those of us who were happy children know that childhood was our golden age, when we could run faster, dream more splendidly, love and hate wholeheartedly, believe with complete conviction, and fear more chillingly the monsters alive in our imagination.

And was Pictland not our nation's nursery? All the enthusiasms of childhood are apparent in the Picts, although they were far from being children. So if by a golden age one means a time when men were fired and filled with a whole-hearted enjoyment of life, an appreciation of sumptuous art, a thorough involvement in the natural and supernatural worlds, and latterly an unquestioning trust in the goodness and power of Christ, then the Pictish era was indeed a golden age.

BIBLIOGRAPHY

PICTISH ANCESTORS

Prehistoric Stone Circles. Aubrey Burl. Shire Publications 1979 and 1988
What Happened in History. Gordon Childe. Penguin Books 1942 and 1965
Morton Revisited. J.M. Morton Coles. *From the Stone Age to the 'Forty-five*. Eds Anne
   O'Connor & D.V. Clarke. 1983
Neolithic and Early Bronze Age Pottery. Alex Gibson. Shire Publications 1986
Iron Age Societies: 500 BC to AD 700. Lotte Hedeager. Trans. John Hines. Blackwell
   Publishers 1992
Society in Scotland from 700 BC to 200 AD. Richard Hingley. Proc. Soc. Antiq. Scot. Vol.
   122 1992
Prehistoric Scotland. Ann MacSween & Mick Sharp. Batsford, London 1989
Bronze Age Britain. Michael Parker Pearson. English Heritage 1993
Scotland Before History. Stuart Piggott & Keith Henderson. Thomas Nelson & Sons 1958
Scotland BC. Anna Ritchie. HMSO Edinburgh. 1988
Scotland: Archaeology and Early History. Graham & Anna Ritchie. Edinburgh University
   Press 1991
Brochs of Scotland. J.N.G. Richie. Shire Publications 1988
Powerful Pots: Beakers in North East History. Ian A.G. Shepherd. University of Aberdeen
   1986

ROMANS AND CALEDONIANS

The Oxford History of the Classical World. J. Boardman, Jasper Griffin, Oswyn Murray.
   OUP 1986
The Northern Frontier of Roman Britain. David J. Breeze. Batsford, London 1982
Later Roman Britain. Stephen Johnson. Routledge & Kegan Paul. London 1980
An Atlas of Roman Britain. Barri Jones & David Mattingly. Blackwell Reference 1990
Scotland's Roman Remains. Lawrence Keppie. J. Donald 1990
The Agricola and the Germania. Cornelius Tacitus. Trans. H. Mattingly. Penguin Classics
   1970
A Battle Lost: Romans and Caledonians at Mons Graupius. Gordon Maxwell. EUP 1981

The Romans in Scotland. Gordon Maxwell. EUP 1989

Agricola's Campaign in Scotland. Scottish Archaeological Forum 12. EUP 1981

Agricola and Germania. Cornelius Tacitus. Ed. J.H. Sleeman. Cambridge University Press 1939

PICTISH HISTORY AND ARCHAEOLOGY

'*Populie bestialis Pictorum feroci animo*'. Leslie Alcock. British Archaeol. rep. International Series, 71 (61–92)

Pictish Studies: Present and Future. Leslie Alcock. *Reconnaissance Excavations on Early History. Fortifications and Other Royal Sites in Scotland 1974–84.* Leslie & Elizabeth E. Alcock. Proc. Soc. Antiq. Scot. Vol. 122 1992

Early Sources of Scottish History: AD 1200–1206. 2 vols. A.O. Anderson. Oliver & Boyd, Edinburgh 1922

Kings and Kingship in Early Scotland. M.O. Anderson. Scottish Academic Press, Edinburgh 1973

Scotland in Early Christian Times. Joseph Anderson. The Rhind Lectures in Archaeology for 1880. David Douglas, Edinburgh 1881

Early Scotland. H.M. Chadwick. Cambridge University Press 1949

Pictish and Other Burials. Joanna Close-Brooks. Pictish Studies Ed. J.C.P. Friell and W.G. Watson. BAR Series 125 1984

The Picts. Isabel Henderson. Thames & Hudson 1967

The Picts and the Scots. Lloyd & Jenny Laing. Alan Sutton Publishing 1993

Pict and Norseman in Northern Scotland. Anna Ritchie. From Scottish Archaeological Forum 6. Glasgow 1974

Picts. Anna Ritchie. HMSO, Edinburgh 1989

Chronicles of the Picts, Chronicles of the Scots and Other Early Memorials of Scottish History. Ed. William F. Skene. H.M. General Register House, Edinburgh 1867

Celtic Scotland Vol. 1. William F. Skene. Edinburgh 1886

The Picts: a New Look at Old Problems. Ed. Alan Small. Dundee 1987. Articles as follows:

    Picts – the Name and the People. M.O. Anderson

    Portknockie: Promontory Forts and Pictish Settlement in the North-East. Ian Ralston

    Clatchard's Craig, a Pictish Hillfort in Fife. Joanna Close-Brooks

    Settlement in Southern Pictland – a New Overview. Gordon S. Maxwell

    The Picto-Scottish Interface in Material Culture. Anna Ritchie

    Early Christian Monuments Displaying Crosses but No Other Ornament. Isabel Henderson

    Pictish Place-Names – Some Toponymic Evidence. Ian A. Fraser

    Patterns in Stone, Patterns in Population. Jim Inglis.

Warlords and Holy Men. Alfred P. Smyth. Edinburgh University Press 1984 and 1989

The Problem of the Picts. Ed. F.T. Wainwright. Articles by R.W. Feachem, K.H. Jackson, S. Piggott & R.B.K. Stevenson. Thomas Nelson 1955

PICTISH ART AND SCULPTURED STONES

The Early Christian Monuments of Scotland. 2 vols. J. Romilly Allen & Joseph Anderson. Rhind Lectures 1903. Reprinted by Pinkfoot Press, Angus 1993

Dark Age Sculpture. J. Close-Brooks & R.B.K. Stevenson. NMS, Edinburgh 1982

Crossbows on Pictish Stones. John M. Gilbert. Proc. Soc. Antiq. Scot. 107 1976

Pictish Vine-Scroll Ornament. Isabel Henderson. *From the Stone Age to the '45.* Eds Anne O'Connor & D.V. Clarke. John Donald 1983

The 'David Cycle' in Pictish Art. Isabel Henderson. From *Early Medieval Sculpture in Britain and Ireland.* Ed. John Higgitt. BAR Series 152 1986

The Symbol Stones of Scotland. Anthony Jackson. The Orkney Press 1984

The Pictish Trail. Anthony Jackson. The Orkney Press 1989

Date and Origin of Pictish Symbols. Lloyd and Jennifer Laing. Proc. Soc. Antiq. Scot. Vol. 114 1984

Later Celtic Art in Britain and Ireland. Lloyd Laing. Shire Publications, Aylesbury 1987

The Declining Pictish Symbol – a Reappraisal. Gordon Murray. Proc. Soc. Antiq. Scot. Vol. 116 1986

A List of Dark Age Sculpture and Inscribed Stones in the National Museum of Antiquities of Scotland. NMS 1981

Excavations of Pictish and Viking-age Farmsteads at Buckquoy, Orkney. Proc. Soc. Antiq. Scot Vol. 108 1976/7

Pictish Art Society Journals 1 to 5. Ed. Niàll M. Robertson 1990–94

Pictish Figure and New Symbol Stone from Barflat, Rhynie. Shepherd and Shepherd. Proc. Soc. Antiq. Scot. Vol. 109 1978

The Age of Migrating Ideas. Ed. R. Michael Spearman & John Higgitt. National Museums of Scotland 1993. Articles as follows:

    Further Thoughts on Some Well-Known Problems. R.B.K. Stevenson

    Remarks of the Liturgical Fan, Flabellus or Rhipidon. Hilary Richardson

    The Book of Kells, Folio 114r: a Mystery Revealed yet Concealed. Jennifer O'Reilly

    The Norrie's Law Hoard and the Dating of Pictish Silver. John Graham-Campbell

    The Pictish Class I Animals. Carola Hicks

    Pictish Cave Art at East Wemyss, Fife. J.N.G. Ritchie & J.N. Stevenson

    Image and Icon in Pictish Sculpture. Leslie Alcock

    Snake Bosses and Redemption at Iona and Pictland. Douglas MacLean

Sculptured Stones of Scotland. John Stuart. Spalding Club, Aberdeen 1856

The Pictish Class I Symbol Stones. Charles Thomas. *Pictish Studies.* Ed. J.C.P. Friell & W.G. Watson. BAR Series 125 1984

The Interpretation of the Pictish Symbols. Charles Thomas. *The Archaeological Journal* Vol. CXX 1963

PICTISH PLACES

Burghead Well. Leaflet. Ancient Monuments of Scotland (undated)
Catalogue of Meigle Museum. Leaflet. Ancient Monuments of Scotland (undated)
Pictish Stones in Dunrobin Castle Museum. J. Close-Brooks. Pilgrim Press, Derby 1989
The Battle of Dunnichen. Graham Cruikshank. Pinkfoot Press 1991
Bennachie and the Picts. Penny Dransart. Bennachie Notes 6 1986
The Enigmatic Symbol Stones of Bennachie. Penny Dransart. Bennachie Notes 8 1987
The Maiden Stone of Bennachie. Penny Dransart. Bennachie Notes 11 1988
Norrie's Law, Fife. James Graham-Campbell. Proc. Soc. Antiq. Scot. Vol. 121 1991
Burghead. Leaflet. Grampian Regional Council (undated)
The Picardy Stone. Leaflet. Grampian Regional Council (undated)
The Art & Function of Rosemarkie's Pictish Monuments, Isabel Henderson. Groam House, Rosemarkie, 1989 and 1991
The Dark Ages in the Highlands. Ed. Edward Meldrum. Inverness Field Club 1971. Articles as follows:
    North Pictland. Isabel Henderson
    The Meaning of the Pictish Symbol Stones. Isabel Henderson
Scottish Place-Names. W.F.H. Nicolaisen. Batsford, London 1976
Foul Hordes: The Picts in the North East. Ian Ralston & Jim Inglis. University of Aberdeen 1984
Guide to the Wemyss Caves. Frank Rankin. Save the Wemyss Ancient Caves Society, East Wemyss
The Solar Stones of Edderton. Douglas Scott. Tain (undated)
Moray Province and People. Ed. W.D.H. Sellar. Scottish Society for Northern Studies 1993
The Picts in Tayside. Alan Small & Lisbeth Thoms. Dundee District Council 1985
The Celtic Placenames of Scotland. W.J. Watson 1926. Birlinn Ltd, Edinburgh 1993

PICTISH NEIGHBOURS

Neighbours of the Picts: Angles, Britons & Scots at War and at Home. Leslie Alcock. Groam House, Rosemarkie 1993
The State of Pictland in the Age of Sutton Hoo. Sally Foster. From *The Seventh Century in North-Western Europe*. The Boydell Press, Woodbridge 1992
The Kingdom of Northumbria AD 350–1100. N.J. Higham. Alan Sutton Publishing Ltd 1993
Vikings in Scotland. Anna Ritchie. Historic Scotland and Batsford, London 1993

THE PICTISH CHURCH

Life of Saint Columba. St Adamnan. Ed. William Reeves. Facsimile reprint by Llanerch Publications 1988

Norman Sculptures and the Medieval Bestiaries. J. Romilly Allen. Rhind Lectures in Archaeology 1885. Facsimile reprint by Llanerch Publications 1993

Ecclesiastical History of the English People. Bede. Trans. Leo Herley-Price, R.E. Latham & D.H. Farmer. Penguin Books 1955 and 1990

Northumbria and the Book of Kells. T.J. Brown. From *Anglo-Saxon England*. 1972

Symbolism of the Celtic Cross. Derek Bryce. Llanerch Publications 1989

Celtic Christianity. Anthony Duncan. Element, Dorset 1992

Bede, Iona and the Picts. Archibald A.M. Duncan. & *Writing of History in the Middle Ages*. Eds R.H.C. Davis & Wallace Hadville. OUP 1981

Columba. Ian Finlay. Victor Gollancz Ltd 1979

Early Christianity in Pictland. Kathleen Hughes. Jarrow Lecture 1970

Bede and the Pictish Church. D.P. Kirby. Innes Review 24 1973

Sacred Stones Sacred Places. Marianna Lines. St Andrews Press 1992

Curadan, Boniface and the Early Church of Rosemarkie. Aidan MacDonald. Groam House Museum Trust 1992

St Columba of Iona. Lucy Menzies 1920. Facsimile reprint by J.M.F. Books, Felinfach 1992

The Pictish Nation: Its People & Its Church. Archibald B. Scott. T.N. Foulis, Edinburgh 1919

Scottish Saints. Dennis Townhill. SPCK 1978

FACTS AND FOLKLORE OF THE SCOTTISH CELTS

The Clans, Septs and Regiments of the Scottish Highlands. Frank Adam. Cassell & Collier Macmillan Publishers Ltd 1908 and 1975

Studies in the History of Dalriada. John Bannerman. Scottish Academic Press, Edinburgh 1974

Popular Tales of the West Highlands. 4 vols Ed. J.F. Campbell. Edmonston & Douglas, Edinburgh 1861

Carmina Gadelica. Alexander Carmichael. Floris Books 1992

The Highlands. J. Close-Brooks. HMSO, Edinburgh 1986

A Highland History. Earl of Cromartie. The Gavin Press 1979

Folklore of Scottish Lochs and Springs. J.M. Mackinlay 1983. Facsimile Reprint by Llanerch Publications 1993

CELTIC HISTORY AND MYTHOLOGY

Celtic Art in Pagan and Christian Times. J. Romilly Allen. Reprinted by Studio Editions Ltd 1993

Celtic Inheritance. Peter Berresford Ellis. Muller 1985, new edition Constable 1991

Irish Druids and Old Irish Religions. James Bonwick. Dorset Press 1894

Legends of the Celts. Frank Delaney. Hodder & Stoughton 1989

The Celtic Realms. Miles Dillon & Nora Chadwick. Weidenfeld & Nicolson 1967

Dictionary of Celtic Myth and Legend. Miranda Green. Thames & Hudson 1992

Celtic Totem Animals. Lorraine McDonald. Dalriada Publications, Brodick, Isle of Arran 1992

A Guide to Ogam. Damian McManus. Maynoth Monograph 4 1991

Celtic Warriors: 400 BC–AD 1600. Tim Newark. Blandford Press 1989

The Druids. Stuart Piggott. Thames & Hudson 1968

The Celts. T.G.E. Powell. Thames & Hudson 1958

Celtic Warriors. W.F. & J.N.G. Ritchie. Shire Publications 1985

Myths and Legends of the Celtic Race. T.W. Rolleston. 1911. Constable 1985

The Pagan Celts. Anne Ross. Batsford, London 1970 and 1986

Celtic Lore. Ward Rutherford. Aquarian/Thorsons 1993

Celtic Myth and Legend. Charles Squire. Newcastle Publishing Company 1975

The Celtic Year. Shirley Toulson. Element Books 1993

MISCELLANEOUS

Scotland's Native Horse. Robert W. Beck. MRCVS GC Books, Wigtown 1992

Dictionary of Symbolism. Hans Beidermann. Trans. J. Hulbert. Facts on File Inc. 1992

The Lost Beliefs of Northern Europe. Hilda Ellis Davidson. Routledge 1993

The Foals of Epona. A.A. Dent & Daphne Machin Goodall. London Gallery Press 1962

The Goddodin. Kenneth Jackson. OUP 1969

Tree of Strings. Keith Sanger & Alison Kinnaird. Kinmor Music 1992

The Desert Fathers. Helen Waddell. Constable 1936 and 1987

INDEX